STREETWISE®
CREDIT and COLLECTIONS

Maximize Your Collections Process to Improve Your Profitability

Suzanne Caplan

Avon, Massachusetts

Published by Adams Media, an F+W Publications Company
57 Littlefield Street
Avon, MA 02322
www.adamsmedia.com

ISBN 10: 1-59337-737-1
ISBN 13: 978-1-59337-737-3

Printed in the United States of America.

J I H G F E D C B A

Library of Congress Cataloging-in-Publication Data

Caplan, Suzanne.
Streetwise credit and collections / Suzanne Caplan.
    p. cm.
  ISBN-13: 978-1-59337-737-3
  ISBN-10: 1-59337-737-1
  1. Credit--Management. 2. Collecting of accounts.   I. Title.
HG3751.C35 2007
658.8'8--dc22

2006032611

This publication is designed to provide accurate and authoritative information with regard to the subject matter covered. It is sold with the understanding that the publisher is not engaged in rendering legal, accounting, or other professional advice. If legal advice or other expert assistance is required, the services of a competent professional person should be sought.
    —From a *Declaration of Principles* jointly adopted by a Committee of the American Bar Association and a Committee of Publishers and Associations

Many of the designations used by manufacturers and sellers to distinguish their product are claimed as trademarks. Where those designations appear in this book and Adams Media was aware of a trademark claim, the designations have been printed with initial capital letters.

This book is available at quantity discounts for bulk purchases.
For information, please call 1-800-289-0963.

CONTENTS

Contents

Dedication

To Siobhan Jones Leach, who taught me about patience and tenacity

Acknowledgments

To my agent Laurie Harper, who is always there, and Sherry Truesdell, who keeps the work going, I am grateful. And to Adams Media, who has allowed me to write on the topics I think are most important, I appreciate the opportunity. But mostly, to the unflappable Larry Shea, who is the master at creating a book; this one is a tribute to your skills.

Introduction

Streetwise® Credit and Collections is designed to be a complete work on the topic of credit and collection, covering the issues from both ends, that is, from the securing of credit for your business to the granting of customer credit.

Ever since pioneer days when traders sought to buy essential supplies with a promise to pay, people have had the need to make purchases on a credit basis. Early American settlers were able to secure the seed to plant their crops and the powder to fire their guns by pledging eventually to pay off their trade imbalances with merchants.

This "promise to pay" is the essence of buying on credit. Whether a transaction involves an informal verbal agreement or a complicated legal contract, at its core is this intention or promise. Issuing credit requires a relationship of trust, whether you are a business granting such a privilege or one that is requesting it. Establishing credit plays a critical part in every business transaction, even if many companies manage it poorly.

As this book demonstrates, extending credit is an art as much as a science. Successful businesses understand this and consequently are able to decide on what terms of lending they will allow, to formalize these in writing, and to adhere to such policies consistently. This book provides you with a step-by-step plan to put effective credit policies in place for your customers and in the process explains the why as well as the how.

For instance, offering credit to customers may act as a spur to business sales; the "no money down and set number of months to pay plan" can attract buyers who otherwise might not have sufficient funds for immediate purchases. Over time these customers presumably will be able to pay for what they have purchased. But if the payments due are not collected on a timely basis (and eventually in full), then offering a customer an installment plan may jeopardize your company's financial future.

Determining a customer's credit eligibility is therefore a necessary first step for your business, requiring in the process a thorough documentation of the pending transaction. Next, following through with requests for payment forms the crux of any credit policy. Finally, collection enforcement may be the step of last resort for your business to take. In other words, the entire process of extending credit costs your business money and requires more time than you might recognize initially.

Further, there are major differences between offering business-to-business credit and granting business-to-consumer credit. In operating your business, you will need to know the specifics of handling each type.

You may decide that you do not want to manage your consumer-credit activities in-house. In that case, the solution is to find a third-party company to provide and administer any consumer credit sought from your business. You can then refer customers to a credit-granting agency that will fund their purchases. You will have to give up a small percentage of those sales to the lender, but you will thereby avoid the risk of nonpayment attached to credit sales.

As a credit grantor, you will need to establish policies that are customer-friendly but nevertheless firm enough to minimize your risk. After all, if you do not get paid for your sales, you won't be in business for long. All companies face a certain amount of bad debt, but by being careful with initial lending and by monitoring your loans periodically you can prevent major losses.

When an account does fall into collection mode because payments have not been made when due, you must act quickly and appropriately. You do not want to offend good customers who are having temporary problems since you want to retain their business. When a customer is making no effort to pay, however, you need to take fast and effective action to protect your interests. This may involve referral to a collection agency or proceeding to small claims court. You might even need to retain a lawyer and take the matter to litigation.

In addition to an ability to set an effective credit policy for your customers, you also will need the skills to secure sufficient vendor credit as well as to borrow the bank funds to run your operations. Your company may be extended credit by other businesses, in which case the rules governing such transactions are important to understand. Fair-credit laws govern the granting of consumer credit and the process of payment collection, so an informed knowledge of these laws is vital if you are selling to individuals.

This book begins with what your business can do to establish the credit needed to maintain adequate cash flow until your revenue grows (so that you might become a credit grantor in the first place). We discuss the sources of capital as well as the vendor credit you will require. We also cover what it takes to enter into international trade as both a buyer and a seller and explain important subjects like exchange rates.

In short, your company will confront a wide range of credit and collection issues at various times. *Streetwise® Credit and Collections* gives you the information and advice you need to make effective business decisions.

1

Why Credit Is a Business Necessity

The Leverage to Start a Business

In the operation of your business, you will be not only a grantor of credit but a seeker of outside sources of capital and, it is hoped, a recipient of credit. We usually associate the obtaining of loans with banking institutions, but it is important to realize that receiving credit from vendors is also a form of loan to your company. And because banks are actually in the business of granting credit, they can serve as good models for learning the basics of how to judge the ability of a customer to pay.

Building a growing business requires capital at the outset, even before there are any meaningful revenues coming in. Often this money comes from the owner's investment, but any business that seeks significant growth will require outside sources of credit. This means that the assets you have purchased can be leveraged in order to fund additional growth, from inventory to wages. "Leverage" means that you use future revenue to secure current needs.

The best example of this type of financing is with the purchase of real property, whether in the form of a personal residence or a business building. You leverage your current cash and future earnings to make a purchase for current use.

Understanding Leverage Ratios

As a business owner in the position of seeking credit, you do not want to borrow more than you can pay back over time (assuming that your profits and cash flow will meet projections). And as a credit grantor to your own customers, you do not want to allow them to get in over their heads, in terms of running up debt that they will not be able to pay back over the next few months or years. Credit problems spring up more often from an inability to pay than from any unwillingness to do so. Using existing collateral to borrow cash is permissible but if the leverage (the debt to equity) is too high, the earned cash flow will not be sufficient to retire debt within its terms. When assets are inventory or material that will be sold, the leverage can be higher than with assets such as equipment or buildings.

Cash Is a Timing Issue

Cash flows through a business on a continuing basis, although there are times and circumstances when the outflow exceeds the inflow. In a new venture, the expense of asset purchases will not be immediately returned by way of cash income. Instead, the funding for your business will likely take the form of owner investment or long-term borrowing from a bank. You will pay back this principal from future profits.

The other challenge your company may face is from the depletion of capital due to a period of operating losses. This type of situation is unlikely to be remedied by any borrowing of funds, since banks will not fund a loan to cover losses. The cash will have to come from outside investment or from the sale of any unneeded assets. The better prepared you are for the cash flows in and out of a business, the better you will be able to meet the credit needs of serving your customers.

In circumstances in which your business cash is invested in inventory, in work in process, or in accounts receivable acquired as a result of sales, the resulting imbalance of funds may reasonably be replaced by bank lending. As the cash begins to flow in, the loans are paid down or can be paid off entirely. Bank funds are then used over the short-term to smooth out the timing of cash inflow. Such borrowing is usually through a line of credit that can be drawn on as needed.

Retaining Profits May Rebalance Cash

When your company has a prolonged period of profits that creates a positive cash flow, it is usually good policy to keep the cash in a money-market account that is readily accessible. Often the first instinct of business owners is to increase the salaries or draws for themselves and perhaps other managers, or to purchase some expensive new equipment. But being conservative with expenses in order to build a cash cushion is sounder business practice. If the new equipment is necessary and will offer a payback over time, consider going to your bank for a loan to facilitate the investment while conserving your internal cash to carry you through possible slow times. A business out of cash is a business out of choices. Overspending is a behavior to watch out for in your customers as well. Customers who are spending lavishly may be using up all of their cash reserves.

Turning Assets into Collateral

Many seasonal businesses build inventory prior to their big selling season. They may buy material over a period of months and try to pay for it when the bills come due, even if that is long before any goods are sold. This practice usually strains the cash flow of your business. Instead the inventory (assuming that it is current and will be sold) can be used as collateral for a loan.

Your growing accounts receivable are also assets that may be used as collateral to secure a loan. All of your noncash items that will convert to cash within six months are eligible. This type of short-term borrowing is undertaken to add cash funding to cover slow times. As inventory is liquidated and customers pay their bills, you will be able to retire your loan. Most banks are willing to make short-term loans where there is a reliable likelihood of early payback.

Only Current Accounts Receivables Are Eligible

Most lenders will require a current aging of your receivables (a chart of what debts are 30, 60, 90 and more than 90 days out) to determine the value of your collateral available to support a loan. Some will verify the credit worthiness of your customers as one of the criteria for the loan limit they are willing to advance. If a big customer becomes a credit problem to you, you are likely to become one to the bank. Train yourself to collect receivables promptly from your customers.

The other issue a lender will consider is the date of your customer invoices. Any charge that is over sixty days old (and assumed to be thirty days past due) will not be eligible as loan collateral. Typically, neither will any other outstanding or future sales to delinquent customers. This policy should be instructional for you since if sixty days have passed without your being paid for goods or services, there is an increased risk you won't be paid. Banks apply these rules, and you should do so as well. You want the next sale but not if the previous one has yet to be paid for.

Using Other People's Money (OPM) to Make Money

A profitable business seeking to grow a larger venture will have a need for cash from outside sources to leverage its concept or skills. In addition to working with traditional lenders, you can negotiate to partner with your vendors for extended terms of payment, which as mentioned earlier is really another form of receiving a loan. As money comes in that you would typically use to pay a vendor's bills, you can—with the vendor's approval—use your capital to continue building inventory in order to increase your future sales. And in turn you can increase your purchases from that vendor as a result of its forbearance.

This strategy works better for a retail or wholesale distribution company whose cash is tied up in short-term investment, that is, in selling products that will be turned back into cash in a reasonable period of time, usually less than sixty to ninety days. Consider the shelf life of your product if you are thinking about asking a vendor for extended terms. Money owed on obsolete inventory is unlikely to be paid.

OPM = Outside Investors

When the need for capital is for purposes of longer-term investment (such as in equipment or technology development), the source to use may be an outside investor who is willing to put capital at risk for the possibility of high return. Bank loans and lines of credit are, according to their stated terms, obligations that must be retired. Investment in a business, on the other hand, is not guaranteed. Rather, an expectation of payoff may be tied to future profitability or to an exit strategy (such as a public offering or sale of the company). This ability to leverage resources is necessary for any business with an aggressive growth plan. The difference between a business investment and a loan is that the former is at risk and the latter is secured by collateral or a promise to pay regardless of outcome.

Your Bank as a Source of Credit

Most banks offer a variety of loan products and credit services that you can use to fund your business. In addition to (typically) longer-term secured loans and shorter-term lines of credit, you may also be able to secure a bank-issued credit card that enables you to make small purchases or fund travel and entertainment expenses; you can then choose to pay the bill in full each month or over time. Careful use of such additional capital can assist your cash flow as well. Remember, however, that the cost of this type of credit is higher than that of most others.

Your Bank May Provide Credit Processing

Most banks are looking for business customers who will take advantage of various services on which lenders can profit. One such banking service consists of the processing of credit cards (Visa, MasterCard, etc.) that your business accepts. You pay a fee of a few percent on each credit card transaction and the purchase money automatically goes into your bank account. A benefit of using a card processing service provided by your company's bank is that it may expedite the deposit of your money from sales. The faster you have access to your funds, the easier it is to handle your own expenses. Always ask about turnaround time on transaction deposits when you are inquiring into a bank's credit card processing rates.

Securing Loans for Working Capital

The most difficult type of business activity to fund is a project that takes a long time to complete and does not offer advance or progress payments. This might consist of a construction job or a large manufacturing project that does not bill until it is finished. A small company is likely to run into problems trying to fund months of expenditures without receiving any significant cash flow from the client.

A Restaurant's Life Blood

The issue of credit card turnaround is critical for many retail operations but particularly for those in the food business. With wages a major weekly or biweekly expense and long-term credit for buying provisions seldom available (because food businesses are often considered high-risk customers), the need for rapid access to cash is of prime consideration for restaurateurs. Some credit-card processors can offer a thirty-six-hour turnaround, which may be worth payment of an extra percentage point. Restaurants often survive by using their cash flow rather than by turning quick profits, so quickly accessing credit card transactions as ready cash is critical. With customers' frequent use of debit cards, the cash may be available in less than twenty-four hours.

Finding the Missing Piece

Linden Electric was a small contractor primarily doing industrial repair and maintenance work. Customers respected the quality and value of Linden's work and often offered the company larger jobs. Linden Electric had to decline these because it could not afford to purchase any increased materials and pay the ongoing wages of its workers until the job was completed. After a casual conversation with its local bank manager led to a contract loan, the business grew by 30 percent a year for several years. The financing was the missing piece. Remember: Receiving credit is a business necessity. Linden obtained financing when its lender perceived the increased opportunity available from the company's clientele. From a bank's point of view, a company that serves a committed customer base is a desirable customer to have.

The answer here may be to finance the entire contract through your bank. There is a Small Business Administration (SBA) program that can serve as a government guarantor for the bank, which would make its loan easier to secure. This type of loan is use-specific (meaning that the use is to fund the material and labor and overhead directly related to the contract used as collateral); it is based on the total value of the contract, and it provides the lender with collateral from any payments received. The lender may require that you have client checks issued jointly to it as well as to your company. As you complete the work, the bank allows you to draw on the credit line to pay your expenses; when you are paid, the funds available are reduced accordingly. Profit-taking may be prohibited until the project is complete, in case of any problems along the way. An unfinished contract is as much a liability as its account receivable is an asset. If your business has underestimated total expenditures, it may cost more to finish the work than there is cash available from the loan.

Arrange to Draw on Progress

When you have a contract that extends past ninety days, whether for a supply agreement or perhaps for a construction job, you want to be able to draw on the loan commensurate with your progress. Paying debt service on the loan from the outset will add costs you may not be able to postpone paying. Arrange a financing agreement that allows you to make draws (including profit-taking) in identifiable stages as you complete your work. This way you can meet your obligations as they become due. The final completion of your work will yield a bottom-line profit you can retain.

Selling an Account to a Factor

In this type of financing arrangement, rather than collecting receivables from each of your customers, the accounts are sold to a third party that then will be paid by the customers themselves. This is known as a "sale of the account," and it is done without recourse, which means that the risk of nonpayment is absorbed by the third party (known as the "factor") rather than by your business.

Your customers continue to make purchases from you, but they send their payments to the assigned factor. You are paid a draw when the account is assigned, after which you pay a monthly interest fee based on the amount of open credit. The fee may be as much as twice the current interest rate of the bank but it includes the cost of credit administration. Your factor may decline some of your customers based on their credit ratings, at which point the determination to extend credit to these customers

Know the Collection Policies of Your Factor

Throughout this book we emphasize that the way you treat your customers, even when they are in collection, reflects directly on your company. For instance, situations arise that may cause a client to skip an invoice or to pay late. If this is a temporary problem, the goal should always be to retain the customer while ensuring that the account is paid in full as soon as possible. Some factors are more sensitive to this issue of customer service than others. You need to know how your factor will treat your customers in the early stages of any collection process. Ask what the factor's policies are and review their customer correspondence, if possible, to make sure the image of your company is upheld as you would expect. Your factor is one of the public faces of your company.

Factors who circumvent good customer relations in favor of tough collection procedures may damage your business. You want future sales, if not completed ones, with these same customers.

reverts to you. Many of the larger money center lenders maintain separate divisions that provide factoring services. This type of financing is typically used by the apparel industry. We discuss this method in more detail in Chapter 24.

Floor Planning Inventory

Large banks and commercial financing companies may provide a type of credit based on the financing of your business's floor inventory. This is most frequently used by the automotive industry and by other big-ticket businesses like furniture and appliances. The inventory is totally financed and secured by the lender, who is paid as it is sold. Your business earns a gross profit on each sale as it is completed. The lender has a completely secured investment in your inventory and may also arrange consumer financing when a product is sold. Banks are often looking to acquire dependable auto loans, for example.

▶▶ TEST DRIVE

Obtaining credit is the most common way a business can leverage its assets and smooth the timing of its cash flow. Ask yourself in what ways your company can use credit to achieve this:

- ⮑ Do you have assets that can be turned into cash?
- ⮑ Can you earn sufficient return to attract investors?
- ⮑ Have you considered financing long-term contracts to provide cash flow?
- ⮑ Can you assign your accounts receivables to a factor for current cash?
- ⮑ Have you developed a relationship with a banker to provide financial advice and additional loan services as well as business credit?

Establish Credibility

The more savvy you are as a user of credit, the better judge you will be of granting credit to others and of handling the effective collection of your money. Your best protection against unsuccessful collection is to understand how much and what type of credit is needed by a business or consumer and how to follow through with a policy that reflects that knowledge. Not all of your vendors will set terms of credit effectively; learn from their mistakes and from their successes with you. Establishing credit from vendors is a low-cost source of capital that can benefit every company.

In the days before and just after the doors first open, your new business is in need of vendors for various types of goods and services. You not only want to find the best value for your money, you are beginning to need open credit terms as well. This means that your vendor ships to you before receiving any cash, and bills the charge on terms of thirty days to pay. Although new companies should expect to pay in advance for most of their startup costs, eventually you will need vendors to give you terms for payments.

Usually the toughest policies come from businesses that have the least competition. For example, utility companies such as your phone service and energy provider often require a deposit before they will give you any service at all. Smaller suppliers who are hungrier for the sale will be far more flexible. The more established the vendor, the more formalized are their credit practices.

You will want to meet with potential new vendors in person, if possible. Invite the principals or sales representatives to your place of business or, if they are located out of town, travel to visit them. Even if your company is new, you want to show how serious your commitment is to making it a success. Establishing credit with a vendor partly depends on your making routine information available, but subjective factors often play a role, particularly if you are a new venture. Your experience, knowledge, and demeanor can influence a vendor's decision to offer credit. An astute vendor will be more impressed by your commitment to your venture than by any business hype. After all, even established companies grow by taking risks from time to time.

Dealing with the Big Players

When you are seeking business credit from national corporations such as American Express, Home Depot, and Staples, you will find that their decisions are often based on the personal credit score of a business owner. You will need to provide your social security number so they can obtain a credit score on you. If your score meets their qualifications (usually a number around 650), you are likely to receive an open account. They may set up the account by starting you with a minimal credit limit to see how you handle it. Paying on time will increase the open-credit line on this type of account, just as it does on personal accounts. You need to know your own credit score and to monitor it on a regular basis. Interestingly, indication of this business line of credit will not show up on your personal credit report even though the latter is its source.

When Your Company Has No Track Record

There is no way for a potential vendor to gauge how a new business is likely to handle credit. What you need to do is make a pitch to the vendor, much the way you would make one to a bank. Write an abbreviated version of your business plan and present it along with any credit application. Make sure to include some reliable references, such as your banker or perhaps an insurance agent you have worked with over time. If you have already secured good financing, mention that fact (you don't have to be specific) because it will add to your credibility. In the early stage of your business you are really asking for trust, so the more open and direct you are about your plans, the more supporters you will attract.

Negotiating Terms

The normal term for business credit is net thirty days, which means the invoice is to be paid thirty days after it is issued. Some companies set the thirty days by the date of merchandise arrival, and most vendors typically follow suit. These terms are open-credit terms, which you may not receive initially.

New suppliers may ask you to pay in advance or by COD (cash or collect on delivery). Begin your negotiations on payment terms immediately. Ask if you can pay fifty percent up front and the balance when the material is delivered. Another option is to pay the balance ten days after delivery or upon completion of any work.

Convey that you want to do business with your vendor but are not willing to pay cash over a long term. Any business that operates without vendor credit will find growth nearly an impossibility. Work with any initial terms for a period of time and then try to secure a better deal until the account is completely open.

When to Ask for More

Don't order once or twice on a cash basis and expect that to be sufficient to motivate a new supplier to be more generous with credit. That may take months or even longer. Any changes in credit terms are also dependent on how much you purchase and how often. If you are going to be a frequent customer, it is the continual contact and the flow of payments made on time that will shorten the time span. An occasional large purchase may be more difficult to negotiate since the risk for the vendor is higher. Treat your vendors with the same courtesy you want from your customers, and you may find success.

Working with Consignment

In a normal credit transaction, once you receive a product or material, you own it, whether you have paid for it or not. You can resell it and do whatever you like with the proceeds, even if the business assumption is that you still have to pay the vendor. Buying on consignment works differently and therefore may offer less risk to your new supplier. In consignment the supplier allows goods to be housed in your location for use or for sale while still retaining a security ownership in those goods.

The vendor will come to your business on a regular basis to check the inventory of its material and to bill you for what has been used or sold, possibly replacing what is gone as well. This arrangement allows

Growing Together

The Antique Barn was a small but quite successful store specializing in early American furniture and pottery. The owner rented a small storefront in suburban Pittsburgh. She always made enough money to pay the rent and utilities and to take an austere salary, but she earned little more because she did not have enough space or inventory to grow sales. When a larger space became available a few doors away, she came up with a clever idea, advertising for people who wanted to sell antiques on consignment. Soon not only was the new storefront filled, but other consignors began working in the shop and attracting new customers. This led to a third move to an even bigger location. The policy that made this arrangement work was that all proceeds for consignment goods went directly to their consignors, with only a fee taken out. Funds received for the consignors' items were never commingled with the store funds. This method enabled each vendor's space to take on the look of a big store while each consignor paid only a small overhead.

you to have instant access to what you need (without having to wait to place your order and have it delivered) yet not be charged for the material that remains on your floor. Your company can act like a bigger business in terms of inventory without having to pay the costs up front. Any material that has been consumed, however, must be paid for promptly. Consignment can be beneficial for many early-stage companies.

Consignment May Offer Fewer Choices

Keep in mind, however, that vendors who offer consignment deals are likely to want to determine what and how much inventory you stock. They commit to a certain amount of saleable goods being housed in your company's location with the hope the quantity will be sold. An outright sale puts money in their pocket, which is their goal. A consignment deal may only be offered for slower-moving products as well as for limited quantities. You also need to know if you will be limited to those product lines you can handle and sell. Consignment often works best when the merchandise is privately owned.

Reasons for Changing Vendors

Every company changes vendors from time to time, either replacing ones who haven't served it well or seeking out new sources of products to use or sell. Sometimes, though, the reason an existing business may look for a new vendor is that the old one shut it off for nonpayment. You want to address this potential concern by explaining to a new vendor why you are looking for an alternate or additional source of supply. It is your responsibility to establish yourself as a reliable business partner. Anticipating the questions that may be asked will put you ahead of the game. So let vendors know how you located them and what you expect. Likewise, you should be cautious as a credit grantor when a new business wants to do business with you all of a sudden, particularly if it has not done so in the past. Find out why its previous vendor no longer meets its needs.

The Importance of a Track Record

New vendors will want to see by your credit report that you have compiled a credit history of some length and without incident. They are interested in how you operate your business during bad times and good. This demonstration of a track record is something you will establish with a variety of vendors; if your record is erratic, it will eventually leave a trail. You might, then, limit the number of accounts you open in the early days of your business, working hard to maintain a good record of on-time payments and good communication. When a vendor agrees to modify terms, giving you additional time to pay, it won't count against you since you have negotiated a new deal and are no longer delinquent on your previous terms.

Find out what your vendor considers a past-due account. After allowing for a delay in delivery of goods as well as for the time it takes to mail out an invoice and receive back a check, many businesses regard forty-five days as a reasonable period for payment due. On day forty-five, a nonresponse from you to a bill may generate a notice or a call. This will give you the kind of attention you are trying to avoid. Be sure your payment is in before someone is looking for it. When your vendor can review months of on-time payments, it is sure to make an impression and likely to encourage a more open account or a larger credit limit.

What to Do When Cash Is Tight

Every company runs into tight periods. Business is soft, customers are very late to pay their accounts, or a major repair is needed that takes much of your available cash. No vendors will be happy to have their payments slowed down because of your financial problems, but they will be more upset if they hear nothing from you.

As soon as you realize that you are not going to be able to meet an obligation, make a phone call. Explain the situation, offer to do what you can, and keep your vendor informed. When the information comes from you early in the payment process, it carries a lot more assurance. Making a partial payment is always better than sending no payment at all. Additional information you can provide is a specific date when you will be mailing a check. You would respond favorably to the same overtures if you were in the position of creditor.

Securing Discounts for Prompt Payment

When you are in a strong cash position or have taken a deposit for an order and can pay for your material quickly, ask the vendor for an extra discount. The time frame for paying and receiving a discount is usually ten days, and the amount of discount depends on the current interest rate (or sometimes on the vendor's own need for cash). This type of discount is typically provided at one percent, but you may get more. Ask the credit manager what he is willing to offer. That extra discount adds directly to your profit. If the discount isn't offered, then pay the invoice according to its normal terms.

When you are paying on a cash basis, you should be asking for a discount as well. Buying on credit costs money (interest to the bank, processing fees, etc.), so if you are required to pay up front for merchandise, either before it is shipped or upon receipt, then some incentive may be expected. You won't know what is possible unless you ask for it, so let the owner or credit department know that receiving a discount is your expectation. Be prepared to give up any such discount if you are granted the credit you would prefer. In any case, receiving a discount for paying with cash rather than with credit affords a good lesson in the value of money.

▶▶ TEST DRIVE

A business requires credit from a variety of sources to keep cash flow going. How effectively do you handle your credit relationship with your vendors?

- ➲ Have you taken the time to establish credibility with new vendors?
- ➲ Do you work with your vendors to establish open terms they are comfortable with?
- ➲ Are you consistent with vendor payments?
- ➲ Do you communicate when a payment will be late?
- ➲ Are you taking advantage of discount terms?

The Difference Between Consumer Credit and Business Credit

Direct credit is granted to a customer more frequently through business-to-business transactions than through business-to-consumer transactions. For one thing, customer purchase amounts in business-to-business transactions are usually larger. Second, because companies buy goods to use for securing future revenue, they use credit as one of their timing devices for managing cash flow. Consumers, by contrast, often use their own debit or credit cards to make purchases or else they finance through third parties. As a result, smaller companies are less likely to manage direct consumer credit.

There are a number of federal regulations that your business must follow in handling credit for consumers. First of all, Equal Credit laws are intended to ensure that no company discriminates on the basis of age, race, marital status, the nature of a person's income, and a variety of other considerations (discussed in Chapter 5). And when it comes time to collect, you need to adhere to the regulations of the Fair Debt Collection Act, a law that governs how and where you can make contact with someone to collect a debt. Considering these complicated legal controls for consumer credit, might it be easier to provide business credit exclusively?

Not necessarily. Other rules of commerce, such as antitrust laws, make it important to treat companies relatively equally (you cannot arbitrarily disadvantage one company over another based on personal bias). And when it comes to the collection side, a business (unlike a consumer) may be protected by a corporate shell designed to shelter individual owners. You may have a long fight on your hands when you try to collect from a business. Companies that have no intention of paying their bills can often hide their corporate assets as well.

For the above reasons, knowledge of credit regulations is important from the day you open the first account with a new customer, whether another business or a consumer. Any misstep on your part will make the collection process more difficult.

You Can't Look a Business in the Eye

Many companies open credit accounts with other businesses without ever meeting the owners in person. The business principals fill out an application, which you check along with available public records to determine whether the information is sufficient and positive enough to give you a level of comfort. The question you must ask yourself is: Are you granting credit to a faceless entity or actually to a person who owns and controls the business? Many smaller, closely held companies reflect the values and intentions of their owner. The account may be established in the name of the company, but business decisions will still be made by individuals. Take the time to get to know the principals of businesses to which you are considering granting credit. You can (and should) check the references of the business, but the reputation of the individual owner in the community is important to know as well. With easy online search capabilities possible these days, you should be able to find out if there is negative information you need to know.

Large and Wealthy Corporations Are Not Always the Best Payers

Many business owners are enthusiastic when they receive new quotes or purchase orders from a large corporation. It is easy to assume that with corporate cash flow and access to capital, all of your invoices will be paid promptly. Unfortunately, this does not always work. Often you will find the reality is just the opposite.

Some *Fortune* 100 companies in the U.S. have a policy of paying vendor invoices in sixty or even ninety days, sometimes taking even longer. This goes for all invoices, including yours—unless you receive a special dispensation. The only way to protect yourself is to make contact with the corporate purchasing or disbursement department and receive specific assurance that you will be treated in a different manner. Large companies sometimes manage their cash flow through the temporary use of their customers' money. Sometimes they use slow paperwork flow as an excuse; other times they offer no explanation than that "this is policy." If all else fails, add in the cost of delayed payments (by which you are, in effect, furnishing credit) to your selling price. This hindrance to your cash flow has a cost to you that you need to recover.

Using Credit as an Incentive

"No money down and thirty-six months to pay!" Such offers comprise a strategy you see in the consumer market all the time. This is a policy intended to increase business sales by motivating buyers currently lacking adequate cash to make an immediate purchase. Business vendors use this device as well, referring to it as "dating," meaning that they date their invoice sixty, ninety, or even 120 days after the shipment of goods. When a business has too much inventory on hand, granting an "incentive in terms" may be an effective way to move the goods to consumers. There are suppliers of seasonal merchandise that ship throughout the year despite knowing that sales will be made only "in season," which is when they actually are paid.

If your business offers such an incentive plan to customers, consider: Will you really be making solid sales that will turn into expected cash or are you encouraging your customers to take on more debt than they can handle? Don't make a deal with business vendors unless you are confident it will eventually turn into cash from your customers for your own company. This is why understanding the financial cash flow of your business is important for making wise decisions concerning your customers. Any incentive strategy must work for your customers as well as for your business. Make sure also that your sales force understands that providing such a mutual benefit is an overriding sales objective. An aggressive salesperson might otherwise make a deal where one shouldn't be made.

Who Carries the Paper?

Even when you are acting as the primary creditor in a transaction, you may not be the one who is sustaining all of the risk. As discussed earlier, you may want to sell off an account to a factor, a situation in which you get a discounted value of the sale and the factor does the collecting. Other loans are available from banks or commercial lenders allowing you to draw on the basis of your accounts receivable but leaving you responsible for collecting the debt. A customer's failure to pay would still be your responsibility and would result in a loss to your company.

Any company in a growth mode will find the funding of growing receivables a challenge to do by way of internal cash flow. One way to ease this strain is to use outside funding, but remember that your credit policy and collecting effort must stay in place. You will have to repay your business loan whether or not your customer pays you.

A Business Credit Application

Each company has its own way of handling an application for business credit. Of the scores of applications researched for this book, no two were quite the same. But there are some common questions that must be phrased properly to secure adequate information to make a good decision. Here are some questions you should ask:

1. The legal name of the company. Although some companies do not use an "Inc" or LLC as part of their operating name (though they should), you want to know exactly with whom you are doing business.
2. The date of the application. This is important to know, since you want to update the information on the application periodically.
3. The legal form of the business. Is it a partnership, corporation, LLC, etc.? Or is it a sole proprietorship, in which case you are really doing business with an individual? If so, ask for the owner's social security number.
4. Number of years in business.
5. Type of business. The more you know about your customers' operations and their need for credit, the more educated decisions you can make.
6. Name of the owner (if more than one, list all). You may also ask for each owner's percentage of ownership.
7. Business address.
8. Other locations where the business operates.
9. Name of bank and account number (you may need this for debt collection).

10. Trade references (at least four).
11. Home address of owner.
12. Phone number and fax number of owner.
13. Web site address and e-mail address of owner.
14. Tax Identification Number.

Your business credit application can be a simple document or as complicated as you and your advisors need to make it. If you are selling to large companies, they are not likely to fill out a requested form, although you can ask them questions and fill out one on your own. Smaller, closely held companies should be required to fill out the form in the owner's own handwriting and sign it as well. The owners are making representations you rely on in putting your money at risk, so such documentation must be requested and retained in case it is needed at a later date. If there are joint owners such as a husband and wife, you might ask them both to sign the application.

Personal Guarantees

Your company needs to review its credit policy and credit application with a legal advisor. In addition to asking the above questions, you want to include language that complies with the laws in your state. And you should add a section requesting the owners to personally guarantee the debt of their company. This means that if a business fails to pay its debt, its owner will be responsible. By signing this, your business customers will be further motivated to pay their bills. If you are a business vendor selling large-ticket items and your risk is high, you may also want to include language that allows you to "confess [file] a judgment upon nonpayment without further notice," which allows you to file a lawsuit. Remember that such laws vary by state and that you will need legal counsel to create a binding contract. In order for any clauses to be enforceable, they must be written clearly into the contract so that the signers know exactly what they are agreeing to.

When Personal Guarantees Don't Work

If a business owner is intent upon defrauding you, there are many ways to ensure this can happen, short of your requesting cash in advance.

Businesspeople can make themselves judgment-proof by managing to control little or nothing in their own names. As a new credit grantor, you may be pleasantly surprised at how friendly and cooperative your new business customers are in signing whatever assurance of payment you request. The owners know they are putting very little at risk, even as you believe you are minimizing yours.

What, then, can you do to protect yourself? One way is to ask the principals if they have ever held ownership in other businesses (the more they disclose, the more careful you should be). Another possibility is to secure a personal credit report even though you are granting business credit. You may even find a personal bankruptcy in a principal's past, which suggests this is a businessperson who knows the game and might use it to your disadvantage. Be cautious and follow your instincts.

Reading a Business Credit Report

There is a substantial difference between a business credit report and a personal one. Because there is a formatted structure in personal reports, virtually every account is reported and a defined credit score is given. This is not the case with business reports. They can be long, complicated, and in the end not easy to decipher. The worth of a company, on the one hand, and its ability and willingness to meet its obligations, on the other, may differ significantly.

Larger, publicly traded companies disclose extensive information to the general public, but their reports may tell you little about how they intend to pay their bills. This latter is usually a function of their business policy, a separate matter from their financial strength.

Smaller, closely held businesses make available far less in the way of information, but there are some key items to check. One in particular to look for: Is all the data on the business application (name, location, when the business started, and name of owner) the same as what shows up on the credit report? Clear up any discrepancies immediately. You shouldn't be afraid to ask any and all questions—ultimately it is your money and your business that is at stake.

What You Will—and Won't—See

The business credit report will include a listing of all pending legal action (including any prior bankruptcies). You need to check if a business' credit history has generated a number of lawsuits. In most states, the public filings of liens to secure assets (typically for payoff of loans) will also be listed. You need to review these details and have someone who understands them (your lawyer, accountant, banker, or in-house credit department) determine if this business customer is a good risk for credit. This report should be reviewed annually to check for changes.

You will also see a payment record reported by other creditors. Bear in mind that this part of the credit record is compiled only from those creditors who choose to respond, which might significantly influence the number. Unlike consumer credit reports in which the records of virtually all regular credit grantors are automatically included, a business credit report is a sporadic occurrence. Its history may reflect collective reports or may be skewed by credit information reported by one agency only. Business credit history is far too extensive for complete data to be available on any one report.

Try Industry-Specific Groups

A number of industry-specific groups manage credit functions as a protection for their members. Although their primary service might be an ability to carry out effective collections, they can also monitor customers' use of a certain service or purchase of a product. Being a member of such a credit association can inform you about a potential vendor's payment history, perhaps flagging a business's suspicious behavior.

Types of Credit: Short-Term and Long-Term

When you sell a single item to a customer, you get paid either at the time of sale or according to the terms of a credit account, which means usually by thirty days. This is short-term credit over a period brief enough that term conditions are unlikely to change for your customer.

Slow Down—Caution Signs Ahead

I have been a financial consultant to closely held companies for the past fifteen years. One of my clients was offered an opportunity by a general contractor to bid on a large construction job as a subcontractor. The general contractor was well-known but was not considered particularly reputable. We had two different credit reports drawn up, both of which indicated some red flags. For starters, the company operated under three different names. Also the amount of litigation against them was high. It seemed that they did not like making final payments. My advice was to walk away, but I could understand why my client did not want to do this. Here was a large contract with a potential for high profit and a chance to get into larger jobs.

My client's lawyer checked out the proper corporate name to use and drew up what everyone hoped would be a bulletproof contract. It wasn't. The job became disorganized and phase draws were only partially paid. My client left the job site before the project was complete, without seeing a dime of profit, though he did recover most of his costs. He immediately had his attorney release him from the contract or he would have been deeper in the hole, as far as putting in his time and materials without compensation.

Suppose you do an ongoing project for a customer who pays in phases over the course of a year or longer. Your long-term credit exposure could be risky because conditions may change drastically from the time you begin until you are fully paid. In order that you be paid for the cost of money you need to fund your portion of the job, you have to factor this additional amount into your original quotation. Make sure the benchmarks that trigger payment are clearly specified and you hold your customer to that schedule.

Getting Progress Payments

Any long-term job should specify payments that are made at regular intervals or when certain phases are complete. This process is very typical in construction and home improvement. You are paid an up-front amount (usually to cover the cost of material) and then as you complete the various portions of the work, you receive successive payments.

If there are changes or add-ons along the way, make sure these are spelled out in writing so there is no question about the total value of the contract and how current and future payments will be applied. A common challenge presented by a business customer is that many people may be able to draw on the credit you've issued to the company. Your responsibility is to maintain signatures that indicate proper authorization for alterations to the original contract.

Asking for a Deposit

There are a number of circumstances in which you want to ask your customer for a deposit at the time the order is placed rather than waiting until delivery. One example would be a special order of goods that you would be unable to return if your customer backed out. Whether you are ordering this product or manufacturing it, you need a special order policy. The customer should put down an amount close to the actual cost of the item so that you are fully covered. The amount of this deposit will differ on a case-by-case basis.

You also want to request a deposit in certain longer-term jobs, such as construction work, in which you must fully complete a discrete phase before requesting further payments. Once you are ready to purchase material, commit workers, and deploy equipment, you need to have money in hand. The amount of the deposit will vary depending on the type of work.

A Deposit Is a Liability

Be careful to use any deposit money for its requested purpose. Paying bills due to vendors or covering a payroll may leave you in the hole just as a new job arises. This is not a legal problem, but it eventually might become an operational one. In your accounting system, receipts that come from customers' deposits should not be recorded as sales; after depositing them in the bank you should list them as liabilities since they represent unmet obligations. When you have completed the work, the money is then earned, and at that point the cash becomes revenue. You should conduct your own internal progress billing to keep track of how well you are meeting your profit goals.

Make Sure Your Policy Is Evenhanded

There are far fewer controls governing the granting of business-to-business credit than for business-to-consumer credit. Individuals are protected under federal consumer laws, which are modified by state. Business recipients of credit are not subject to the same level of governmental regulation. The best policy in granting credit is to set up objective standards and stick to them consistently, lest others in your business see you deviate for a few customers and think the rules can be easily bent. Salespeople anxious to make a sale might then offer credit terms you are uncomfortable with, leaving you having to deny the customer. Misunderstandings are avoided if your terms of credit are standardized and no one can modify the policy except a financial person in charge. Business customers familiar with your credit policy are more likely to meet your standards.

TEST DRIVE

You must know the rules and the business strategy of extending credit to another company. Consider the following issues when establishing your credit policy:

- ➲ Will easier credit terms increase your profits (not just sales)?
- ➲ Can you afford to fund growing receivables?
- ➲ Do you require a fully completed business credit application?
- ➲ Do you understand how to read a business credit report?
- ➲ Are you fair and evenhanded in applying your policy to businesses?

Opportunities Through Foreign Trade

As if payment collection were not daunting enough in ordinary circumstances, you face additional considerations, even obstacles, when you do business in a foreign country. It is often worth the effort, though. The marketplace for goods and services abroad can be a fertile field, for the United States with just five percent of the world's population produces about one-quarter of the world's output. That our goods enjoy premier status in many industries indicates that much room exists for business growth through exporting.

In many fields, moreover, production outside the United States comes with such cost savings that importing can be a great source for labor-intensive products, thereby keeping your business competitive. This holds true not only in trades like textiles but also for components that can be integrated into your products.

If your company takes the safe and easy way by avoiding these foreign opportunities because of perceived risks or fear of an unfamiliar process, your competitors may gain an advantage and leave your business in the dust.

Despite the risks, there are tools you can employ to better manage such issues as currency volatility, different terms of credit, and the cost of pressing your case in foreign courts.

Foreign trade opportunities can be divided into three categories:

1. Your business purchases goods that originate in foreign countries.
2. Your business provides special material that is fabricated in a foreign country and returned for you to sell in the U.S.
3. Your business sells your goods (and perhaps services) in foreign markets.

In this chapter, we consider the various credit concerns and strategies you need to know when doing business according to each of these scenarios.

Scenario 1: Buying from a Foreign Firm

Most small businesses involved in foreign trade engage in this first option, buying standard goods whose material and labor have been provided by a non–United States company in a foreign market. Such foreign companies are often found in Asia, but they can be from Latin America or Africa as well.

The risk here is in making sure your goods are produced to the specifications needed by your business. If you are a small company buying from a large, respected company, then your risk is low. However, foreign markets also include small cottage-industry firms that sell to small U.S. businesses.

The best way to protect yourself is by drawing up a well-written and detailed purchase order. However, even this precaution cannot always protect you against goods that do not meet specifications or quality standards. In this case, your only available recourse is to hire legal representation in the foreign country and litigate. As you can imagine, this is almost always cumbersome and very expensive.

Three Ways to Mitigate the Risk

When purchasing goods from a foreign supplier, there are some things you can do to make a transaction less likely to end badly:

1. Factor in currency fluctuations. It is recommended that your payment be quoted in U.S. dollars. This passes the risk of currency fluctuation to the foreign seller. Unless your purchase is very large or the term of delivery is very long, most sellers will bear a short-term risk. If not, particularly if the risk of loss due to currency movement jeopardizes the profit on the goods bought, then a currency hedge may be necessary. If you think the value of the currency will rise, convert your dollars to the foreign currency at time of purchase and hold them as a hedge.

2. Purchase through a respectable U.S. importer. The downside is that this strategy adds another layer of markup to the price.

Also there may not be an area importer available for the product you are purchasing.

3. Agree that payment is due (and made) only after delivery and inspection. This is the best method because it carries nominal additional costs (even if there is a premium for extended payment terms). Unfortunately, most foreign businesses want to be paid before shipment.

Letters of Credit: Providing Assurance

In a foreign market, your bank's name may not be recognized by a vendor, especially if you are working with a small community bank. The first matter to find out is whether your vendor will accept a "letter of credit" (LOC) from your bank (known as the "issuing bank"). Letters of credit are financial instruments providing assurance that a U.S. (or global) bank is your payer. In effect, they substitute the bank's creditworthy name for your business's unknown credit standing. Or an importer can instigate a trading process on your behalf by having its bank provide a letter of credit. Then once the vendor has developed some track record with your company, it may be more willing to sell you an open order (one without the cost and additional paperwork of a letter of credit). Similar to vendor credit, the order is shipped and then invoiced on agreed-to terms.

The First Steps in Obtaining a Letter of Credit

If the vendor will not accept a letter of credit from your bank, you may need your bank in turn to have an internationally recognized bank (which will probably be a correspondent bank—a larger, money-center bank used as a silent partner by the smaller bank) either issue the letter or function as an "advising bank." This means that your bank provides assurance to the advising bank that your company can pay. This service requires an extra layer of paperwork and redundant fees. So if the vendor will accept a letter of credit from your bank, your cost and time to deliver this letter is minimized. Fees vary but they are usually one to three percent of the amount of the letter of credit, with extra fees for amendments.

Using Letters of Credit

The letter of credit will be accepted (that is, paid) only on submission of documents. These usually consist of a draft (sort of an international check), the shipping documents, and other required papers. The bank will not inspect your goods or even determine that what is shipped is what you ordered. Shipping has to be on a common carrier (not delivered by your vendor's truck) so that there is an objective document to verify that shipment has been made).

The letter of credit (which mirrors the terms of your purchase order) must specify:

- The amount of the letter of credit
- Whether payment is "on sight" (the most prevalent terms) or by delayed payment (say, sixty days after shipment or negotiation)
- Description and amount of goods
- Type of shipment
- Destination point
- Currency (U.S. dollars or other)
- When title passes ("Free On Board," "Shipping Point" or "Free on Board, Port of Entry")

This last detail will determine who provides insurance. The letter should also specify if there is to be one total shipment and payment (which extinguishes the letter of credit) or if partial shipments and payment (totaling the amount of the contract) are permitted. There should also be a termination date to the letter, in case no goods are shipped. Otherwise, the letter will stay outstanding and in force until negotiated or returned uncashed. If this deadline needs to be extended, it can be accomplished by an amendment.

If you as the buyer need to know that quality standards have been met, then the letter should specify that an independent inspector (in either the country of origin or at the destination) must perform the quality and specification assurance. The inspector's report (which is usually done at the expense of the buyer) then becomes one of the documents required for payment.

What Documents Do You Need?

The documents to provide for negotiating payment in a letter of credit transaction are usually the following:

1. Original letter of credit.
2. Draft for payment under the letter (either a sight draft paid at the time of presentment or to be paid a specified number of days after negotiation).
3. Copy of an invoice (optional, since the terms should be specified in the letter of credit).
4. Shipping document (usually an onboard bill of lading or air bill).
5. Other documents, such as inspection documents or (if required) certificates of origin or warranty documents.

Again, the accepting bank (either the issuing or the advising bank) will not do anything but inspect the documents to see if they are provided. They will not ascertain the validity of any document. If a fraudulent document is provided, the bank will pay regardless and leave it to you to seek recourse from the vendor or shipper.

Standby Letters of Credit

Increasingly standby letters of credit are being requested in business transactions, and not just for international trade. This practice basically substitutes a bank's credit standing for that of the buyers. Standby letters can be an inexpensive way to establish credit until a vendor will provide goods or services on open order. However, these letters do nothing to protect a buyer. The vendor can draw funds with a simple draft (or perhaps also with a statement, which can be used in later litigation if the vendor made false draws). The bank will pay upon presentment of the draft (and any required statement), even if the bank suspects that the vendor did not act in good faith. The only way to stop payment is to seek an injunction against having the bank pay; in that case, you as the buyer would have to present an overwhelming case to a judge that blatant fraud is involved.

Standby letters of credit must have a termination date, which is usually after a year. However, they can be automatically extended on this date, provided the bank notifies the vendor (on behalf of the buyer) thirty days before the termination date that the letter will not be renewed. The vendor has the right, at that time, to deduct the funds to cover any exposure that exists or will normally exist by the termination date. It actually is best to provide periodic letters of credit and forgo the automatic renewal.

How Banks Protect Their Interest

After issuing a letter of credit, a bank will want assurance that when the vendor presents a draft for payment, the buyer will have the money (cash) to make the payment to the bank. This is understandable, since the bank is committed to make the payment to the vendor if all of the terms of the letter have been met.

Nine times out of ten, this assurance involves providing the bank with cash collateral (via a deposit account under the control of the bank) for the total exposure to the bank. And the bank will continue to hold this collateral until the letter of credit exposure has been terminated by surrender of the original copy of the letter of credit. Full and final draw may also extinguish the letter of credit, but usually final draw requires the original copies supplied with the documents. If the termination date has passed and there has not been full draw, the bank will wait a reasonable period of time to make sure the documents are not in transit. There may be a clause in the letter of credit that states the termination date and the last day to present drafts and documents.

The bank may also provide a line of credit for the buyer, and thus it may make available a reserve under the line of credit to permit funds for the letter of credit payment. Customers with such lines of credit are those with excellent credit, a track record of good prospects, and good financial management.

Some companies purchase goods as part of a contract with another company. A contract loan (one written to provide funds to handle a single contract) through the bank (possibly one insured by the SBA) could provide the funds to pay the letter of credit when the components purchased from overseas are delivered.

What Bank Should You Use?

If the need to provide a letter of credit is an infrequent occurrence, your present bank, even if it does not have the staff or expertise to negotiate the drafts, can work through its correspondent bank that does. Working this way may cause an extra layer of fees, but this may be preferable to trying to find the right person at a very large bank to handle your situation. The fees should not be double, since your bank may cut its own fee (having less paperwork to do) or waive its fee altogether (due to its overall valuable relationship with you).

However, if you find the need to have frequent or large letters of credit, especially those that overlap), then perhaps you should open a relationship with a large international player.

As pointed out earlier, most drafts are paid on sight (on presentation and negotiation). If you need time to move the goods through your pipeline, you can ask the vendor for a time draft (that is, one payable after negotiation). The vendor can then sell the note at a lower price in the financial marketplace (the note at the lower price will then become the commercial paper of the large, well-known bank) and the vendor will get his money immediately. The vendor might add to his price the time value of this money (the discount), but you are, in effect, receiving trade credit. Again, however, your collateral will be tied up until the bank pays the draft.

As already mentioned, if your payment is in any other currency than U.S. dollars, you need to protect against a rise in price of the cited currency, probably by purchasing the currency immediately or by buying a future contract.

One final thought, before you get started on any foreign purchase: It is a good idea to ask your vendor for a pro-forma invoice at the start, just to have in writing what is expected of you upon shipment and delivery.

Scenario 2: Providing Material to Be Fabricated in a Foreign Country and Shipped to You

A good example of this type of foreign trade would be a U.S. company making exercise equipment that contracts to have a digital control fabricated in an Asian country. Some of the chips are proprietary and must be shipped to a foreign assembler, put together, and shipped back to the U.S.

All the aspects of a letter of credit can protect you in this type of transaction, except for the fact that your costs for the goods shipped to the foreign country are at risk. This risk comes not just from the credit risk of the foreign company that is doing the fabrication or assembly but also from unforeseen elements, such as civil unrest in the country, weather, and earthquake hazards.

You can buy insurance against the civil unrest, but Acts of God are difficult, if not impossible to insure against, at least at a feasible price. You may even be able to get a reverse letter of credit from the assembler to guard you against loss. But this may be a costly maneuver.

If the amount of the risk is immaterial, you might be better off just to self-insure—and hope for the best. You may have more at stake, though, if the component is an integral part of a finished product under a large contract and you have other costs associated with that contract. If this product has to be pre-positioned in the marketplace, for example, you could be out marketing and warehousing costs. And this exposure can be even greater if other material has to be simultaneously fabricated and combined with the piece that is assembled overseas. A small problem, delay, or failure to produce in the foreign market can snowball into a loss on the entire lot.

Scenario 3: Your Business Sells Your Goods or Services in Foreign Markets

In this situation, the main way to protect yourself against credit risk to the foreign purchaser or distributor of your goods (other than receiving cash for the order) is to require a letter of credit.

All aspects of the letter of credit discussed under Scenario 1 apply but in mirror image. Since your company will be receiving the letter of credit (as its beneficiary), you need to review the steps in that process.

If you do not use or cannot obtain a letter of credit from the purchaser, then you must use due diligence verifying the creditworthiness of the customer and the trade practices in the foreign country. Your situation may be one in which the sale amount is too small to warrant the extra cost and time delay of a letter of credit. Or you might test the waters with a small shipment. But if the amounts grow larger, you may also want to use letters of credit or use the U.S. Export-Import Bank, discussed next.

The Export-Import Bank and Your Business

The Export-Import Bank is a useful institution that exporters and their bankers can access to validate foreign trade transactions. Ideally, a seller can build on this to graduate to more conventional terms.

The Export-Import Bank, an agency of the executive branch of the U.S. government, has backed exports ranging from less than $100,000 up to the tens and even hundreds of millions of dollars. With an average transaction amount of $1.3 million, many small companies as well as multinational corporations use this resource.

An Export Credit Insurance Policy for small business exporters is available to encourage those new to exporting. This policy is used as:

1. A risk-management tool to insure against nonpayment by foreign buyers.
2. A way to extend competitive credit terms to foreign buyers.
3. A way to arrange attractive financing with the exporter's lender by using insured receivables as additional collateral.

The insurance policy covers:

1. Commercial losses due to insolvency and default (ninety-five percent coverage).
2. Political losses due to war and revolution.
3. Cancellation of import or export license.
4. Currency convertibility problems (or frozen currency) up to 100 percent.

To be eligible for the insurance policy, an export transaction must:

1. Consist of products with a minimum of fifty-one percent U.S. content. (Special terms are available for specific environmentally related products or services.)
2. Be completed in 180 to 360 days (a policy term is for one year) with a buyer in an eligible country.
3. Not be protected by a confirmed letter of credit.

To qualify, an exporter must:

1. Be a small business as defined by the SBA.
2. Have export credit sales for the previous two years averaging not more than $5 million.
3. Have at least one year of successful operating history and a positive net worth.
4. Perform a credit investigation of the buyer.

There are many other details about this program too numerous to list here. More information can be obtained from the Export-Import Bank *(www.exim.gov)*, the SBA, and the U.S. Chamber of Commerce.

Obtaining Credit Information on Foreign Firms

Obtaining credit information abroad, especially on smaller companies, is admittedly harder than in the U.S. Here are several sources that can help:

1. Business libraries. Several useful publications in this field are expensive to buy, but they can be researched through many large libraries with business divisions. Jane's Major Companies of Europe and Dun and Bradstreet's Principal International Businesses are two good sources, particularly for information on larger companies.

2. International banks. These banks have vast amounts of information they are willing to share to help their corporate clients. This resource is available for larger firms.

3. Foreign embassies and consulates. These institutions are anxious to promote trade and can offer valuable assistance.

4. Purchased credit reports. Dun and Bradstreet (DB) and Graydon International can offer reports on foreign companies, just as DB does on businesses in the U.S. However, the information can sometimes be dated.

5. Government agencies. Information on the stability of countries and even on industry trends in a particular country can be gleaned from the U.S. Department of Commerce and from other governmental agencies promoting international trade.

Other Information You Must Have to Go Global

You should be aware of several factors not strictly related to obtaining credit assistance when beginning to do business in a foreign country:

1. Do some research on business practices in the country. Often the art of negotiation and the timing and closing of a deal differ widely from what you have experienced in the U.S. In many countries, a large amount of time must be spent in laying the proper foundation for a business relationship. In Japan, for example, a good deal of ceremony is involved just in exchanging business cards. (You should receive your counterpart's business card in both hands and fully view it with respect, not just shove it in your pocket.) In Mexico, preliminary introductions should include inquiring after the family of your prospect, even when you have just met a businessperson.

2. Be aware of political and religious aspects of the country. In some countries strong religious affiliations predominate, so you should ascertain the religious holidays there. Just as businesspeople from other countries learn that not much business is conducted in the U.S. between Christmas and New Year's, you should be aware of other nations' holidays and not expect

to have shipments or business transactions take place on or around such days.

3. Although letters and e-mails can be used to communicate, transmitting via fax is best. Faxes are written documents, have a fast transmission period, leave a receipt that the communication was delivered, and can be used to send information even to remote villages.

4. Be courteous and friendly. Don't use slang that could be misunderstood, and personally sign all communications.

If your business practice is to treat your buyers and vendors with respect and sensitivity, to keep your promises, and to give the other side an incentive to work with you (for example, by offering prompt payment and quality at a fair price), not only will your business succeed in the U.S. but internationally as well. A big world full of opportunities awaits you out there.

▶▶ TEST DRIVE

Domestic credit alone is a complicated subject, but global credit comes with an entirely different set of challenges altogether. Are you prepared to take the step into foreign trade transactions? Ask yourself the following questions:

- ⮑ Do you know the cash requirements of a foreign purchase?
- ⮑ Does your current bank issue letters of credit?
- ⮑ How does a standby letter differ from a general LOC?
- ⮑ What can you do to check references of an international customer?
- ⮑ Are you familiar with the services of the Export-Import Bank?

Understanding Consumer Credit Laws

When you grant business-to-business credit, you will find that the criteria for making decisions and taking collection action are fairly broad and allow you to set your own rules. This is not the case when you are dealing with consumer credit. A number of federal laws govern the process, regulating the granting of credit to begin with and continuing through the collection process.

Be Aware of the Laws

The federal government oversees a vast set of acts intended for consumer protection, variations of which have been amended by the states. These range from the Equal Credit Opportunity Act, which addresses the criteria for determining whether to grant a customer a credit account, to the Fair Debt Collection Practices Act, which regulates the contact with an individual over a debt. The purpose of these laws is to protect consumers from unfair and discriminatory practices that existed in the past and that are still occasionally ignored. Violation of these laws may subject you to a number of civil sanctions and fines. This chapter includes a discussion of the Equal Credit laws. Appendix Three contains the text of the Fair Debt Collection Practices Act, which I strongly suggest you peruse. Further, you should review these laws with your company attorney.

After considering the complexity of understanding and administering consumer-credit laws, your company may decide not to grant direct credit to consumers. Consumers can use other forms of credit or debit cards with you without receiving direct credit from your company. Explore these alternatives first. For some products or services, however, customers expect you to offer payment plans and here the choices are limited.

Steps to Take

Begin by making certain that you are using a nonbiased determination of who receives credit and who is denied. You must learn what criteria you can legally use. In addition, you need to know what information you are allowed to report to credit bureaus and how to do so. Very clear laws regulate what is allowed in collecting a debt. These cover how and when to contact the debtor, how to verify that the person in fact owes the debt, and how to resolve the matter. You must also comply with laws regarding any errors in billing and actions to take to correct such problems when they are brought to your attention. Although laws against collection abuse are directed at collection agency violators, you would do well to follow them as guidelines. Penalties for credit discrimination may be directed at you as a direct creditor.

Applications for Consumer Credit

The questions you need to ask of a consumer are quite different from those you would ask of a business. You should require a social security number to assure you are granting an account to the correct person. In the interest of preventing identity theft, you should check a photo ID when you take a customer's credit application. Consumers should be able to secure some form of photo ID, even if they do not have a driver's license.

Information to request includes the following:

1. Full legal name
2. Full address and phone number
3. Number of years at location
4. Whether ownership or rental of residential property
5. Number of dependants
6. If at location less than two years, list the immediate past address

7. Source of income

8. Name of employer

9. Position or title

10. Years at job

11. Salary (gross per hour or month)

12. Other sources of income (only if you wish to consider these in accepting the account)

13. Other open credit accounts

14. Car payments

15. Social security number (a must!)

Your application must include language asking the applicant to give your company authorization to request and use consumer-credit reports in your credit evaluation process. You need written permission for this authorization.

You may be able to find a preprinted credit application form. Prior to using this in your business, however, have it reviewed by your attorney. Some forms do not conform with current federal law or the specific laws of your state.

Checking Credit Reports

Very extensive credit reports are available through three major credit entities: Experian, Equifax, and TransUnion. If you are a member of one of these bureaus, you can generate a report online in only a few moments. Although you have a right to review these reports on consumers, you must give a valid reason for accessing them. You will also be required to report on your credit experience with your clients. The rules regarding how and what you report are covered by the Fair Credit Reporting Act. These are regulations you need to review.

Consumer-credit reports contain an extraordinary amount of information that can verify a customer's current residence and current and past employment. All public filings including any past bankruptcies and account charge-offs are listed. A charge-off is an account that was deemed uncollectible and written off. You will find your customer's open credit accounts listed, including the level of open credit and the current amount owed. Payment history for the past twenty-four months is also recorded and whether payments were made on a current basis. You will see the total amount of consumer debt. Any negative action taken by a creditor will be listed on the report.

Credit Scores

Each credit-reporting agency assigns a score (a number usually ranging from 400 to 800+) to each report. These numbers, drawn from a large review of reports and weighing various factors, are predictive of a consumer's future credit payments. For the granting of standard credit, scores between 600 and 650 need more review, those over 650 are considered reasonable, and those over 700 are desired credit customers. Scores in the very high range around 800 may not necessarily be the best, possibly signifying that an applicant has received little credit in the past with no indication of how she would handle a large amount of credit. Applicants with very low scores of 450–550 are usually too risky for any independent business to carry unless it is set up to do so (such as operating a rent-to-own business).

Some elements that affect the actual score are:

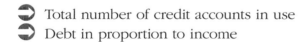

➲ Total number of credit accounts in use
➲ Debt in proportion to income

Not All Credit Is Equal

Secured debt such as a mortgage is not considered in a credit score, although the account information will be listed on a full report. Utility accounts are also listed but not considered in calculating debt ratios. Credit charge cards held in an owner's business name will not be included in determining a personal credit score. Businesses such as banks and large retailers have very specific rules about the range of scores they will accept. However, your company does not have to adhere to any specific rules other than the ones you set. If you know your customers well and want to take a risk, the decision is up to you. A consumer's credit score is only a number, and you can read the credit report to find out details.

⊃ Amount of available credit in use
⊃ Late payment history
⊃ Charge-offs (accounts never collected)
⊃ Length of credit history
⊃ Number of recent credit inquiries and new accounts

The Equal Credit Opportunity Act

Under federal law, there are a number of regulations you must follow both when responding to credit requests and when making decisions about the individuals to receive credit.

Personal factors you cannot characterize or consider include:

⊃ Sex
⊃ Age
⊃ Marital status
⊃ Race
⊃ National origin
⊃ Religion

Although you may ask some questions regarding personal information, such as seeking a person's date of birth for purposes of identification (since common family names may cause mistaken identity), you may not discriminate on the basis of age in offering credit unless an applicant is under the age of eighteen. You are expected to make your credit decision on the basis of a person's past credit history rather than on extraneous issues such as race.

A Review of the Elements of the Act

The Equal Credit Opportunity Act, known as ECOA, is meant to ensure that all consumers are given an equal chance to obtain credit. It does not require that everyone who applies be granted credit. Purely financial facts such as a customer's income expenses, debt, and credit history are valid considerations in not granting credit. The regulations cover the following issues:

1. When a customer's application for credit is made, a creditor may not . . .

   ⤵ Discourage an applicant because of age, race, national origin, marital status, or source of income.

   ⤵ Ask for information concerning race, sex, religion or national origin. You may ask about immigration status.

   ⤵ Ask about marital status other than whether an applicant is married or unmarried. Other details are not permissible.

   ⤵ Request information about a spouse except in cases when a couple is making a joint application, the spouse will be added to the account, or the primary credit seeker is relying on the income or alimony of a spouse.

   ⤵ Ask about plans for raising children.

   ⤵ Ask about alimony, child support, or other spousal separate maintenance agreements, unless the applicant is relying on any of these for income to meet credit standards.

2. A creditor may ask . . .

   ⤵ About marital status in the community property states of Arizona, California, Idaho, Louisiana, Nevada, New Mexico, Texas, and Washington.

   ⤵ Whether an applicant is paying alimony, child support, or separate maintenance payments.

3. When making the credit decision, a creditor may not . . .

   ⤵ Consider gender, race, marital status, religion, or national origin.

   ⤵ Base a decision on whether there is a phone listed in the name of the applicant.

   ⤵ Consider the age of an applicant unless:
      a. the applicant is too young to sign a contract in the state
      b. an applicant over age sixty-two is being given a favorable balance, meaning that they are eligible for adequate credit
      c. there is a significant drop in income due to retirement

4. When evaluating income, a creditor may not . . .

➲ Refuse to consider public-assistance income equally with other income.

➲ Discount income due to gender or marital status. When evaluating a couple, each income is counted at 100 percent.

➲ Discount or refuse to consider income from a part-time job, a pension, an annuity, or social security.

➲ Refuse to consider alimony or child support, although you may ask for verification of such income.

5. Applicants have the right to . . .

➲ Have credit in their own birth name or in the name of a spouse.

➲ Receive credit with a cosigner other than a spouse.

➲ Get credit without a cosigner if they meet eligibility standards.

➲ Retain their own accounts after they change their marital status or reach a certain age.

➲ Know whether an application was accepted or rejected within thirty days of filing a request.

What to Ask?

Questions that you may not ask on a credit application include ones of sex, race, religion, or national origin. You may ask if applicants are married or unmarried but not if they are divorced or widowed. Additional questions about a spouse may be asked only if you are being asked to add this person to the account.

And there are questions about total household income that may be asked only if the applicant is asking that an additional resource be considered as income for the purpose of receiving the credit. Alimony and child-support payments are included in this gray area. When establishing consumer-credit policy for your business, you need to check with an attorney to make sure you are in compliance with state and federal law.

Explaining Why Credit Was Refused

Under the Equal Credit Opportunity Act, you must accept or reject any application for credit within thirty days of the application. If you reject an application, you must state specifically why you are taking that action. If you deny credit based on information from a credit report, you must furnish the name of the company issuing that report along with the reason for your denial. Indefinite or vague reasons are not acceptable. Any applicants refused credit on the basis of a credit report have a right to see that report in order to dispute any items reported in error. If you are closing or limiting a customer's account, the same rules apply as far as the need to give a full explanation of why you are taking such action.

All of these requirements are meant to ensure that all consumers have equal access to credit. This is the primary reason you must set your own consumer-credit policy in advance.

What Rights Applicants Have When They Suspect Discrimination

If any applicants feel they have not been treated fairly, they may appeal to you for a review. At that point it is critical you recheck your process to make sure you have followed the law. As a creditor you may then proceed to the attorney general's office in your state or even take action to federal court. Whether you win or lose, this will be a costly battle. If your denial of credit is demonstrated to be part of a pattern of discrimination against any group of individuals, the injured parties may join together and file a class-action suit. Set up your consumer-credit policy according to accepted standards so you can prevent these complications.

Can You Use Third-Party Financing?

The easiest way to make credit terms available to your customers without needing the structure of a credit department is simply by accepting credit and debit cards. This is sufficient for the needs of most small companies. In fact, many service companies that did not previously offer this charge option have found themselves billing for work done and then waiting for weeks to get paid. Offering your customers the chance to put product

Inside Track	Putting High-End Items Within Reach

Karlin's Kitchen and Bath Design Center was an installer of high-ticket new gour-met centers and luxury baths. They had potential customers who desired their work but couldn't quite afford it. To facilitate sales to them, the company estab-lished a relationship with a mortgage company that found home equity loans of good value for new customers. The mortgage broker appreciated the referrals, and as a result Karlin's could sell higher-price designs to more of their customers. The only challenge for this business was that often they had to submit invoices to the mortgage company for draws against work completed. This would not have been necessary had these customers borrowed a line of credit against the equity in their homes.

charges on their personal credit cards can save your business the cost of bookkeeping and make the funds readily available. The cost to consider is the one to three percentage points charged by credit-card companies. You can also use this same system to accept debit cards, and the charge is slightly smaller.

You can also make use of finance companies that take applications from your customers and make loans for specific purchases, such as for carpet or furniture. Your customer borrows money from the finance com-pany and makes payments to them. You receive the proceeds from the purchase. There is seldom any additional cost to you because you are a good source of referral business to the finance company. Your customer pays the established cost of the credit.

Collecting Through Professional Firms

Throughout this book we focus on handling credit and collection func-tions in-house, since many companies choose to become directly involved in these issues. If you are a consumer-based business with an occasional credit problem with customers, you need to find a good professional agency early in the game and refer most of your collection work to them. You can still send out a customer statement and perhaps a payment reminder. But because the regulations governing consumer-credit col-lection are so strict (and professionals have learned how to be effective), in this case it may be more prudent for you to outsource your collection process from the start. If you are a small consumer-based business, outsourcing collection functions might lower your administrative costs and increase the percentage of recovery.

Debt Collection from Consumers Is Complicated

If you are concerned about complying with all the regulations under the Equal Credit Protection Act, you also need to review the details of other federal laws concerning credit. These range from the Truth in Lending Act to the Retail Installment Sales Act to the Federal Debt Collection Practices Act. Some of the rules apply to you, as the direct credit grantor, and others apply only to any third-party collector you hire.

When you are selling to individuals rather than to other companies, you must follow a particular set of strategies. How well do you know the rules? Consider the following:

- Have you looked at the applicable consumer laws?
- Do you know what you can and cannot ask on a consumer-credit application?
- Can you interpret consumer credit scores?
- Do you grant credit in compliance with the Equal Credit Protection Act?

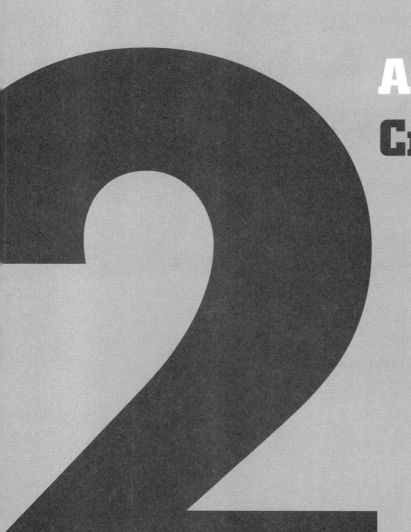

2

An Effective
Credit Policy

How Much Credit Can You Provide?

From the day you begin offering credit to customers, you must consider all of the aspects of your credit policy, starting with how much credit to extend and on what basis (the terms of the account). Be well aware of the total cash flow due you at any time. Your labor or the product you sell is the lifeblood of your company—make sure it is safe. Money not collected is a direct bottom-line loss.

How much credit you can afford to extend to your customers is a very serious question for any company, no matter how long (or briefly) you have been in business. You have bills to pay as well as wages that are due, and these obligations must be met in a timely way. If your accounts receivable are running too high and your bank account is running too low, meeting your obligations won't be easy to do. Cash businesses such as most retail stores are easier to operate than those that hold a lot of open credit. The only danger with a flush cash-flow business is that when cash is coming in you can mask downward trends, which may not be good for the company in the long term. The airline industry is flush with cash in a sea of red ink. They receive money now for flights that may be months away, so the cash crunch isn't felt. This cash flow falls into the category of deposits.

A growing company that offers credit may find itself short of cash as sales and expenses grow and payments are delayed. So you need to start the process to determine how much credit you can safely finance with a realistic cash-flow statement. If you have bank financing in place to draw on, you can extend more out in credit, but you still should not increase your risks.

Beyond the actual need for cash, a second consideration is the management structure that you require to administer an effective credit department. Checking new applications, setting reasonable limits, and watching accounts that are getting overdue is an important job. If you cannot afford to put some serious emphasis on this function, you cannot afford to be a credit grantor. This is a role that needs to be filled by a professional who is given some authority, rather than assigned to an office manager, clerk, or even to yourself.

An Ohio-based industrial distributor called me to talk about his business, which he described as "close to bankruptcy." "I don't understand it," he told me. "My accountant tells me we have been making a profit, but I can't pay any of my bills."

I made an appointment to spend an entire day at his office, but it took me less than forty-five minutes to discover his problem. His sales ran around $45,000 per month, but his accounts receivable totaled almost $200,000. Worse yet, the majority was over ninety days; thirty-five percent had balances that were less than the original invoice total, meaning only partial payments had been made and the rest of the money was unlikely ever to be collected. Writing these amounts off could actually have caused this company to fail, yet this situation could have been prevented if someone had been careful with the credit aspect of the business. The company weathered the problem but not without substantial pain. An aggressive collection effort brought in cash but ruffled many feathers including those of his sales force. Some customers realizing they had been taking advantage of their payments due paid quickly, while others resented the collection request and took their business elsewhere.

Who Will Handle Credit Checks and Decisions?

Having a designated manager in your company to handle the review of credit applications, credit reports, and references and then make the credit-granting decision is good policy. A company with clearly defined lines of authority is likely to create and support a credit department without question. A company with power centralized in the office of the owner will find this to be a problem. This latter situation is particularly the case in a sales-driven organization. The individual sales associates (who are usually more intense if they are commissioned) may appeal to a higher authority (the owner) to allow their customers to raise their level of purchases even if doing so takes them over their established credit limit. The question is this: Who will review existing credit information to make sure that increasing a customer's credit limits is a safe decision? These issues need to be handled with careful thought and consistency, and any nonconforming deals shouldn't be made on the spur of the moment. Never set up your sales force as the adversary of your credit department. The two areas need to work together.

Credit Training Is Important

A variety of organizations exist that do training in office procedures. These range from management associations to community colleges to private, for-profit trainers. All types of administrative issues are covered, from time management to credit management. You might even try your local credit bureau or credit-management associations. Any of these can provide seminars on how to set up and effectively run a credit department. Such programs are likely to include advice on authority and how to set up procedures for decision making. Why establish the function of credit manager if no one will pay attention?

Know What Your Customer Is Buying

Setting an initial credit limit with a business involves more than taking into account the basic information on a credit report. You start with the assumption that the company you are selling to is a legal entity that has assets and resources to operate a business. The next consideration is how much of your product or service they will use over a specific period of time. For example, a restaurant that uses $5,000 worth of seafood each month may need credit from their supplier only slightly above that limit. They turn their sales dollars quickly and should not have to go beyond a thirty-day need. When their purchases grow too high, they are falling behind, buying supplies beyond their current needs. Money that should have been used to pay for the food is going somewhere else.

A furniture store that sells a variety of products including yours may have items in stock for sixty to ninety days before a sale. With monthly sales of $3,000 from your product, this customer may need a $6,000 limit. Any more credit and their cash is likely to be diverted from paying your bill to pay others.

Knowing what your customers are buying and how your products or services move through the customer's own business operations is a key element in setting a credit limit, and in monitoring it as well. The success of most small businesses is based on understanding what a customer wants. Add to that a knowledge of how much credit your customer needs and you will be a valuable asset to your business.

An Override Policy

Many database accounting programs allow you to be alerted when new sales take customers over their established credit limit. This should trigger a stop to a customer's sale until the current account and the new purchase amount have been reviewed and someone in authority has decided that overriding the limit is prudent business. This is not something you should allow to happen without a responsible person in the company being alerted. The reason to set a limit on credit is to limit your exposure, so that you don't increase a customer's limit thoughtlessly. Even good, steady customers can get in over their heads so that you as the creditor are paid slowly, if at all. A quick phone call to a customer to ask for a payment or to find out what has generated this increase in credit activity may be all you need to do.

Making a Temporary Adjustment

What do you do when a steady customer suddenly places a very big order? You don't want to have the credit denied without thought and lose the sale. This is the time for a friendly phone call and a quick judgment about what is going on. The script may go something like this:

> "Bob, we just received your last purchase order, and we appreciate the extra business. But I notice that it will take your open account to over $20,000. I just wanted to discuss this with you."
>
> "What do you need to know? Haven't we always been a good customer?"
>
> "Of course, and I'm happy to see the growth in your account. I was just wondering if we could expect payment on this new order in forty days, which is your normal cycle."

You want to be gracious and show your customer that he is valued but also that you monitor the open accounts. But perhaps you will want to do this order on a trial basis.

> "Bob, I'm increasing your credit limit for this order. In a few weeks let's discuss what your future needs will be. We are glad to be a part of your success."

You've kept the customer and his business and protected your own interest. A customer who gets turned down without comment is likely to look for a new and more cooperative supplier.

Personal Guarantees

If your company did not start out with its customers by securing written credit applications with personal guarantees attached (discussed in Chapter 7), does that mean you have no chance of getting such a guarantee at a later date? Not at all. Perhaps you have a customer who has a credit line of $5,000. Early on, this amount seemed to meet her needs, but recently you have needed to authorize larger amounts to cover incoming orders.

Now might be the time to call the business owner to thank her for the recent business and ask for ways that you can continue to grow together. At the same time, bring up the subject of credit limits and how you would like to raise hers to cover all of the expected needs. (If you have a formal credit department, communicating with customers about current and future requirements might be one of its regular tasks.)

Then you might request some updated credit information and ask your customer if she would be willing to sign a personal guarantee. Most small-business owners will understand this request. They almost certainly have signed personally at the bank and with other vendors as well. Simply let your customer know that this extra guarantee raises your comfort level and that of your lender.

Periodic Recheck and Review

You should maintain a credit file on each one of your customers that contains their original application (and any signed guarantees) and a copy of their credit report. Any trade credit references that were sent to you should also be included, along with copies of any letters you sent them stating terms, limits, or asking for payment. Your money is at risk, and you want to document everything you can.

Let Customers Know You Pay Attention

What is the value of personal guarantees? The reality may not be as relevant as the perception. When you as a company principal make individual contact with your customer to discuss credit and personal guarantees, you are then placing the issue of credit and payment on a one-to-one basis. All businesses make regular choices over which bills to pay and you want to do what it takes to get to the front of the line and stay there, as far as your customers' priorities are concerned. A conversation that shows that credit is one issue that receives your personal attention may aid this process. A customer will often find it easier not to pay a big impersonal company than one where she knows the people and has personal relationships—such as with you.

Some credit-reporting services will send out alerts whenever there is a meaningful change in the status of a company. This could include any filings of lawsuits or liens (particularly tax liens) that have occurred. When it comes to your larger-credit customers, subscribing to such a service can provide some protection. Business sales and restructuring are going on all the time. The rush of airline bankruptcy filings, for example, hurt vast numbers of small vendors.

For each of your credit accounts, you must have a policy that requires someone to review the file and recheck the credit report. A slowdown in payments should trigger this action as well, because once a company has gotten delinquent, future payments may become increasingly delayed or in doubt.

An astute online researcher is able to check for any public filings without the cost of paying for a new credit report. Such a search would pick up lawsuits or tax actions. You can also subscribe to online credit services that will let you review many credit reports for a flat monthly fee. If when you examine a business customer's report the credit information matches your record of payments, then no action is required on your part. A noticeable variance in activity requires further attention. The earlier you catch up with any new trends or obstacles, the smaller your exposure will be and the safer your money may be as well. The business environment changes rapidly, and you want to stay ahead of the curve.

Recheck Trade References

One way to verify whether your customer has remained creditworthy is to contact the references listed when the account was first opened. Ask the contact about your customer's credit limits and whether payment terms have been met. Learning that "Company A is no longer a customer" tells you that the time has come to take a closer look at the account. Try sending the following letter to your customer, and after you receive updated information, conduct a credit analysis as if this were a new customer:

Company A
Attn: Accounts Receivable

Dear Sir/Madam:
We are currently in the process of updating our credit files. This is our standard procedure and not a result of any changes in your account with us. We are enclosing a copy of a credit update form and would appreciate it if you would fax or mail it back at your convenience.
Sincerely,

John Smith
Controller
ABC Supplies

Always Consider Customer Service

The job of a credit department is to meet the needs of providing cash for your business while still being customer friendly. The credit department is not the collection enforcer. Whether you are responding to a customer because it has been a while since you have performed a review or because the account indicates erratic payments, you want to be polite, earnest, and thank the company for its business. The reputation of your company is built on how you treat people, and this includes customer treatment by your credit department.

When to Raise and When to Lower Limits

Example: You've had a business customer for a few years that buys regularly and pays its bills on time. You have an internal credit limit on the account, and though the business comes close, it never exceeds the amount. Perhaps now is the time to raise that number and use this raising of the credit limit as a customer incentive for further business. Try a letter as follows:

XYZ Corporation
Attn: Purchasing

Dear Sir:
We at ABC Manufacturing appreciate the opportunity to be of service to your company and the efficient way you handle your account. We want you to know that we are able to provide a higher credit amount to your company should the need arise. Please feel free to call us if we can be of assistance.
Sincerely,

ABC Manufacturing
John Smith
Controller

Having good customers is a necessity for any company, and the credit department has a part to play in customer satisfaction.

In other cases you might want to lower the risk you have with a business by reducing its credit limit. Here again you still want to keep the customer's business. Make sure that your communication contains a message such as this:

Triple A Construction Company
Attn: Credit Department

Dear Jim:
We conduct an annual review of our financial results including taking a look at our outstanding receivables. We notice that payment on your

Inside Track

Courtesy Counts

I had a contractor business client who was doing a major home renovation scheduled over four months that turned into a year. Several times during this process my client fell behind in making payments to its suppliers. Of all the collection letters he received, the one he remembered was similar to the letter just presented: It dropped his credit limit yet was still courteous and friendly. Everyone got paid in the end, and the supply company that was supportive is now my client's largest vendor. Your goal is to collect your money and keep your customer. I am always amazed by very rude collection letters sent over very little money. That makes the polite ones stand out. And I have not seen rude letters secure any better results than ones that are courteous while remaining firm.

account has been late a number of times. Cash flow is one of the toughest areas to manage in a company, and we have determined that our level of outstanding credit is too high at this time. We are taking action on this matter as follows:

We have reduced your credit limit from $10,000 to $6,000 as of January 1st. We hope you understand our reasoning and will feel free to call us if you have special needs. We will review this account in six months.

We value your business and hope we can continue to prosper together in the future.

Sincerely,

John Smith
Controller

▶▶ TEST DRIVE

Have you started to formulate the elements of your company's credit policy? Ask yourself if the following issues have been decided:

 How much credit can you allow?

Are you rechecking a business credit report to make sure you are minimizing risk?

Are you handling customer communication politely?

Can You Cover Your Costs?

Being a direct credit grantor is always a risk. Any cash that you don't receive in your hand at the completion of a sale or a project doesn't become a sure thing until the account is paid in full. You want to run your credit policy with the recognition that cash flow is a balancing act. You cannot risk the future of your company by taking unnecessary risks.

When you developed a business plan for your company, you may have included a pro-forma statement indicating how sales revenue would cover the costs of operations. In a statement of cash flow, you break down this sales revenue into cash sales and collections from accounts receivable, which together comprise your total available cash (unless you borrow or invest additional capital).

Out of this cash flow, you have to pay for labor, materials, and overhead expenses such as rent and utilities. At the end of each month, you carry over your remaining cash (either positive or negative) to use as the starting cash for the next period. If you are not collecting your credit accounts on a thirty-day basis, you are likely to have a shortfall in paying your own bills. Some of your expenses (such as wages) will be paid immediately and others will be paid over time. The longer it takes you to collect on your accounts, the longer it will take you to pay your expenses.

When setting up your own credit guidelines, your first determination is this: Will your cash sales and those credit payments you are fairly secure about receiving be enough to pay for all of your costs? If not, you might be running your business for the benefit of customers rather than yourself, in which case you better change the strategy quickly before there is no company to run. Cash flow may take a few months to stream in, but if it doesn't happen within a reasonable time you will face a credit crunch. Money you borrow directly to fund receivables is owed by you rather than by your customers. If they do not pay, then you must do so.

Constant Cash for Constant Needs

Joe Gallagher ran an industrial painting company that worked on water towers throughout the eastern United States. The customers were mostly industrial and municipal water authorities. The jobs were big, and there wasn't a good deal of competition. Perhaps the reason for that was something Joe learned the hard way: Ongoing expenses for this work were high, and the payment cycle was slow. Men on the road needed expense money plus their regular wages, and they often worked overtime. These labor costs were paid weekly even though business customers traditionally paid only one progress payment and a final one after job completion. The lag could be up to ninety days. The business grew, and the profits were good on the income statement, but the cash was so slow that Joe ran out of it, his bank lost confidence, and the company failed. And once the company wasn't operating, a number of the customers refused to make their final payments. Make sure your ongoing cash flow is sufficient to pay your ongoing needs.

The Difference Between Secured and Unsecured Credit

When a bank lends you money, it usually secures this with collateral such as your inventory and equipment or perhaps some real estate. This gives them the right to foreclose or repossess your assets to liquidate their loan. This lowers their risk, because they have eventual recourse.

On the other hand, your business as a vendor to another company is not typically secured by any collateral. If your customer refuses to pay, you have no right to take any of its assets—unless you go through lengthy and sometimes costly court proceedings to secure a judgment against the company. You can then execute a judgment against tangible properties. That is, if there are no liens ahead of yours.

One way to change this status is through a consignment deal in which you retain ownership until a product is sold. You may not be able to act quickly enough to grab proceeds after a sale, but you could take back all remaining inventory on hand and so lessen your loss.

The point here is this: For the most part, credit is about good intentions and not the force of law. Knowing your credit customers well and working with them to keep their accounts current is a far more effective use of time and effort than implementing a punitive and tough collection policy. Don't let it get to that point.

The Value of a Personal Guarantee

We have referred to the strategy of adding a personal guarantee to a business credit application, or of asking for one at a later time when reviewing a business customer's credit. Such a guarantee has more of a psychological effect on the individual taking responsibility for a debt to your company than any actual value in law. In fifteen years of business consulting, I have seen only a handful of cases in which the legal enforcement of a personal guarantee resulted in meaningful cash.

If a company is owned by an individual who alone signs a personal guarantee, the only assets you can attach (and then only after *all* legal proceedings have concluded) are those in the individual's own name, rather than any owned jointly with a spouse or partner. Although a bank often asks for a spouse or a partner's signature (which they only sometimes are able to obtain), you are unlikely to do so without looking as if you don't trust a potential customer. The credit applications of large credit grantors such as office supply and construction supply companies require only a single signature.

And regardless of any signature you have, it still takes a lawsuit to turn a claim into a legally binding judgment. You will have to cover attorney's fees and filing costs in advance, and your debtor has the right to defend and appeal. Depending on the circumstances, this can be time consuming as well as costly. And then you have to *collect* your judgment. This doesn't mean you shouldn't include such a request for a guarantee; just don't consider it as legal assurance.

Securing a Confession of Judgment

There is an even higher level of protection you can seek before granting credit to a new business customer. Along with signing a personal guarantee, the customer agrees to sign a "confession clause," which gives you the

> ## You Need Legal Advice
>
> When it comes to the legality and language of guarantees and confessions, you need to thoroughly review your options with your company lawyer. If what you have in writing does not conform to the laws of your state (which vary), you will be unable to enforce either a guarantee or a confession of judgment. As is usually the case, if people are intent on not paying, they can find a way to slide out of most actions filed against them, or at least delay these by a legal defense or appeal. Your attorney can advise you on the governing laws in your state and the period of time it takes for claims to proceed through the system.

right to file a judgment without having to take further legal action. I have seen this clause invoked at times in the construction industry but in few other places. The same rule for a personal guarantee applies to a single signature. If the confession clause is not signed by both parties holding joint property, you can collect the judgment only on any asset held by the party that signed. A judgment can be executed against money or property of any value that is then sold to satisfy the creditor. You usually send a sheriff physically to attach the property you plan to take. If you have a business customer's banking information, you can also go directly to the bank and lay claim to a cash balance.

Consumers Do Not Sign Confession Clauses

With the exception of bank loans (including mortgage notes), consumer credit does not include a confession clause, for the reason that it is not legal under the laws of most states. Because an individual account holder is personally liable, confessions of judgment are not applicable on nonbusiness credit applications. Most consumer protection laws are meant to assist individuals from being taken advantage of by sophisticated creditors, which means that a collection lawsuit has to be filed before a judgment can be issued. This process allows individuals to protect themselves by means of invoking a formal defense in any legal actions taken against them. They will get time to respond to a collection suit in case there are reasons that the credit was not paid such as failure on the part of the company.

Evaluating Trade Credit References

On the business credit application you ask for the names of a customer's trade creditors. Customers will normally supply you with the names of current accounts, so don't expect much in the way of negative comment. What you want to take note of is the length of time customers have had open credit and the highest amount of their credit limit. Does this limit seem sufficient for the types of products or services being purchased? If it seems too low, perhaps an applicant is being watched, and you should do so as well by granting a smaller starting amount.

You also might try a random check of another industry supplier that would seem to be a logical creditor even if it isn't listed. Typically you fax a form for the business's credit department to return. You may uncover some information your applicant did not want you to know. Make your form look reasonably random, not specifying that this business has been used as a reference.

Checking Personal Credit References Requires Permission

Before you can review the credit report of an individual and request further references, you must have signed permission to do so. In the case of a business, the information is more open and public, but indi-

---

No Information May Not Necessarily Be Negative Information

Sometimes a trade reference may not be forthcoming with information. A responding company may be reticent about reporting any negative information in their files that could cause you to deny credit to a mutual customer. Most companies these days worry about being sued and so report only minimal information.

Or it could signify a competitive tactic on the part of a business, if you both sell or supply similar goods or services. You might therefore consider little or no response as a neutral rather than negative piece of information. Rely on that which you can establish, not what you assume. If information is scarce, return to your original customer and ask for more.

---

viduals have a right to protect and control their privacy. With the recent explosion of identity theft, some people as protection freeze their credit reports from all review. A lack of permission might also preclude checking on a customer's employment and landlord history.

Checking a Bank Reference

You do want to know where your customer banks, since this could become critical information in a collection action. But recognize that banks hold their account information in confidentiality. So all you are likely to find out is that a customer has an account with a bank, along with general information on the average balance retained and whether a borrowing relationship has been established. Make sure you have your applicant's approval before approaching any bank with a request for a reference. You should also keep copies of checks you receive to know where customers do their banking, particularly if a situation has recently changed. Ask business customers for the names of their bank officers; some companies have a particularly good relationship with their bank, which is a good sign. You may be able to make a call to find out more about the company and its owner.

Out-of-State Credit

For your local customers, you should drive by their places of business and actually see how they are doing. If you have sales representatives in the area, you can ask them to conduct site visits and provide information about the business location. They can look at displays or inventory levels and evaluate the physical condition of the premises. This can be a very instructive procedure.

You can judge your customers' level of success by whether they keep their places of business in good repair and well-staffed. On the other hand, you also want to know if they seem to be spending unnecessary money on extravagant offices or luxury autos. Those may be signs not so much of success but of excess, which may tell you to proceed cautiously in granting credit.

Talk to Your Banker about Credit

If you are among the fortunate companies to have astute bankers as a resource, use them. Discuss with them how they make credit decisions and learn what you need to know about their process. Typically, a bank takes into consideration the cash flow of a business, its history with credit, and a matter they call "character." This last refers to the personal ethics of the business owner. Your banker, who will be impressed with your diligence, can teach you what signs to look for in a customer and how to make informed decisions.

For business customers separated by physical distance and with whom you have little contact, you need to take time to check a full credit report, including local real estate records to discover if a business owns its premises. Make an effort to gather a reference from the local Better Business Bureau. Find out if there have been complaints about a company, particularly about its handling of refunds, which can indicate its financial condition. You need to do all the research you can to prevent any credit loss. Collecting past-due accounts from another state may prove costly because of tracking down local references. For the most part, sending letters and making calls from your out-of-state business will not generate results, so have your existing collection agency provide research information.

Asking for Financials

If your business customers are requesting substantial amounts of credit, but you haven't been able to obtain sufficient positive references, the next step is to ask for a copy of their recent financial reports. Some privately held companies may refuse this request on grounds of confidentiality, which is understandable; such documents contain information they do not want competitors to see. From your perspective, however, if you are going to risk your own company's financial future by extending terms to another business, you are entitled to sufficient information to make a qualified decision. Always be gracious and friendly with a business even when this request is denied. You want to try to keep your customer and a possible sale if you can do so safely. And consider how reluctant you might be to release your financials. Nevertheless, impress on your customers that you are making a financial investment in their companies and need to be protected.

What to Look For in Financials

Most business owners in looking at financial statements go directly to the profit (or loss) section. This is an important factor to consider, since profitable businesses should be able to pay their bills as they come due.

There is an additional section to review, one located on the business's balance sheet. You want to compare current assets (cash, accounts receivable, and inventory) with current liabilities (accounts payable and current loans due). The resulting sum describes the solvency of the company, meaning its ability to meet current obligations (such as the money owed to your company) out of cash flow from collections and sale of inventory. If you know a business well, consider how current and salable its inventory is. Some companies never write off old inventory no matter how unlikely to sell.

▶▶ TEST DRIVE

Credit always involves risk, but you can minimize yours if you consider the following:

➲ Will your costs of granting credit be covered?
➲ Can you secure a personal guarantee that will be effective?
➲ Do you know how to evaluate trade or bank references?
➲ Are there other indicators of business creditworthiness?
➲ Do you know what to review in a company's financial statements?

Allowing Customers to Buy According to Their Need

When you are selling to consumers, you don't want to appear as if you are motivating them to get into debt over their heads. (This is true even though most of the risk is held by a credit card company.) Selling to another business puts you in more of a partnership position. You want the sales of a customer's business to grow along with yours, but to the extent that you put its cash flow at risk, you are at risk of not being paid yourself. At the same time, when you show support to a new venture, you are more likely to be rewarded with long-term loyalty.

Prudent companies purchase items and services that help them run their businesses more profitably or serve their customers more efficiently. This is the way you should be learning to operate your own company. What you learn about the effective use of loans and vendor credit for your own business helps you in offering credit to your business customers. And in turn their success enhances yours.

Knowing What Your Customer Is Using Your Product For

A customer who purchases something on credit from you that its business will turn quickly into cash does not need the extended level and terms of credit that another company needs to purchase items for inventory that take a longer time to sell. In practice, when your customer gets paid, you should get paid. This means you should understand the use and value of your own product or service to your customer and grant credit limits accordingly. A client who uses credit from you to generate working capital is likely to have such a strategy eventually catch up with him, so that you may not be paid at all.

First you must understand the general credit requirements of your industry and of your market, and then learn the specific needs of your customer base. Make sure that your credit policies are in synch with this knowledge. If you have to fund exceptionally large receivables, the cost of your own debt will affect your bottom line.

Knowing Industry Cash Flows

A restaurant sells off most of its perishable goods in a matter of days, and their cash comes in quickly; even credit-card purchases should be in their account within forty-eight hours. If you are a food supplier who is not receiving regular payments, your money may be at risk.

If you are selling material to manufacturers, they may require weeks to process the shipment and more time to produce finished goods. Then they sell their product, ship it, and finally collect from their own customers. The entire cash-flow cycle may take sixty days or more, during which time their payments come to you from working capital or bank funding rather than from collection of receivables.

Perhaps one of the most financially complicated and challenging industries is in home remodeling, in which a contractor receives a deposit equal to or exceeding the costs of materials for the job. Even with this prepayment, a contractor seldom offers any deposit to its own suppliers. Only when its progress payments come in will the contractor begin to pay its supply bills. You may be paid from a contractor's deposits for new jobs instead of with payments from a job you supplied.

Credit Limits Should Recognize Needs

Let's consider the first situation just discussed. A restaurant with sales of $1 million may have food costs of thirty-five percent, which means its annual food purchases are $350,000 or $29,000 per month. If you are supplying twenty percent of its food, this would total slightly less than $6,000 per month. That should be your credit limit, because if the business owes you for more than thirty days of food it is using your money to pay its rent and wages.

The same formula applies to the manufacturing company. If their material costs are $600,000 per year and you are supplying fifty percent, that is $300,000 and a 60-day credit limit may take you as high as $100,000. You might want to be paid more quickly, but your collection would be constrained by the reality of your customer's normal cash-flow cycle.

The toughest call to make is when you know your business customer has been paid in advance or along the way, yet you have not received your share. This is where open communication and the exchange of financial

Giving Things Away Is Easy

If your credit policy is too generous or even sloppy, you may find that sales come very easily. Customers who know they won't be forced to pay on time—or even at all—will be happy to take all the credit you have to offer. They won't worry about price because it doesn't matter. By the time you get around to shutting down a customer's account, the business could be making purchases from a new supplier. You then have no leverage to secure payment. I have known companies in this position on account of poor record-keeping and lack of attention. Sadly, such companies are often funded with the owner's personal funds, money he has worked hard to earn in advance. Or an owner works harder to complete more jobs because so many of these do not ultimately pay.

data between businesses come into play. If your customer's credit is funding growth, you may both prosper. If the business practice is thereby backfilling old debt, the outcome is unlikely to benefit either of you.

Special Deals Require Special Terms

There are a variety of reasons why a company might offer its customers a special deal, whether in the price of products or services or with credit terms. It could be just to generate sales to keep employees busy. Sometimes it is good business sense to cover payroll. Or it could be motivated by a need to move perishable items. This category doesn't refer necessarily to food that will spoil; it may include items that are seasonal, such as Christmas decorations or a current fashion trend that might not be around the next year. You may have gotten a large return from a customer and need to resell it. You may have gotten part of your money as a restocking fee. There are two ways to generate a quick bump in sales to existing customers. One would be via a sharp price cut and the other would be by offering a more liberal payment plan. Offering sixty instead of thirty days to pay could seal a deal.

Cutting prices automatically means that you're cutting profit margins, which you might want to avoid. What you also want to avoid is encouraging customers to purchase more than they can effectively use or resell just because they don't have to pay for it right away. Customers whose

Buying at the Right Time

Some states impose an annual tax on the value of inventory, often called a "floor tax." Companies in those states strive to keep inventory at a very low level during the month of taxation. At one time my company bought leather from suppliers in Wisconsin, one such state. I learned quickly that I could get the best price and be allowed to exceed my credit limit if I bought material from my Milwaukee supplier before the floor tax month. My supplier did not normally like to change any terms, but they invariably did so during that period in the year so that my company could work the payments into our cash flow. This supplier had an exceptionally good controller who knew as much about my business as I did, and he gave me as much time for payment (though no more) as he assumed I needed. He was usually right.

enthusiasm leads them to raise their ordering limit with a product they can't use will in the end either seek to return it or have difficulty paying you. Just because your interest is in moving goods that might not sell quickly, remember that you must get paid for them for a sale to be complete. Simply shifting the burden to someone who is otherwise a good customer can be shortsighted. The next order may not come because a customer is still delinquent on a "special deal."

Secondary Protection: Using Outside Credit Resources

Perhaps you sell construction equipment and call primarily on small contractors growing their companies. You are able to finance single-item sales for a few months, but what happens when you start to call on customers who wish to make large purchases? This could be a time for you to form an alliance with a leasing company that can step in with financing for a sale bigger than you want to handle. Don't try to cut yourself into their fees; simply make the financing alternative available to your clients as a way of facilitating the sale.

Here's another scenario: You are providing a new accounting system or software product that will improve productivity and increase profits, but the payback will not be for a year or even longer. This could also work with a leasing arrangement. Or perhaps a bank could set up special financing that allows you to sell the product without having to finance it internally.

There are many businesses for which small sales are easy to handle in-house but larger deals need the participation of an outside lender. Locate a few such credit resources and develop an alliance so you can call on them when you need them. Realize that if a lender turns down a financing deal, most likely you would be prudent to do the same. Finance professionals have access to reliable information and good instincts as to the creditworthiness of a plan.

Growing Customers Need Growing Credit

Every business wants to find itself in a market in which sales are good and growing ever better. One way is to expand your sales efforts over a wider area to handle many new business customers at once. This lowers your credit risk in having any one customer owe you too much money. The downside is the cost of handling the accounts. The maintenance of your accounting system is a lot of work, requiring good organization and continuous efforts.

An alternate strategy is to work with fewer but more aggressive companies whose rapid growth can take you along with them. Once you develop a working relationship, you can then plan sales efforts together.

The challenge of such a scenario is that your need to grant larger credit terms to single customers will be stretched. A customer that increases its business with you also increases its short-term need for credit. As a result of sharing the risk, any sneeze by your customer may give you a cold. Working this way is an effective strategy only if you know the principals of these other companies well and have a good understanding of their financial strength. In that case you would need to review the other companies' financial statements to be sure you both would benefit from a shared effort. Since you would be a central part of your customers' growth, they should not object.

> ## Having One Large Client
>
> Small manufacturers or suppliers often long for a single large business customer to jump start their sales revenue. Wouldn't it be wonderful to have a large order from Wal-Mart so that your items will be sold in every store? Perhaps not. The Arkansas company has a reputation for being a ruthless customer when purchasing products from other businesses, although they have been trying to soften that image. Wal-Mart makes demands on how product should be packaged, requires large shipments at one time, and often takes over ninety days to pay its bills. They also require an unlimited return policy, so you might find half your shipment unpaid for and back on your dock. Don't play in this game unless you have some experience and preparation. The thousand-pound gorilla can easily step on your toes. And when they're gone, so is your business. Slow growth with a wider diversity of smaller customers may be a safer plan.

Reducing a Limit or Requiring Cash

Being proactive about credit limits means you make sure these limits reflect the needs and capabilities of your customers. There are times when your customers' needs are less (they are no longer selling some of your products) or their finances are a bit stretched. Just as when you raised their credit limits to allow more purchasing, this might be a time to reduce it to lower your company's level of risk. As always you need to be gracious and polite, since you want to retain a particular customer's business. Try a letter like the following:

ABC Distributor
Attn: Tom Jones, Purchasing Director

Dear Sir/Madam:
As a company that takes pride in our level of customer service, we appreciate our years of business with you. A recent review of your account shows that you are purchasing in small quantities yet taking a bit beyond our normal terms to pay. To adjust your account to current conditions, we have reduced your credit limit to $3,000, which we hope will be sufficient to serve your needs.

| Inside Track | Taking a Bath on a Major Project |

A small remodeling company I work with that specializes mainly in kitchens and baths was asked to do a major project. When they were designing the job, the homeowner said he was securing bank funding to pay for it. That didn't come through, but he did make a large down payment, and he assured the company he could pay upon job completion. My client finished with almost $40,000 still owed them, which totaled most of the expected profit in the job. A mechanic's lien was eventually filed, but it took some time to see any real money. This work could have been financed through a second mortgage, but my client did not want to make that demand of their customer and instead took a big loss when the expected cash did not come in. When it comes to a big job, you and your client are partners . . . when their funding is insecure, so is your payment.

Should you want to discuss this matter now or in the future when you see greater activity with our company, please feel free to call me.
Sincerely,

John Smith
Controller

This letter reducing a business customer's credit limit was written to its purchasing department, although it could have gone to the owner or the accounting department. Regardless of where it is directed, a number of people are likely to see it. They may not be able to have you paid more quickly, but they will remember the tone of your letter. And if some day they go on to work at another company, the positive impression you leave may be of value. Most people try their best in business, and it seldom works well to treat them poorly. And in most cases it is unlikely to get you paid any faster. Once you lose any customers, it is very difficult and expensive to get them back.

Requiring Cash or COD Terms

Take the step of requiring cash or COD terms after a review of a noncreditworthy customer's need for new or continued credit. When customers are buying little and paying late, you can not give them credit. The loss of volume reduces your profit and the cost of financing cuts even further into what you will make. In this case, you are unlikely to salvage your losses, but your letter should try. For example:

ABC Supply
Attn: Accounting Department

Dear Sj135

ir/Madam:
Periodically we review our accounts, and recently yours has come to my attention due to the number of late payments. We value the business of all of our customers, but we cannot keep our prices competitive and our level of service high if we are not being paid in a timely fashion.
I regret at this time that we can no longer serve you with an open-credit account. We would appreciate a chance to continue our business relationship and to revisit this situation when conditions improve. Please feel free to call me to discuss this.
Sincerely,

Jane Smith
Controller

▶▶ **TEST DRIVE**

The credit limit you set for your customers must reflect their needs and abilities to pay. Are you getting the information you need to make these decisions? Ask yourself the following questions:

➲ Do you know how much product your customer is using on a regular basis?

➲ Are you handling sales terms to make sure terms of payment are being met?

➲ Do you have relationships with lenders or leasing companies to finance your growing customers?

➲ Do you take action to lower your risk when a customer does not perform?

Put Your Policy in Writing

Let's say that yours is a small company and that you and one or two accounting assistants—with whom you are going to form a credit committee—are going to make all the credit decisions. Do you still need a formal policy? The answer, for several reasons, is yes. First, you need to make sure you set and maintain a limit on the amount of customer credit outstanding, as well as handle the written requirements correctly and in timely fashion. And second, you need to maintain the documentation required to take any formal action should the need arise.

You will face a series of issues in determining your credit policy. Once the decisions have been set, they should be published for current and future employees to follow. Don't just leave them on a shelf; make sure they are read and carried out. Here are some issues to consider and policies to put in place:

1. Will you require signed original applications on file before opening any account? If so, all items must be filled out completely and the signature of any person whose name is on a personal account, or of all owners of a business, should be secured.

2. Will you require a full credit report or credit score on file? If so (and you should), have you established the minimum score you will accept? Any exceptions to policy should be noted in writing.

3. Will you ask for a personal guarantee? If so, ask for this consistently.

4. Will you check all personal and trade references before opening an account? There are standard questions to ask when doing so, and all answers should be retained in writing and kept on file.

5. Who will make a customer credit decision and set the credit limit? Will there be a signed form? You may want to require a second signature to verify a decision.

6. How will you notify a customer of a new open account and of its terms? These should be established in writing and in the proper form, and you need to retain a copy.

7. Will you have a policy regarding postdated checks? Will you accept these as cash or only as payments? (A cash transaction signals completion; payment plans are a plan for future cash before the deal is complete.) If you accept them, you must notify the customer when they are being processed.

8. How often will statements be sent? This should be at least monthly.

9. When will an initial collection process begin and what steps will be taken? Who will be responsible for contact? The credit decision maker needs to step in from day one.

10. When will you turn an account over to a collection agency or to a lawyer? Have a specific time or triggering action (when a customer phone has been disconnected, for example) and move quickly.

11. If claims of returns, defective material, or poorly done jobs are raised, who will handle the resolution? Assign the task along with a time frame for settling it.

12. Will you accept partial payments or payment plans? What level of authority to approve this will you require? Don't just allow checks to come in for any amount and be posted.

13. When will you put an account on hold?

These are areas of major concern for any credit department. Your department may also have some issues specific to your company, such as:

1. Who is authorized to override a credit limit? Does this require a signature? You certainly need to have someone take responsibility for doing so.

2. Are special terms set up as a separate account? This will cover special sale merchandise, so as to avoid confusion with regular credit terms.

3. Do you require deposits, and under what circumstances? Are any deposits refundable, and under what circumstances? Your customer should see this in writing.

4. Do you require signed contracts for each new order? Will add-ons or changes also require a signoff? Always the best policy is to put policy in writing.

Use the Features of Your Accounting System

Virtually all automated accounting programs allow you to set a credit limit for any customer. This is done at the time a new customer is entered into the system. The objective is to flag an account when it goes over a credit limit. If you fail to set up this feature properly, the warning will not come up or it may default at the same place for all customers. Credit limits are meant to add security. Take the time to enter the exact credit limit that has been assigned for each customer. When an invoice is posted that takes an account close to or over the limit, make sure that the appropriate people are notified. Use this tool to keep credit awareness high. You don't want to turn down new business, but you do want to reduce risk.

Post Notices about Deposits

If your place of business is one that most of your customers frequent, you need to post company policy on the wall in a very prominent place. Later in the chapter a number of issues about general terms of credit are covered, but the issue here is specific to deposits on special orders. A sign might read:

ALL SPECIAL ORDERS
REQUIRE A 50% DEPOSIT
THAT WILL NOT BE RETURNED

You are unlikely to be able to return a product made to a particular customer's specifications, nor should you be out the money because you were trying to serve a need. Make sure that your customers understand this policy on special orders.

Confirmation of Deposits and Change Orders

A further way to assure everyone is on the same page with regard to policy is to confirm an order or job by letter. Here's an example of a letter to send when accepting a deposit for an order:

Ms. Roberta Jones
Anywhere, PA

Dear Ms. Jones:
We received your check for $2,500 as a deposit on the cabinets we are having custom built for your family room. This is a special order from our supplier that may not be cancelled, and therefore your deposit is nonrefundable.
We know you will be pleased with the work, but we want to be assured that you understand the terms of this order.
Sincerely,

Joe Smith
XYZ Remodeling

If an original order is changed, you also need to confirm that by letter:

Bill King
Project Manager
ABC Construction

Dear Mr. King:
We are enclosing copies of signed change orders that your field employees have authorized on the job site. Please be advised that these are being incorporated into the original contract and all terms and conditions of that agreement will be in force.
Please notify us of any further changes you anticipate.
Sincerely,

Jane Smith
Controller

Letters Granting Credit and Stating Terms

The credit function or department of your company should be seen always as a customer-friendly place. This perception begins with the first letter sent that opens the credit account. At that time it is a good idea to have this initial letter signed by the credit manager, so that the customer knows whom to call if there are any problems. I cannot emphasize enough: Payment decisions are very often made subjectively. A business with limited funds pays their favored vendors first (and sometimes only them). You want your company to be high on the list. Your letter should include four elements.

1. A welcome and thanking of the customer for the opportunity to do business.

2. An announcement of the specific amount of credit that will be available.

3. Your normal business terms, along with an explanation of when an account would be put on hold.

4. An invitation to contact you if there is any problem with an invoice or any other matter in which you can be of assistance.

Establishing a Personal Relationship

The salesperson isn't the only one who needs to interact with the customer. All communications from your credit department should invite your customer to be conscious of your terms, and should convey that you are willing to discuss problems before they cause an account to go into default. Developing this business relationship is your goal. Make the credit-granting aspect of your customer relationship as personally connected as the sales end:

ABC Supplies
Attention: Bob Jones
Your City, USA
Dear Mr. Jones:

Boston Manufacturing Company is pleased that you have chosen us to be one of your new suppliers, and we are happy to open up an account for your company. Your current order will be shipped as soon as it is completed.

After reviewing your application and credit request, we have set up your open account for a credit limit of $12,000. Any orders that exceed this amount will require prior approval.

Our terms are one percent ten days, net thirty days. Most of our shipments are quoted F.O.B. shipping point. Please consult your quote or ask your salesperson about any changes to that.

We expect payments within thirty days, and we will charge a late fee of one percent per month for any past-due amounts. Please bring any questions or concerns about your order or your invoice to our attention immediately so we can assist in finding a quick resolution.

Again we appreciate your confidence in us and look forward to a long and mutually beneficial business relationship.

Sincerely,

Barbara Adams
Credit Manager

Follow Initial Letters with a Call

Although the typical point person in business-to-business transactions is from the sales department, the credit department has an important role to play as well. Follow up a welcome letter with a phone call. Verify that your letter was received and volunteer to answer any questions your customer might have. Ask a few questions about who will process payments for your account and, perhaps, how this person will handle paperwork. Find out whether the customer needs anything extra sent with the invoice, such as a copy of the packing list. Begin to create an atmosphere of cooperation and, it is hoped, of a future without credit or financial problems. Invite customers to call you if they run into any problems, since ones you know about, you can usually solve.

Print Your Terms on Invoices and Statements

Most computer-generated invoices have space to insert information such as purchase-order numbers and other specifics of the charge. This should include the terms of the sale. Make sure these details are listed on each invoice and are correct. If your terms change for different customers, you can set the default in the accounting system to bring that information up according to the purchaser. And when you make a sale according to special terms, take care that such an agreement is reflected on the invoice sent. When you sell on the basis of "net sixty days," make sure this condition is included on all of your paperwork. And check that this time span is reflected on your posting, so the invoice does not appear as past due after thirty-five days.

There should also be a clause on your billing that states you will charge a late fee or interest on invoices that are not paid according to terms. You have established a formal policy, so make it evident to your customers and adhere to it. Also make sure that your late fee and/or interest rate does not exceed your state's limit.

Post Credit Terms and Return Policies in Your Place of Business

Whether you do business with the general consumer or only with other businesses, there are a variety of settings in which deals will be made. Customers will contact you online, via phone, postal mail, or e-mail, in response to a salesperson's visit, or in person at your place of business. Wherever the contact is made, you want to be clear about your credit and return terms. List these terms on all documents, not just on invoices, including your order confirmations. Any special marketing promotions should state terms that are part of the promotion.

If you do much of your business at a physical location, post your terms in a visible place and make sure they are large enough to be noticed and read. Here are some issues that require a notice:

- Do you accept personal checks?
- Is there a limit for the use of a credit card? A minimum?
- What is the charge for a returned check?
- Can merchandise be returned?
- Will cash, credit, or store credit only be issued for returns?
- Is there a restocking charge?
- Will late fees or interest be charged on past-due accounts?

Signs about Credit Policy

Here are some signs that clearly state credit and payment policies you may want to post:

WE ACCEPT CHECKS
FOR THE AMOUNT
OF PURCHASE ONLY
(You do not want to be used as an ATM for a customer.)

NO CREDIT CARDS
ACCEPTED FOR CHARGES
UNDER $25.00
(The fees for a small charge can eat up all your profit.)

RETURNED CHECKS
WILL BE CHARGED A
$25.00 FEE
(Charge whatever the bank charges you.)

ONLY MERCHANDISE
PURCHASED WITHIN THIRTY (30) DAYS
MAY BE RETURNED
(You will never resell last year's model.)

STORE CREDIT
WILL BE ISSUED FOR
ALL RETURNS

(Store credit will minimize your transaction loss by keeping the money in the company.)

A 15% RESTOCKING CHARGE
WILL BE DEDUCTED
FROM RETURNS
(With returns, you must check merchandise, retag, and restock. There is a cost to these.)

LATE FEES ARE
CHARGED ON ALL
PAST-DUE ACCOUNTS
(This is especially important to state on invoices but posting it in clear view is a good idea as well.)

An Official Return Policy

When merchandise leaves your business, you might consider it sold, but (depending on the business) a portion might very well be returned. Your first challenge is to make sure items are returned in sellable condition. If you can put a return back in stock, it costs very little. Most retail companies charge little or nothing for returns. But some items represent a problem due to repackaging, for instance. Here is where you might want to institute a fifteen percent restocking charge. And you want to reserve the right to refuse a return because of condition.

Special orders are an entirely different issue. Can you resell such products at all? Will you have to discount them drastically in order to do so? Your policy on returns should reflect the level of difficulty they cause for your business. And you must state these terms when an order is placed. Depending on the size of the deposit, you may not want to take an item back at all. Here are some choices to offer:

 Special order items cannot be returned.

 Restocking charge of twenty-five percent (or fifteen percent) on all returns of merchandise.

When Every Order Is Special

The company I spent much of my working life operating was an industrial-safety manufacturing business. We designed and produced high-heat clothing and gloves. Working with special orders was almost standard for us, since most of our work was to customer specification. Although we advised purchasers that nonstandard items could not be returned, we would still have an occasional tussle over it. The worst moments came when a shipment would be returned without authorization, and the customer would refuse to pay. I never found a foolproof solution, but I did begin refusing to produce an order for nonregular customers without first receiving a deposit. And I aggressively worked on the collection of monies owed for unpaid orders. My paper trail grew over time to reflect precisely what was ordered and what the terms were.

➲ All returns will be issued in company credit—no cash refunds. (You can still charge a restocking fee if you are not returning an item for cash.)

Customers do have the right to full disclosure. You have the right to set reasonable company policy only as far as you give people proper notice. Do not give them a chance to claim that they didn't know. That could end up as a claim in a dispute. Educate your salespeople to point out the terms when they make a sale. And make sure they get written authorization to modify any terms of a sale.

Can You Charge Interest on Past-Due Accounts?

The simple answer to this question is yes. But as pointed out earlier, there is a difference between a consumer account and a business account. As with many aspects of consumer credit, there are state limitations as to how much interest you can charge on past-due consumer accounts. Check with your lawyer, your state attorney general, or your state consumer-protection office. You may be able to charge a late fee on the account—and interest as well. Appendix Two provides information on legal state interest rates.

Posting Payments

When an account is in default, the customer is making less-than-full payments, and you are charging interest, the account ledger can get very confusing. Your best strategy is to post all payments from original invoices and only charge additional interest on the remaining invoice balances. This makes it easier to see how much of the actual charges have been paid and provides better documentation if you do enter into a collection process. You may be challenged on your fees and interest but not on your original invoice charges. You want to be able to track all activity on the original charge so that you know exactly the amount of principal owed you.

Late fees come into play if you are incurring the cost of a collection agency or a legal action. If you are still collecting a past-due account in-house and your customer offers to pay the principal amount, the best advice is to take the money that is owed to you and not hold out for penalty fees. The first voluntary offer is often the best one.

When it comes to past-due business accounts, there are few legal limits as to what to charge in penalties or interest. A common amount is one to one-and-a-half percent per month. If you turn over an account for professional collection, an agency or lawyer will add substantial collection fees as well as retain a portion of the principal as a part of their fee. This is the cost of the service. Remember this when considering an offer to settle.

▶▶ TEST DRIVE

Credit policies must be established consistently and conveyed clearly both to your employees and your customers. Ask yourself:

- ⮲ Have you written a formal policy? Have you circulated this among employees who need to know?
- ⮲ Are you advising your credit customers on all of your terms?
- ⮲ Are terms listed on invoices and statements?
- ⮲ Are your terms posted in your place of business?
- ⮲ Do you have clear policy on deposits and returns?

Purchase Orders and Contracts Must Be in Writing

Although verbal agreements are usually considered legally binding, they can be honestly misunderstood and may not be solid evidence in legal proceedings. The best way to make sure that all parties involved understand a purchase or contract agreement is to put the deal in writing. And have the document signed by both sides in order to signify common understanding.

Consider this situation. A customer calls you on the run and places a substantial order. You are pleased to have the business, but make sure you ask for a purchase order when the customer returns to the office. Ask for this to be e-mailed, faxed, or snail mailed so that it is in writing. Use your own organization as an excuse: "We need to check stock and quantity in so many places that only a P.O. really works well here." Whatever it takes, an order in writing is always preferable to a verbal request. Once you enter that order, a confirmation should be generated and immediately mailed to the customer.

The same goes for a job contract that defines the scope of work. What is expected from your company should be covered in writing so that both customer and provider have agreed to a single set of expectations. Each of you will have an identical document to refer to in case of any misunderstanding of work done or of the price. This provides protection for both parties. When you have no common understanding, it becomes clear when the specifications are expressed in writing. Then you can make modifications to the contract until the understanding of terms is mutual.

The Details of a Contract

The following are issues covered by a written contract:

The Subject—The exact subject of the work must be described in full. "Replacing the toilet" should be spelled out in detail: "Work covered in small downstairs powder room consists of removal of existing toilet fixture and replacing it with a new Kohler Model 1234." You should leave no room for mistakes.

A Contract Requires a Lawyer

You may be able to use the same contract for most of your clients or projects, assuming variations apply only to customer names and details of products or services. If using standard boilerplate, the model should be drawn up by your lawyer. And anytime you need to add or remove any specific terms, review by an attorney is advisable. When a contract works out well, your initial consulting of a lawyer may seem like an unnecessary expense, but on occasion of misunderstanding and dispute, you need all the legally binding documentation you can obtain. The process of drawing up a legally binding contract in writing forces you to negotiate with your customer over any terms or changes. However, unless a job is enormous and complicated, don't leave your lawyer to negotiate with the customer's lawyer. Such an approach becomes expensive and sometimes counterproductive.

Price and Payment Terms—Your contract should state the full price due (including applicable taxes), the date of payment(s), and any penalty or interest rate if payment is not made when due. Any cancellation terms need to be noted, or if no cancellation is allowed, that should be stated.

Delivery Dates—If the contract is for work to be performed, this item refers to the completion date; otherwise the date references the delivery of goods. Do not use the words "time is of the essence" unless you can meet an exact date specified, since such language could be cause for dispute if dates are not met. A collection claim against a customer could then prompt a counterclaim, and a misunderstanding with a customer as well. If a client has specified due dates for additional work, list these as well.

What Constitutes a Default—When a contract covers a scope of work or a lease covers a term of rental, certain types of failure could cause the contract to go into default. What constitutes a default should be spelled out on the contract. Payments would likely cease if such conditions arise. You would no longer be eligible to receive payments, and your customer would no longer be liable to make them.

Guarantee and Warranties—If any guarantees or warranties exist, their provisions should be spelled out to allow for eventual financial recourse. You must also identify any goods or services being provided "as is" or sold with limitations.

A Sample Purchase Order and Confirmation

You want a customer to fill out a purchase order that specifies all information necessary to execute a contract according to both sides. The order should include a date and tracking number. The quantity of goods must be listed as well as the agreed-upon price. All terms such as freight charges and payment terms should be included. The document must be signed by a customer who is an authorized purchaser.

This is the type of form you should use. Be sure to note any missing information from a purchase order you receive.

PURCHASE ORDER

From: ABC Company   Date: January 1, 20––
         Main Street   Order #60606
         USA

To: XYZ Supply
        4th Street
        City, State Zip Code

Quantity	Item #	Description	Price ea	Total
11	9999	widgets	6.00	66.00

FOB: DELIVERED   John Smith
Terms: NET 30 DAYS   Authorized Purchaser

*Purchase Order # to appear on invoices, packing list, and all correspondence

A Sample Confirmation

Many accounting software programs include a feature that enables you to generate a confirmation response automatically after a customer places an order. This is useful because it allows another opportunity for buyer and seller to determine that they are both in agreement with the purchase item, the delivery, and the terms.

Order Confirmation
XYZ Supply
4th Street
City, State Zip Code

To:
ABC Company
City, State Zip Code

Your Order **#60606**
Was received on   January 10, 20––   calling for 10 widgets
                                                    unit price$6.00/ea

We expect to ship on   February 1, 20––

F.O.B. DELIVERED
Terms: NET 30 DAYS

Thank you for your order!

If There Are Discrepancies, the Document Prevails

If your business is about making, selling, or installing products that are at all complicated, you want to create as meticulous a document trail as possible. If you do not have a software system that generates automatic confirmations, you need to design one of your own. And use it! You want customers to notify you of any problems before you ship. That way there are no returns or credits necessary, and your invoice can sail through to payment. Nonreturnable items become the final responsibility of the customers if they are put on notice of what is being shipped. From purchase to confirmation through invoice and statement, what is written and retained is the most powerful argument.

Keep Track of Invoices, Payments, and Credits

The best accounting system is one that electronically tracks a purchase or sales order through the phase of generating an invoice. This means that when an order comes in, it is booked in order entry as a sale. When it is fulfilled and shipped, the electronic information is turned into an invoice with added shipping information. The order is then recorded on the customer's account. As a result of this process, the data at each step remains the same, which ensures accuracy. If you generate your billing manually, make sure you check the paper invoice against its original purchase order. Order errors at any step delay payment. Any details you miss means your customer has to verify information twice.

Also make sure that billing is done in a timely way, since the payment clock only begins ticking when an invoice is received. Even if you record invoices with a date prior to printing and mailing, many customers pay on the basis of when they are received. That day becomes the "date of record" in terms of which payment is scheduled. Customers who don't receive invoices for weeks are unlikely to alert you. Invoice generation and mailing is your responsibility, and it is a critical issue as far as your cash flow is concerned.

Track Payments Against Original Invoices

One of the challenges in working with an internal accounting system is in keeping customer accounts up-to-date and accurate, so that you know when payments have become past due. There are times when a

When Can Payment Be Expected?

The optimal scenario is to receive cash thirty days after the date of invoice. Most companies bill with terms of "net thirty days." If you delay your billing a few days, you are setting this cycle back. Consider that the mail is likely to take a few days in each direction, which can add five to seven days. You need your cash, and an efficient way to get it is to submit bills as soon as work is complete or products are shipped. You would do well to note when your customers usually schedule their payments and set up your accounts receivable system to alert you if that time has passed without payment receipt.

large project is billed or a particularly big shipment of goods is made, resulting in a larger invoice than usual. Your customer may not be able to pay the entire bill at one time and instead sends a partial payment. Make sure that after the amount paid is deducted from the original invoice amount, your system records the remaining balance in relation to the original invoice number and date. So when you send a statement of the customer's account, it will accurately show that as of the original date of invoice, a balance still remains. The invoice remains forty-five or sixty days old even though a portion has been paid.

If you post a partial payment on your system without tying it to an invoice, the printed statement will reflect the original invoice as fully unpaid. That is likely to generate a call from the customer that may delay paying off the actual balance due. Take time to be accurate with your billing, and you will increase your cash flow.

Issue Credits Quickly and Post Them Where They Belong

If a discrepancy in documentation arises due to a partial shipment or an authorized credit, make sure the paperwork is updated quickly, posted from the original invoice, and sent to the client. Then when you issue a statement, the proper amount due from the invoice will show as owing. You need to verify an incorrect invoice before authorizing it for payment. You might want to credit an invoice containing any discrepancy, particularly if regarding price, and issue a new invoice with the original date.

Issuing a Statement

On at least a monthly basis, you should send all of your customers a statement of their account. The document would list all open invoices by their date and number, including any balances that remain open on these. This can be issued easily by any of the commonly used accounting software programs, such as QuickBooks or Peachtree. The statement must contain the dates of open invoices, the number of the invoice, the purchase order number, and perhaps a description of what was shipped or completed. The purpose of sending out such a document is twofold:

➲ You want to verify with customers that your internal records match theirs. The sooner you agree on how much is owed, the sooner you can work out a payment arrangement.

➲ You want to send a notice that will be attended to. Even though a customer statement is a routine document for most companies, it must be processed by an individual for whom it serves as a reminder.

A monthly statement looks like this:

ABC Supply
Main Street
City, State Zip Code

Statement for June 30, 20‒‒
Due from XYZ Corporation
First Street
City, State Zip Code

DATE OF INVOICE	INVOICE NO.	PURCHASE ORDER	AMOUNT DUE
3-14-06	011	3667	3,400.00
3-27-06	026	4655	1,400.00
4-15-06	077	5001	1,000.00
6-1-06	101	3477	1,000.00
		TOTAL DUE	6,800.00

PAST DUE	PAST DUE	PAST DUE	OVER
1–30 DAYS	31–60 DAYS	61–90 DAYS	90 DAYS
1,000	1,000	1,400	3,400

An Essential, If Uncomfortable, Job

A client of mine who did high-end apartment and office plumbing always had large invoices outstanding. This happened even with customers who had good payment histories. It turned out that the nonpaying customers had complained about the jobs, to the point that my client avoided them for weeks while their money went uncollected. I encouraged my client to deal with these situations so either we could reduce the price or make demands for full payment. The lack of action on my client's part stopped any payment processing by his customers. They were waiting for him to resolve their concerns.

Interestingly, once a customer was called and some adjustment made, a check came in fairly quickly. My client's was an uncomfortable job worth doing. Customers may withhold payment as a way of getting your attention. Make sure that you address your customers' concerns.

Change Orders Must Be in Writing

When you are midway through a job and a customer increases the quantity of product to be shipped or increases the scope of work, you need to capture that request in writing. Do not simply add the extra amount to the original purchase order or contract. If you do not take the extra step of getting the request in writing, you can expect a future payment problem from your customer. This could reflect merely an administrative problem or your customer could try to avoid paying extra charges. Or you might run into a lack of agreement on charges. What begins as a paperwork discrepancy could wind up jeopardizing all the profits on an order or job. Any items that modify a contract could call the entire order into question.

What Should You Require?

One method you might use to capture a change order is a one-page addendum to the contract referencing the original scope, the change, and the new cost. For example, you could write a new purchase order that uses the original invoice number with a variation (such as "Order 1234 – req. 2") and notes the additional quantity and change of value in the total order. The fact is that some companies track the value of their issued contracts or purchase orders; if the invoice your company sends exceeds this amount, your payment may be held pending verification. Writing change orders in this way is also a good budget technique. Since your aim is to make sure your cash flows without any interruptions, documenting your customer's total purchase expenditure is sound business practice.

Contact Reports on All Billing Inquiries

Your customer account report should track any calls or written inquiries about an invoice, whether concerning the total amount of a charge, the quality of work, or a product that was sold. Once the issue has been resolved, add a note to this effect to the customer history and make sure that any agreement to changes or promise to pay is highlighted. Each time you have to go back to do research is another delay in getting a bill into your customer's payment cycle.

The Larger the Company, the More Complicated the System

Business is in a technology race in which larger companies now have the resources to automate a good part of their accounting functions. For them, this is a good thing, from a cost perspective. Fewer people are needed to process more transactions. If you are a vendor, this situation represents a challenge in meeting their standards. Employing a simple system such as Quickbooks can help if you have knowledgeable users. Even using a manual system works if it is well-organized and you are disciplined. If you are serving larger corporate clients, however, you may want to consider a purchase of software that keeps up with your transactions and contacts. Remember, your collections are your cash flow.

Record All Statements and Letters

If you send monthly statements to your customers (which you should), note the date of these on your account records. You need to know when you have made contact with your customers in the process of billing and verify all accounts receivable. Your statements should include a request to "please bring any discrepancies to our attention, immediately." Never let small matters that can create a discrepancy between your balances and your customers' records keep you from issuing payments.

Any customer letters sent to your company having to do with invoices, balances, or any requests for proof of delivery must be entered into the customer record, and hard copies retained for future reference. Know exactly where you are in your customers' payment cycles.

Sending out an invoice and expecting to be paid works only in part. You must organize and document all paperwork from customer orders to shipment to receipt. Is your system in place? Ask yourself these questions:

- ➲ Do you require signed contracts or purchase orders?
- ➲ Do you issue order confirmations and state your payment terms?
- ➲ Do you track all customer payments and credits?
- ➲ Do you issue change orders and make sure they are signed by the customer?
- ➲ Do you track all customer statements and correspondence?

3

Putting Policy into Practice

Make Sure the Billing Is Accurate

Your financial relationship with a customer begins with a new sale, at which point the clock begins to tick on when your invoices turn into cash. Be a reliable and timely partner in the process, and you will make many of the collection issues easier. When you are dealing in the retail consumer business, the transactions are mainly in person. The business-to-business sale, however, is more complicated.

In many business-to-business transactions, the actual sale takes place via phone, mail, e-mail, or on a scheduled contract release date. You do not hand a product to an individual in exchange for cash, credit card, or a signed sales slip. Why is this distinction important?

Because at the completion of the sale, you often do not have instant verification that your charge for a product or service has been accepted. And the product or service might not be accepted. It is often in the time lag and with the exchange of documents that the first sign of a discrepancy is noticed. And, if you don't agree on the charge or the terms of sale, there is likely to be a problem getting paid. You must find a way to adapt to your customer's system.

Learn What Constitutes an Acceptance

One of my clients is an electrical contractor who works as a subcontractor on larger building projects. His company often works on long-term jobs and in the interim receives progress payments. Receiving the final payment at the end of a job is always the toughest period because both the customer and the prime contractor (often with an architect or engineer) have to approve the final sign off.

It is the responsibility of someone in your company to know what the final process is in a business transaction. Will the company pay for partial shipments or does it require a complete order before an invoice is accepted? Must you secure a specific signature from a manager or supervisor? Companies set up a process to manage their own businesses; you need to learn what it is and meet their requirements.

Determine Your Customer's Process

When you are setting up a new customer account, a critical piece of information to request is what your client requires in an invoice and where it should be sent. You may need to include items such as the following:

⮑ The purchase-order number and any requisition number or release

⮑ The quantity shipped and individual item price

⮑ Contract completion percentage with details (in the construction industry, for example, a ten-percent retainer deduction is common)

⮑ Full shipping address (if different from billing)

⮑ Terms of sale

⮑ Date of shipment (particularly when it is not the date of invoice)

⮑ Name of authorized purchaser

⮑ Signatures for sign-off

There are many details of a sale that your customer may require itemized on an invoice. Your customer's accounting system might need the inclusion of full information in order to generate a payment voucher. It's in your interest to tailor your billing system to meet your customer's needs. Missing information delays payment. In a rapidly changing technology environment, your own accounting system needs to match the level used by your customer.

How Many Copies and What Attachments?

Some businesses use a cumbersome system that allows them to verify in several locations different elements from multiple invoices submitted for payment. This may require that you submit paperwork with multiple copies and delivery tags. This is information you need in setting up an account so you can proceed through the authorization process quickly. Working closely with customers to ensure you know all the billing requirements enables you to ask additional questions, such as who is assigned to process the order, how long it normally takes to receive

> ## Ask about Transmitting Electronically
>
> Increasingly, large and even midsize companies are using paperless accounting systems. When you are ready to invoice, you just electronically enter your customer's accounting system. This avoids the delay of mail and the potential for human error either in misdirection or posting of the charges. There is a cost to you in acquiring and installing compatible software, but the efficiency is worth it. Accessing electronic systems online, you can determine immediately if your invoice is accepted. Additional paperwork, such as purchase and change orders and sign-off forms, can also be electronically entered into an accounting database.

payment, and where to call in case of delay. When invoices are met by silence, you need to know where to search for answers.

Check for Errors

One of the primary reasons why payments are delayed is due to billing errors. An invoice has to be double-checked to find out exactly what is wrong, and it may not get back into the payment queue until all questions are answered. Effective collection begins with accurate billing, so make sure your accounting process is tight and effective. Use a system that cuts down the chance for mistakes.

Proof of Delivery

A quality billing procedure generates a signed paper trail designating that a product is delivered or work is complete. The different forms produced depend on the method of shipment.

1. Signed packing slip—when material is picked up at your place of business by the purchaser or a representative of the purchaser
2. Signed bill of lading—when a shipment is picked up by a common freight carrier. This shows the total number of cartons and the weight that is being transported.

3. Signed proof of delivery—provided by United Parcel Service (UPS), Federal Express (FedEx), and other carriers that deliver small packages to businesses.

4. Electronic tracking proof—an overnight carrier can track packages electronically, which you can access online to confirm proof of delivery in real time.

5. Signed completion order—When you finish working on a project, create a document for your customer to sign accepting the work as completed. The more complicated the work, the more detailed such a document needs to be.

You do not need to enclose such documents when you are billing a customer (except when specifically required), but you should keep them with all other sales documents, beginning with the purchase order. This will make it easy to refer to them if necessary. Some systems are able to scan all documents and keep them electronically as files attached to your customer's account.

Make Sure Your Customer Is Satisfied

It is bad news to phone a customer to inquire about a delayed payment, only to hear (for the first time) that the business either did not receive the material, found it unacceptable, or did not like the job you did. In the first place, your getting paid will be delayed until this concern is resolved.

Mistakes Do Happen

There are times when a company you are doing business with does not in fact know whether it has received a shipment you've sent. Perhaps someone put the package in the wrong place and did not find a receipt or the packing list was not sent to the accounting department. A good collection process begins with verification that invoice and material were both received and have been processed for payment. This verification is the first matter to determine when you are researching a payment trail. Do not assume everything is in order until you have received complete verification.

Inside Track	Keeping on Track

Sometimes a customer's dissatisfaction is expressed for the first time in answer to a collection lawsuit. This happened to me quite recently. I was working on a project with a local media person with whom I met from time to time over a period of four months, making progress even if slowly. I thought things were going well, although this woman was difficult to work with. My fee was paid via an advance retainer, with the balance due as we completed the work. The labor started dragging, and our working relationship became less energetic as we proceeded. I felt I was due an additional payment, which I requested, since we continued the work even if the pace had slowed.

The response was a demand for money back from me, with a complaint that the work we had accomplished was unacceptable. I don't believe this was true, but I should have gotten more verification along the way as to whether the client was satisfied. In the end I did not lose the funds the woman had paid, but neither did I receive the additional payment. I learned from this not to handle slow-moving projects casually. When there seems a loss of momentum, act on that perception or the wheels will come off the track.

More important, you have an unhappy client who feels its problem has been neglected. Try to make follow-up calls after every major customer transaction. Even if such practice is not typical of your industry, you might want to consider it. Not only does this method resolve any customer disputes or errors, but it is good sales policy.

Customers want to know they are valued after making a sales transaction. Providing such customer service is good for future business as well as for receiving customer referrals. A pleased customer might have additional work to award your company or a desire to purchase more product. You won't know this until you do your follow-up and ask questions. Then you may find out things about your company that you didn't know. Listen to your customers, for their feedback is important.

Minor problems might be resolved by showing some attention. A color variance may not be as important as a customer feels it is when no one seems to care. A small missing part may correct a problem that could grow if left unattended. All customers and clients want to feel they are important to your business, so take the time to see that they are satisfied.

Handle Disputes in Writing and Issue Credit

Once you find out that customers have a dispute or find a discrepancy with your company, you must document their claim and your behavior to correct the problem. And you need to determine what actions they are looking for from you.

Begin by stating your understanding of the problem in a letter such as this:

ABC Corporation
Attention: Accounts Payable

Dear Ms. Jones:
We understand from your purchasing department that our shipment of valves on your Order #6656 (our Invoice #1234) contained several valves that were incorrectly manufactured and will not work in your operation.

Kindly advise us how many pieces were unusable and we will arrange to have them returned and a credit issued. If you prefer, we can replace the parts as well. We strive for a hundred percent satisfaction from our clients and would be happy to make any adjustment that will meet your requirements.

We appreciate your business, and we are ready to resolve this matter quickly. We are sorry for the inconvenience.
Sincerely,

John Smith
XYZ Valve Company

Establish the Facts

As soon as you know what a customer's problem is, confirm the issue in writing so that each of you is clear about the discrepancy and under-stands what options are available to resolve the problem. It would be foolish to allow a $5,000 invoice to go unpaid because a credit or replace-ment worth only a few hundred dollars isn't taken care of. Ask specifically

> ### The Customer Who Can't Be Satisfied
>
> When there is a dispute with customers who will not agree to any offers to resolve the problem, it is a sign they do not want to pay. If you can reclaim your merchandise, do so. If this payment is for work completed that cannot be retrieved, get ready to pursue the fees. A customer intent on settling an obligation will find a way to accept a credit and call it even. Someone who has no interest in this is indicating that she does not intend to pay. Document all your efforts to find a mutually agreeable solution.

what a customer is looking for in resolving the issue. Then confirm that agreement in writing as well.

ABC Corporation
Attn: Ms. Jones, Accounts Payable

Dear Ms. Jones:
Confirming our recent conversation with your purchasing department, we will not be replacing the items in our last shipment that did not meet your specifications. We have been asked to issue a credit instead, which we will do immediately.
Please advise us if you have any questions with regard to this matter.
Sincerely,

John Smith
Controller

How Much of a Discount Can You Afford?

We all want to receive the full profit due us. Sometimes this isn't possible, perhaps because of your error on a job or because of a misunderstanding between the client and you. You need to determine how much of an accommodation you will give in real dollars to settle the problem and launch the payment process. A refusal to pay as a result of a dispute can keep a larger amount of money out of your hands for a long time.

You want your good customers to know you stand behind your work, so that they will continue to purchase from you. A stalemate with any customer in a dispute means no money at all for you. Time won't make such a problem go away. Make an offer and, once it is accepted, issue a written credit. Then when you issue a credit, you should process an invoice for payment.

How Much Is Enough?

There is no standard answer to this question. If the customer's complaint is without substantial merit, offering a ten percent discount to secure a quick payment makes sense. Consider how much you would pay to a collection agency or a lawyer. Collection agency fees usually range from twenty to thirty percent depending on the dollar amount and the length of time passed.

When a complaint has some merit, even if you think your customer is overacting, the time has come for you to make your last and best offer for a resolution. The bottom line for you is to cover your costs, so deduct the typical markup on the job and offer to take the net amount. Let your customer know your reasoning here, and perhaps your compromise will secure his or hers.

Criticism Is Tough, but Nonpayment Is Worse

Here is a point that needs emphasis: Even when you feel a customer's complaint or dispute is greater than it needs to be, you have to find a mutually agreeable solution to move the payment process forward. In most circumstances, collection cases should not be taken to litigation; an example is when a dispute will cost as much in lawyer's fees as you are likely to collect. And in the end you will probably make a compromise anyway. Save the professional fee, bite the bullet, and offer whatever will work. Not all customers are reasonable.

Letters to Confirm the Outstanding Amount Due

Once you have decided to agree to what is due on an outstanding invoice, you need to confirm that amount in writing. This is the last chance for your customer to make any claim that hasn't already been raised. Send the letter via registered mail. Here's an example:

ABC Corporation
Attention: Accounts Payable

Dear Ms. Jones:
We are enclosing our corrected invoice #1234 covering the valves shipped to you recently. You will note that we have reduced the quantity by three to account for the material that was not accepted by your quality department. The amount of this invoice is $4,680.00. We would appreciate your prompt payment of this amount.
Sincerely,

John Smith
XYZ Manufacturing Company

 ▶▶ TEST DRIVE

The moment you make a sale on credit, the collection process goes into effect. Don't let it be slowed down by errors or disputes. Ask yourself the following questions:

- ➲ Do you know whether your customer needs further information to process your invoices?
- ➲ Do you track and verify shipment?
- ➲ Are you sure that the customer is satisfied?
- ➲ Do you resolve disputes so that payments will be made?

Keep Your Source Documents after the Charge

You've made a sale in which you were paid by someone other than your direct customer. It may have been a bank, a consumer credit company, or a leasing company. You're out of the deal, right? Not necessarily. To protect yourself in case of a challenge at some point, you must keep track of this sale by documenting the transaction.

When you accept a credit card payment from either a consumer or another business, you need to maintain records beyond saving the credit card receipt. This is as simple as retaining a cash register tape (or any other point-of-sale document), an underlying purchase order, or a work order. Such a document specifies the charges in more detail than does a credit card receipt.

You need to keep your original documents for a number of reasons. Perhaps the merchandise will be returned or exchanged. You might want to refer back to the initial sale transaction for further information about exactly what was purchased and under what circumstances, including the date and price. You might have sold your product on a "no return" basis or in "as is" condition. You might want inventory information in case the tag or sticker on the return item is missing. Returning the item puts it back into your inventory. You should track this transaction so that your system recognizes a return and puts it back with the available inventory.

If a dispute arises over a charge, you want to have as much backup information as you can. You want to know exactly what was sold and at what price. One credit card scam (among the many out there) involves a purchase of sale merchandise that is then returned for full price. Protect your interests by issuing and keeping sales documents and by requiring customers who wish to make a return to bring back their own copy.

Customer Data Has Value

Regardless of what type of business you are running, having information about your customers, such as who they are and what they purchase, is an important tool. A credit card receipt does not provide much future marketing data, so additional order information, including who the customer is, can be useful. If you don't have a computerized system to col-

---

> ### Think of Customer Data as a Company Asset
>
> Should you decide to sell your business, realize that one of your most valuable assets is your customer information. The new owners will want to know who is buying your products or using your services so they can use that information as a basis to grow their new company. In operating a business, the cash flow from third-party credit grantors, such as banks and other financing entities, might be the most important source of current cash flow, but in fact the information behind that cash can prove profitable at a later time. Don't let your customer data go unnoticed. And the more effectively you can store, sort, and use the data, the more valuable it is.

lect and maintain this data, do so manually and create a database from it. You can add a software program to a counter computer to generate data instantly while you are ringing up a purchase. In knowing exactly what is purchased by what customer, you can create promotions that are specifically targeted.

Electronic Documents Work Well

This book makes frequent reference to the need to collect important source documents, beginning with the purchase order of an original contract. Perhaps the image that comes to mind is the unhappy sight of hundreds of folders of papers that need to be moved from drawer to drawer every year and then stacked in boxes after a few years. The backrooms at many businesses are filled with dusty piles of these boxes. But the days of this paper nightmare are over.

You can buy a software package that will convert your new and existing documents into electronic files. Existing hard copies can be scanned and new documents can be produced electronically regardless of what form they're in. All document files can be moved to electronic folders that are attached to customer records. If and when the day comes that you need to convert an entire file to paper, all you do is print it.

With Contract Financing, Proper Documents Must Be Submitted

When you or your customer receive a loan to finance some long-term work, the lender will specify the type of documents that must be submitted for payment. That a third party is underwriting the expense of the work you are doing is a benefit to you, but you will not be able to access that money without submitting the proper paperwork. Your original contract should spell out all the details you need to take care of.

When Your Business Is Being Financed (Contract Financing)

If you have a large contract that will take time before the work is completed and your company can be fully paid, your bank may be able to make a loan to finance this work. Receiving the working capital you need to pay wages and expenses would seem to be the immediate answer to your cash-flow problem.

But it isn't quite that simple. You have to provide progress invoices to your client and submit these documents to your bank as well. The lender will allow you to draw funds on your line of credit to pay for materials and labor. If your client is paying you installments on an ongoing basis, you will have to send these payments to the bank to pay down your loan. The bank will never be out the full amount of the project, just the cash needed to do the work. You pay interest only on the funds you are borrowing as working capital.

Each time you reach a benchmark completion in your work, you should provide a detailed invoice for approval by the client, whether you expect a payment or not. You want to keep your draws from the bank in accord with the stage of work you are completing. And you want to use this loan money to pay the actual costs you incur. You will be waiting to receive most of the overall profit until the end of the job, but in the meantime you obtain operating markup to pay overhead and promote internal cash flow.

At some point the entire project is completed, payment in full is due from the client, and you pay off your bank loan. To protect yourself from any delays or deductions at the end, make sure you have copies (with sign-offs) of all the interim documents. Those that have not been executed at the time the work is ordered or completed will be difficult to re-create.

Watch Out for Roadblocks

On many jobs, particularly involving construction work, there are materials to order and subcontractors to schedule. Subcontractors might be required in the early stages of the work, so you need to verify they will be available. Check to make sure deliveries are on time and on the availability of materials and manpower. If you near the end of your work but a task or work by a subcontractor is delayed, your money will be delayed as well. Plan your needs and verify that everything will be on-site when scheduled. You need a project manager to coordinate the various functions.

What Happens If Your Client Does Not Pay?

In the case of contract financing, the bank is lending you (the contractor) money on the condition that you will use the expected payments from your client as the primary source for the payback. You as the contractor are the one who carries the risk with the loan. Because you need your client's final, in-full payment to meet your bank obligation, you need to work closely with her every step of the way to make sure she is satisfied. If you do not receive the final payment from your client, your bank will look to you to pay the balance on the loan. You are the actual borrower. On the other hand, even though you retain and disburse the working capital as the job proceeds, you are in effect providing credit to your client.

When Your Client Is Being Financed (Third Party Financing)

The most common use of this third-party money involves construction jobs. Your client (the property owner) borrows funds from a bank to complete a project that typically will add value to her home or commercial building. The loan on the project has a total value, but payments in stages will pay for work in progress.

You as the contractor are likely to be asked by the lender to take an active role in establishing the client draws by furnishing a description of the work to be done and in what order it will be completed. At the end of each stage the lender will order an inspection, and if the work is determined to be complete, the bank will release a payment to you. The final payment may consist of a retainer amount (a ten percent holdback from each stage) along with the balance of the funds.

This type of loan belongs not to you but to the property owner, and the bank will be responsive to any concerns of their actual customer rather than to you. You will need to satisfy your client, working with her to motivate the bank to release funds.

When Your Client Has Secured the Financing

When your client borrows money from a third party to pay for work you are doing (client financing), the risk for you is different than in contract financing. Even when the lender acts as your disbursement agent while you are completing the job, the ultimate relationship is between the lender and borrower (the property owner). Your only risk is if you don't complete the work according to your original specifications, in which case the lender might delay or decrease some of your payments. Once the job is complete and signed off, your financial responsibility ends. Obtaining that lender sign-off is therefore critical for you.

At the close of the job, the lender will look only to the borrower for payment, and any delinquencies will be handled between borrower and lender. You are out of the loop, unless there is a later claim made against the quality of your work. Your lawyer can help you create a stream of paperwork that lessens any of your risks once a completion agreement is signed.

Know the Terms of Your Clients' Loans

Not all home-improvement loans are created equal. Some mortgage programs, particularly those that are guaranteed by the government, work to the disadvantage of the contractor doing the job. Their intent is to protect the consumer, even if it does not seem that way. They might result in a long lag in payments and a holdback in excess of ten percent, which is not released until job completion. Know the program your clients are using before you sign a building contract with them; that way you won't be surprised if full-payment checks are not forthcoming. Make sure their mortgage plan is reputable and that your draw schedules are specified in the loan documents and written into your client contract.

An Unfounded Claim

A partner and I did a series of seminars on investing in real estate. These seminars were full-day programs including lunch and handouts, and we had a number of guest speakers. All our attendees seemed to enjoy these events and learn from them. Imagine how surprised we were when Discover Card notified us of a claim a young woman had made that the seminar wasn't as we had advertised.

We wrote back enclosing a copy of the program and describing the background of all the speakers. I mentioned that the claimant had attended the entire seminar, stayed through lunch, and taken her handouts. Notably, she had filled out an evaluation form without writing down any complaint. I saw her claim as a way to get something for free, and I included her evaluation form with my response to the credit card company. We prevailed in the end, but until that time I had not even known such a claim could be made.

Credit Card Disputes Can Result in Charge-Backs

The sale is made, the deal is done, or the work has been completed; your customer has paid you, the vendor, with a credit card. The money has been transferred to your account, and you have spent it paying bills. This transaction may still not be over. Your customer might try to return the product so that you have to refund his money. But what if your credit policy allows no further claim, and you do not return money? A cardholder has the right to dispute any charge on his account, and if the card company decides he has a fair claim, you may still lose the money from the sale.

How does a charge-back work? The cardholder notifies the issuing company that (he feels) a charge was made in error or a product or service was not as promised. The credit card company puts a hold on the charge and contacts you as the vendor to get your side of the story. This is when your documentation becomes important. You will be able to state what the charge was for and attach any substantiation or documentation you have. Unless there has been a serious failure on your part, the customer charge is likely to stand. But don't be surprised if a charge-back happens to you. More frequently credit card customers are filing complaints about goods or services and seeking a refund. And all credit card companies allow their customers to dispute a charge.

Form Alliances with Funders to Access Credit

Lenders—whether a bank, a mortgage company, a mortgage broker, or a leasing company—are always looking for good borrowers. If your customers are potential contacts for lender financing, you might consider facilitating a match between lenders and your customers. This is particularly opportune when the item you sell or the work you do can be used as collateral. Knowing the resource you can provide, find a lender (or perhaps two) who will be happy to receive your referrals.

If your customer base is diverse, you might want to outsource more than one financing option. Once you get a chance to know the credit strength (or weakness) of a client, you will know whom to make a financing referral to. That will make it easier and quicker for your client to find a willing lender.

If your customer base is more difficult to finance than is the norm— for example, if your customers are younger, more overextended, or lower-income—then you must locate a funding source that works effectively with such cases. Be careful not to bring in predatory lenders. You should be able to find reliable and hardworking people whose expertise is in finding or providing creative lending. Work with them to enhance your offering to your client.

▶▶ TEST DRIVE

Third-party lenders are a way to receive job payments as you need them and eventually in full. However, there are some requirements you need to keep in mind:

⮕ As a vendor, have you retained the paperwork from sales to your customers?

⮕ Do you know what project information must be submitted to lenders to secure payments?

⮕ In the case of contract financing, are you aware of your loan risks if your client doesn't make scheduled payments to you?

⮕ Have you considered that a customer return or complaint may result in a reverse of payment from a credit card company?

⮕ Do you have lenders who are ready and eager to work with your customers?

Send Regular Statements

Ideally you have many credit clients with the cash flow and office organization that enable them to pay on a timely basis all invoices you issue them. It is likely, however, that some of your customers regardless of intent to pay need a bit of prodding. Here is where an effective system can help.

Your computerized accounting system should be able to compile monthly statements to all customers that show their sales, payments, and remaining balances. It is important you print out and check these documents to make sure all transactions have been posted correctly. Then you must transmit the statements for customers to check against their own records and alert you about any discrepancies. The sooner you know of any problems, the sooner you can make adjustments. Always include a disclaimer on your statement requiring that any claims or errors be brought to your attention within thirty days. This may not be heeded, but it will at least be in print.

The Elements of a Statement

The following are items you need to identify on your statement of account:

1. Date of sale (all current transactions that remain unpaid up to this date)
2. Balance as of beginning date (including any unpaid invoices from previous periods)
3. All new sales
4. All payments covered (posted from invoice amounts)
5. Any partial payments made
6. Any credit issues, for any reason
7. New balance as of current statement date

Most systems allow for some customization in the invoice format; make yours as simple as possible. You want it to be readable. Your customers should be able to track their balances by your information. Post payments against the invoice they correspond to, rather than randomly, so the debits and credits listed on the statement listed will match.

When Should You Add Interest to a Statement?

If you have advised your customers in advance that you will be charging interest on unpaid balances, when should you add this amount to a statement? From a purely financial (and legal) standpoint, you can do so as soon as an account is thirty days overdue (if your terms are "net thirty days"), but from a business and customer-service standpoint, I would recommend against this. In the first place, if your customer does not know what the additional charge is and does not expect it, adding an interest charge will make the statement balance show a different amount from the customer's internal account. Checking this discrepancy could cause a delay in payment by a customer. This might be just an excuse for a late payment, but it is a good idea always to give your customers one less reason to withhold a payment.

If an unpaid balance is only an occasional event with a particular customer, you might want to waive the charge or at least notify him by letter that his account is subject to this interest charge. Perhaps your trigger should be sixty days (or even ninety) overdue so that you allow time for mail delivery and the differences in companies' operational cycles. Your goal is to get paid in full as well as to retain the customer, not just to earn a few extra dollars. Although a service or interest charge is compensation for a customer's use of credit, in my experience few business customers pay such a charge in full.

Can You Do This Via E-mail?

Increasingly companies are transmitting invoices and statements electronically. The result is a huge savings of time (in printing and preparing for mail) and money (in paying for postage). Often all you have to do is make a notation in a customer's account and all communications beginning with the invoice can be transmitted online. Each time you call up a customer's account to produce an invoice, statement, or reminder, a document is generated in electronic format. Make sure a customer's name matches the address information on screen when you open up an account on the computer and direct every communication to the proper company department.

The First Friendly Request

If an invoice goes unpaid beyond the normal term and you want to bring it to your customer's attention, don't do so with a sledgehammer! Try to make the first notice as offhanded as you can while still letting your customer know you take the time to follow up on payment records. (Not every business owner does.)

You might consider sending a copy of the statement attached to a short memo headlined "From the desk of ... " On the note simply ask, "Has this payment been overlooked? I would appreciate your attention." Make sure you sign it.

A statement marked with circles and handwritten notes looks like an afterthought. A clerk might well throw it away without showing it to a higher-level person. Simply bringing the oversight to the personal attention of the company owner or manager may prompt action. Find a polite and effective way to do so. This would be an occasion for direct electronic submission.

Making a Demand for Payment

There are many steps in the process before your request for payment should turn into a demand. Once you turn normal credit procedures into collection, you cease being a valued vendor to a customer or company

---

Do You Know Who Schedules Payments?

In many companies, payment schedules are produced by someone in the accounting office. Depending on the cash flow of a business, the release of payment checks may be more random than you think. Necessary items like wages, utilities, taxes, and loans are covered first, and any vendor invoices are paid when the rest of the cash comes in, very often on the basis of calls and supplier importance. Including a note to the CEO on a statement may elevate your standing to the front of the line. Being considered a valued resource will speed up the process as well. Become a reliable business partner who is being paid to keep the relationship with the customer going. Effective collecting is as valuable a skill as customer service.

---

and instead become an adversary. By that time you should have stopped granting any additional credit, and so you are not making new sales. It is always more desirable to make payment an incentive rather than a threat, which means making an effort to promote your value to the customer as an ongoing supplier and to hold open the possibility of granting future credit. Your best strategy is to send reminders that manage to keep the business relationship intact.

Start with a Strong Notice Giving a Specific Period of Time

The demand letter should not be threatening. That isn't the way to start what you hope will be a cooperative effort by your customer to pay down her obligation to you. There could be many reasons a payment hasn't been made, though by the time you are ready to send the first request, the possibility of oversight on your customer's part is less likely.

What you want to do is emphasize that the money is due now and in full, and that you will wait a short period before taking any further action. The request should sound like this:

ABC Supply
Attn: Ms. Jones

Dear Ms. Jones:
We are enclosing our statements and copies of our invoices that are now past sixty days old. As you know, this is beyond the terms we allow and must be corrected. We will expect your check no later than ten days from the date of this letter. If we haven't heard from you, we will assume that your plans do not include meeting your obligations.

We value the relationship we have with our customers and hope this will continue.

Sincerely,

John Smith
Controller

Making Contact Via Phone

Making a collection call is usually not an easy task, nor is it one that should be assigned randomly. Particularly when an invoice is only just beyond the due date, this early call should be informational in purpose. You don't want your own business to look desperate for cash, nor do you want to convey suspicion that the customer is intending to pay. This is not a call for the business owner to make, which would leave too serious an impression coming from that level. An efficient controller or office manager should be able to strike the right tone and should be encouraged to handle this task efficiently.

The question to ask your customer is: "When is this invoice scheduled for payment?" This assumes that the invoice has been received and that there is no problem with the product or service or with the charge. The caller needs to be customer friendly and very gracious. If the invoice has been held back due to a problem, your representative needs to be ready to offer assistance in finding a solution. If the customer is paying on a forty-five-day or even sixty-day cycle at this point, you need to know that.

Are You Getting Past the Gatekeeper?

Any salesperson knows that the critical step is to get past the front desk and face-to-face with the decision maker. Plant employees may love a new product, but only the purchasing department can make the deal. The business side works the same way. There may be several levels of personnel handling the paperwork but only one person who makes the decision about payments. You want to track your customer's procedure until you make contact with the head of the department that handles invoice payment.

At that point, find out who the decision maker is and begin to copy everything to him and even to address your letters there. Some organizations, particularly ones that run into cash-flow issues, put some effort into blocking demands from going up the chain of command to the person in authority.

A Temporary Hold on an Account

Depending on your credit terms (and cash needs), you need to decide when to put a temporary hold on an account that is past due. Send out an extra copy of the statement of account along with a letter that reads as understated as you can make it. Even at this point your objective remains customer retention, including furthering the sales you worked hard to obtain.

ABC Corporation
Attention: Accounts Payable

Dear Ms. Jones:
We are enclosing a copy of your most recent statement showing a past-due invoice that has now exceeded forty-five days. Although the amount owed is small, this balance has placed your account in arrears. It is our policy to place a temporary hold on all accounts over this limit.
This can be quickly cleared up via a phone call alerting us of any problem regarding a pending payment. We assume this nonpayment is an oversight and look forward to a quick resolution. We value your business.
Sincerely,

John Smith
Controller

You want to keep the customer active, and the cash flow continuing; your professional demeanor at this point of collection is critical. Be as collaborative as you can as long as you believe the company has good intentions. But monitor the situation closely.

Mid-Month Statements

Some businesses do not write checks on a regular or organized basis. They see statements and circle the bills to be paid. Why not jump to the front of the line by sending statements in the middle of the month instead of at the end? Or, you may want to send them out twice each month. I had one client who always received a rush of payments right after statements went out, no matter when it was. In the case of clients whose accounts went over a certain amount, he sent out extra reminders randomly. Perhaps client nonpayments are truly over-sights and clients just need prompting. Dare to take as personal an approach to invoice collection as you do with sales.

Having a Salesperson Help to Collect

Salespeople usually do not like to double as bill collectors; they are generally not good at it. In my extensive conversations with people in sales, they invariably convey that they do not consider the collection process as part of their job, even though many of them stand to lose money if a bill isn't paid. If you use salespeople to help collect payments due, consider this: Do you want to possibly offend your customers (and reflect poorly on your business) by using personnel not trained in collections, who would thereby be as ineffective as they are uncomfortable and awkward at the task? During a collection visit, I actually overheard a salesman say, "We don't pay our bills either."

If you are expecting salespeople to handle credit collection as part of their job, they should be trained in credit management. Inform them of the billing and collection process and even involve them in setting credit limits for their customers. Ask them to talk about general business conditions with customers so if the time comes for them to ask about a past-due account, this doesn't come out of the blue. An excellent salesperson should be able to do this easily.

Six Sample Letters

Here are some sample letters for establishing initial contact with customers who haven't paid their bills. Your assumption at this point is that the payment obligation has been overlooked or that there is something to resolve. You want to be in the role of problem solver.

The Reminder Letter
ABC Supply
Attention: Accounts Payable

Dear Ms. Jones:
We notice that your account is carrying a past-due balance of $1,865.40, which is now forty-five days old. As you know, our terms are

net thirty days, and we would appreciate your attention to this matter in the near future.
Sincerely,

Bill Smith
Controller

Missed Invoice Inquiry

ABC Supply
Attention: Accounts Payable

Dear Ms. Jones:
We received your check for $304.00 today, but we notice that an older invoice in the amount of $1,865.40 remains unpaid and is beyond our terms of net thirty days. We will look for payment soon since your account is now past due. We thank you in advance for your attention to this matter.
Sincerely,

Bill Smith
Controller

Invoice Not Received?

ABC Supply
Attention: Accounts Payable

Dear Ms. Jones:
Invoice #6742 in the amount of $1,865.40 was sent to you on February 2, 2006, but we have not yet received payment. We are surprised since your account is always handled so promptly. If you did not receive this invoice, please let us know. We would be happy to send a copy. We value your business and look forward to receiving your check promptly.
Sincerely,

Bill Smith
Controller

Sending a Statement

ABC Supply
Attention: Accounts Payable

Dear Ms. Jones:

We are enclosing a copy of your recent statement, which shows four invoices that are currently past due. Won't you please give this your immediate attention by expediting a check to us? Open accounts require payments within our terms of net thirty days.
Sincerely,

John Smith
Controller

Partial Payment Received

ABC Supply
Attention: Accounts Payable

Dear Ms. Jones:

We received your check for $750.00 and appreciate your payment. However, the original invoice was in the amount of $1,865.40, leaving a balance of $1,115.40 that is now past due. Please advise us when we might expect payment for the balance of the invoice.
Sincerely,

Bill Smith
Controller

Is There a Problem?

ABC Supply
Attention: Accounts Payable

Dear Ms. Jones:

We were expecting your check in the amount of $1,865.40 to cover your invoice dated February 2, 20--. However, we have not heard from you. Since your account is usually kept current, we are surprised.

Is there any problem with the invoice or with the material shipped? We would be happy to discuss it with you or provide assistance in working out a payment plan. Give me a call at your earliest convenience to discuss this matter.

Sincerely,

Bill Smith
Controller

Assume the Best

The message you are conveying in your first set of reminder letters is that everything in your business relationship is normal and you expect it to remain that way. What you are looking for here is cooperation; this is always the easiest and cheapest way to collect your money. And it's the best way to keep the customer as well.

You also want your customers to realize that you will begin proactive steps on collecting as soon as it is required, and that you will continue to monitor the situation and take appropriate action if it isn't resolved. Fair, reasonable, and consistent behavior makes everyone comfortable. Encourage a customer with a temporary problem to communicate with you.

▶▶ **TEST DRIVE**

From the time payment comes due, you must monitor your collections and take action to send notices and reminders. Are you consistent in your actions? Ask yourself the following questions:

- ⮕ Are statements checked regularly for accurate balances before sending?
- ⮕ Is your first request for overdue payment friendly and courteous?
- ⮕ Do you know whom to call and what to say in the initial collection process?
- ⮕ Do your salespeople take an active role in the collection process?

Take the Time to Research

Sometimes payments are not made because customers have not received the exact merchandise they ordered (or expected) or the services provided were not found acceptable. The sooner you learn of any dispute and can settle the issue, the sooner you will collect your cash. A minor paperwork glitch can provoke a major misunderstanding that takes time to negotiate.

Perhaps an excuse sounds unlikely ("We never received that shipment"), since you have sent packages on a regular basis to the same address. When you start to collect a bill, first make sure you have provided the requisite goods or services and the customer has no counterclaim.

You should address any issue raised by your customer quickly and deliberately. Call the freight company for proof of delivery or talk to associates who handled the account. Assume your customer has honestly described a discrepancy that, once settled, will result in full payment to you. Promptly send the written results of your investigation to your customer for review and action.

Even if it sounds like an excuse, as long as your customer has an objection, you will not be paid. Find out whether she in fact has a claim before you move into collection mode.

When There Is a Complaint on the Work

You bid a job, did a fine piece of selling, and won the contract. You received a deposit and along the way collected additional payments. Now that you are down to the final check, there is a complaint from your customer that is a reason for withholding funds, at least from his perspective. Periodic work sign offs might have prevented this situation. Are such customer sign-offs legally valid in the event of a later dispute? No, but they serve as a way to jointly review the work with your customer to determine any potential trouble spots.

If you have been notified of a dispute, ask your customer to submit the problem to you in writing. You need to limit the issues to specific concerns you can respond to individually. Then you can either deny the complaint, redo the job, or issue a credit.

Just a Few Numbers Off

When I was running my own manufacturing company, we made a fairly expensive shipment of specialty clothing to an electronics plant in eastern Pennsylvania. When we followed up on the invoice, the company claimed it had not received it, and consequently we weren't paid. Starting with the earliest paperwork, I discovered that the purchase order numbers were reversed when the original production order was written. So all documents, including the packing list, contained the wrong order number. The shipment was received by the company and materials put into inventory, but the paperwork mistake kept the order from being signed in as completed and cleared for payment. Straightening out the mix-up caused a delay, but eventually we were paid. There are many good reasons to have a common database driving your business, but it essential that the initial input be correct, as it will repeat throughout the process.

Collect All Backup Documents

The information required to resolve a payment dispute could be extensive. Begin with the original purchase order or the initial job order to learn exactly what was ordered or expected. Follow through by examining any paperwork concerning materials, manufacturing, or installation. Determine whether your company failed to perform, giving your customer a reason to be dissatisfied and to refuse to pay. Be sure to review all internal and external documents from beginning to end. If you find the error was on your side, make contact with the customer to discover what would satisfy him at this point. For instance, if he did receive the wrong items, offer to take them back and provide the correct ones.

Check E-mail Records as Well

Many companies are now communicating electronically, although this means that sometimes the document trail is a bit hidden from view. The growing number of businesses that have installed more sophisticated computerized accounting systems are able to create electronic document files containing all order information, from price quotation, order entry, and shipping address to e-mail correspondence. If your business still uses hard copy files, you can print out any e-mail exchanges and attach the documents to the rest of the order paperwork in a customer account.

A Question of Timing

When there is a dispute over payment, ask yourself: When did the customer bring the problem to the attention of your company? A complaint that is expressed at the time of the first order has some credibility, and if you are the one who allowed it to be ignored, you could have a long dispute on your hands. So make sure any dissatisfied communication from a customer with your company, whether via phone, mail, or e-mail, is brought to the attention of management as soon as it is received. A salesperson who tries to smooth over a customer complaint without the knowledge and intervention of higher-level personnel is compounding the problem. Some salespeople who are motivated by their commission check are unhappy when money is subtracted from a deal. So they delay bringing up the possibility of a cost adjustment to the responsible people in the company and instead try to talk their way out of a dispute with a customer. Change the culture of your company to foster a problem-solving environment.

Keep your entire file intact, whether paper or electronic. I highly recommend that you install a good electronic accounting system. These can be very reasonably priced ($2,000 to $3,000 for two to five users) in terms of the value they bring to your business.

Establish Your Side of the Story

Once you face a fundamental disagreement with a customer over an amount owed or whether a bill will be paid at all, you need to gather the complete facts. Begin by looking through all relevant documents and speaking with anyone who was involved in the sale, delivery, installation, etc., contacting the customer in particular. Take notes describing the date and substance of your conversations.

Then as a result of your investigation, write up the entire situation. What was ordered or purchased? What was shipped or what work was completed. Describe the nature of the dispute, when it was brought to your attention, and what has been done to solve the problem thus far. If the dispute takes time to resolve or ends up in a lawsuit, your memory will never be as fresh as now. If any facts critical to the case are known exclusively by one employee, you might ask this person to write a report, dating and signing it. Any small claims case or arbitration is usually decided on the basis of the strongest documentary evidence. The more documentation you retain, the better your case.

Compromise When It Makes Sense

Any business owner who has been through the collection process, which takes time and money, knows he doesn't always end up with a check. With any serious dispute, the lawyers who take over the legal action will likely recommend at some point that you accept a settlement. Wouldn't it be better to make a deal before you've incurred the legal costs and expended significant effort?

Consider what would be reasonable for you to accept based on several criteria:

- How much are you out-of-pocket on costs? (What have you actually paid to others for goods or labor?)
- How legitimate is your customer's complaint? (Did you fail at some part of the job?)
- How serious is the customer's intent to pursue the dispute?
- Do you have all of the documents you need (proof) if this case goes to court?
- Can you turn this situation into a positive solution for both sides?

If you have a substantial amount of your own money invested in the order or contract, the customer's claim is weak, and your documents are strong, be prepared to turn the case over to an attorney. If you're willing to stop short of a fight that might bring maximum return, consider how much you are willing to compromise and open the door to a settlement. Start with a phone call that presents an opportunity to negotiate. You want to ask for an opening offer, rather than be the first to lower the price and allow your customer to wear you down. Don't negotiate against yourself.

Whether by letter or phone, begin by asking your customer, "What will it take to resolve the problem with Invoice #1234? I'm sure we both would like to get this amount off the books and move forward." You can gauge by the answer whether you both can come close enough to a settlement number to close the deal. Any business relationship that ends this way is uncomfortable for both sides. But a dispute that ends without either of you having to pay a third party is some success.

The Value of Current Cash

When you are working with customers who aren't willing to pay their bill in full, remember that only the cash they offer you at present is sure; holding out for more later might mean that you end up with nothing. Your customers could have disappeared or become insolvent by the time you secure a judgment against them. And you may not be the only one they haven't paid. So you should seriously consider the offer of a partial settlement in cash when it is made. Arrange to pick the check up, have your customer wire the funds, send them overnight, or charge them to a credit card. Take the money when it is offered.

Get the Agreement of the New Terms in Writing

Once you have arrived at an amount that both you and your customer agree is fair (or equally unfair), you must put the agreement in writing to complete the deal. You essentially are stating that in exchange for payment of the agreed-upon sum, you agree to release any and all claims arising from the disputed business transaction. Make sure that you include in your agreement

Failure (or Inability) to Pay Is Not a Dispute

My recommendation that you compromise on or discount a price in order to collect on a bill pertains to situations involving a dispute over goods or work. Those customers who will not or cannot pay their bill even though your work or products were completely satisfactory present a different matter altogether. This latter case of financial irresponsibility raises a credit issue that should be handled through the enforcement process, which the upcoming section on "Aggressive Collections" addresses. In terms of the present discussion, by contrast, compromise in an order dispute is an effective tool to solve the problem. If the collection of your money is in jeopardy due to a work claim in contention, the sooner you need to see at least some of it.

how the payment should be made and when it is due. When the transfer of good funds is completed, then your claim is satisfied. Make the proper adjustments in your accounting system to designate the account as paid in full. In most circumstances this shows as a loss to your business.

The Confirmation Letter

Your customer may want a letter stating that his or her payment is accepted by you in "full satisfaction." This means that you release your claim on the unpaid amount as soon as the agreed amount is returned to you in good funds, meaning that the money has been transferred to your account. You can render the agreement through a letter like the following:

ABC Supply
Attn: Mary Jones

Dear Ms. Jones:
As per our agreement this morning, we are deducting thirty percent from your current bill. Therefore your payment to us of $2,500.00 will satisfy the entire invoice, and your account will be satisfied in full. We are expecting your check no later than June 30, 2006, or this offer will be withdrawn.
Sincerely,

Jane Smith
Controller

Do not leave a compromise offer on the table for too long. You have made an offer for the receipt of cash. If it doesn't come in by a stipulated date, go back to collecting the full amount.

Some Disputes Are Ploys to Not Pay

When customers complain over very little, or they don't start making any complaints until they are asked to pay and then will not look for a way to settle the account, the dispute is not about the work or the product—it is directly about money. Companies with financial problems learn this technique early in the game and use it as a dodge as long as they can. When you see this is the case, you need to go into collection mode as quickly as possible. Offer a small concession to mitigate a customer's stated concerns and then provide a very short time period to settle the account. Be clear that collection enforcement action will kick in the day after the deal is no longer operative—and then execute this. You are likely to have an angry former customer but you aren't likely to have money in hand any other way. And this isn't a customer you want to keep.

Dealing with a Bounced Check

A check will be returned for insufficient funds for a variety of reasons. There are companies that always "play the float" by writing checks even when the money isn't actually in their account. When the funds they expect (or hope for) don't arrive in time, their account is overdrawn.

Some banks hold deposited checks longer than others. Your customer may well have funds on deposit, but these are held as uncollected because they are from out of state and incoming checks are not being honored.

So the situation may be innocent, or it may be deliberate. Either way, you must take action on your end at once. Some banks will automatically put the check through a second time without any action from you. Others will return the check to you immediately, so you can redeposit it. If there is a second failure to clear, the check cannot be presented again. Do *not* return it to your customer, but instead send a letter offering a chance for restitution. It should be short but very direct.

This Could Be a Criminal Offense

In most states if customers come in to your place of business, make a purchase, and pays with a worthless check, they could very well be guilty of a criminal offense. If the check presented to you is not redeemed within fourteen days (for any reason), you should turn it over to the authorities. They will usually respond directly to the writer of the check and most likely will recover your money. Bad checks are not a simple matter but rather a serious offense. You need to handle them seriously from the beginning. Never return the actual check to the customer unless he brings cash in exchange.

ABC Supply   *via certified mail*
Attn: Owner (or CFO)

We are sending a copy of a check that was returned by your bank unpaid as a result of insufficient funds. We expect you to correct this situation with certified funds within five (5) days. Otherwise we will be required to turn the matter over for appropriate legal action. You may contact us to discuss this if you wish.
Sincerely,

John Smith
Controller

A business letter should always be courteous and polite, but this is a situation in which your customer was less than honest, so you need to sound serious, even ominous. With that bad check in your hands, you have some leverage, so make use of it.

▶▶ TEST DRIVE

There are times when customers withhold payment because of a problem with the product or service they received. Are you handling these disputes quickly and effectively? Ask yourself the following:

- ➲ Have you researched both sides of the claim?
- ➲ Do you have all documents, from purchase order to shipping proof?
- ➲ Have you attempted a reasonable compromise with your customer to settle the account?
- ➲ Do you deal quickly and firmly with a returned check?

Call the Customer Yourself

Sometimes it becomes evident in a collection case that your customer has no ability or intention of paying her bill. Now your efforts must turn to becoming aware of and enforcing your collection rights. There is every reason to be stern but no reason to be rude. Rudeness is often the technique a collection agency employs, but then they are not considered direct representatives of your company.

If your controller, office manager, or someone else in the office has been handling collection calls, now is the time for you to take over the job personally. Make sure the person who has been in charge knows when to turn the case over to you. If you are the owner of the business, you need to be the one communicating with the principal of the other company; the problem cannot be handled by staff members. Or if you are dealing with a nonpaying consumer rather than with a business, you want him to realize how serious this problem has become. Most customers, whether other businesses or consumers, understand that the money involved is personal to the owner. They also understand that there is a point of no-return when the account will be turned over for collection.

The Meaning of an Unreturned Phone Call

Some people are harder to reach than others, but with the widespread use of cell phones there is no reason a person should miss your phone call or voice message. Through caller ID and call blocking, on the other hand, anyone can avoid a call she does not want to take. Using being in a meeting as an excuse only works for a while. It's safe to assume that a party not willing to talk to you is also not willing to pay you. Be relentless for a few days and then prepare to take further steps.

When You Speak, Look for Solutions

When you do reach a nonpaying customer on the phone, don't use the opportunity as a way to vent your frustrations or anger over the fact money is due you. This is an opportunity to gain information about the financial situation of your customer so you can decide on your next course of action. If you are convinced your customer would like to meet her obligations but is unable to do so at the present time, try to find out

> ## When to Leave a Detailed Phone Message
>
> A business experiencing temporary cash-flow problems faces increased external pressures. I have seen competent office staff leave jobs because of continual collection calls. So it is neither fair nor constructive to berate staff members because their employer will not return a call. Explain what the call is in reference to: "There is an outstanding balance that has become serious." You can leave a deadline for a return call. "I must hear from Mr. Jones before close of business tomorrow or I shall have to turn the account over to my attorney." No idle threat or ugly talk is required, just the facts of the matter. And you might want to thank the call taker for his help; he is likely to appreciate your courtesy. Perhaps your courteous manner will move him to prevail on Mr. Jones to call you back and so avoid future discomfort. I have known of cases in which an office manager campaigned for an account to be paid because she appreciated her treatment by an aggrieved business owner.

what circumstances will change the situation and how soon such changes might happen. Collection can be a slow process that involves gaining your customer's cooperation so you can arrive at an informed decision. Using a business manner, let your customer know that you are calling to get answers or else you will have to take action.

Ask for a Payment Schedule

Even when full payment is long overdue, obtaining a partial payment is a good first step. Now some of the obligation has been met with cash, which in turn leaves a smaller amount your customer has to retire. Such a solution might help his cash flow.

Try to work out a specific arrangement for the balance of payments. Ask your customer how much he is able to send monthly to pay off the remaining balance. If you have determined you are dealing with a consumer or a business owner who genuinely wants to pay, consider that he might have other pressing financial demands on him. If you demand more than he can reasonably handle given his cash flow, you will only increase the chance of failure and a later need to take action. Ask for an amount that realistically fits his budget. That way you are more likely to receive payments each month until your account is paid in full. You can ask for interest to cover your accommodation, but consider getting back the principal a win in the end.

Be Flexible and Reasonable

One question you need your customer to answer if you are to agree to forestall further action is: "How long will it take you to pay the balance?" There is a gain in receiving regular payments, but you must set a closing deadline as well. Many companies don't realize that an ongoing collection effort costs money to administer, which you don't want to be doing for more than a few months. The way to accomplish this payoff is to set an ending date: "The balance is to be paid in full by December 31, 2007." Agreement to this termination date should be confirmed with the understanding that the debt goes to collection at that point.

If you have worked with your customer to arrive at a sum that fits with her cash flow, the obligation should be retired in the agreed amount of time. If the full payoff doesn't happen, you have an enforced collection on your hands.

Send Out Demand Letters via Registered Mail

After proceeding through a round of unsuccessful calls, your next communication with your customer is straightforward. Your only question now is when you are going to get paid, and so your language should be quite a bit stronger. The solution you are looking for is receiving a check. Although negotiations can still go on at this late point, don't wait for them. Any letter transmitted should be short, direct, and sent by registered mail.

ABC Supply   *via certified mail*
Attn: Accounts Payable   *return receipt requested*

Dear Ms. Jones:
Your invoice #6656 is now seventy-five days old, and we have not received a single payment. We are demanding payment in full of $1,865.04

When Does The First Demand Letter Go Out?

There is no hard and fast rule about when the first demand for payment should go out. If an account goes over sixty days without any communication, the likelihood of your collecting it without an agency or lawyer is reduced. If your customer is answering your calls, you might be a bit more patient. But if promises have been made and not kept, then a demand is in order. The longer the period without response, the less money you are likely to collect. You make contact to put yourself at the front of the line. Your first attempt to collect is by means of cooperation; the next step is to get attention by asserting your rights as a creditor.

within seven (7) days of this letter. We urge you to respond to this demand, or we have no choice but to take further action to collect this amount.

Sincerely,

John Smith
Controller

Copy the Letter to a Third Party

As an indication of your seriousness, you might note in your letter that you are sending a copy to your attorney or a to collection agency representative. At this point, you are likely to be sending the account out for collection shortly, so alluding to this might have an effect. Some consumers and businesses really do try to avoid an "on the record" collection action. Consumers understand that debt collection goes on their credit report and affects their score; a company is aware that such an action becomes a permanent part of their credit history and can impair future credit.

One Final Request Before the Account Is Turned Over

If your customer has not responded to any of your efforts, the time has come for you to turn the account over to a collection agency or lawyer for further action. Send out a final certified letter (with a return receipt requested) stating your impending step, directing it to the accounting

Inside Track   When Your Message Finally Gets Through

As a business consultant for the past eighteen years, I often work with small companies going through financial problems. In some cases office managers or bookkeepers will have taken it upon themselves to "protect" a business owner from all bad news, including intercepting calls and letters from irate creditors. Sending a final letter via certified mail to the business owner has produced surprising results quite a few times.

In more than one such case, the owners called my clients to apologize and to arrange to pay the amount owed before any action would be instigated. They claimed they had never been told about previous demands for payment. I have seen this situation enough times to know it is a possible scenario. Your final letter should be a serious attempt to contact the person in charge at the highest level.

department you have been communicating with and to the president of the company. At this point you will be paying a percentage of the account to a collector, so spending a few extra dollars to make sure everyone necessary is notified makes sense. The letter should be very explicit.

ABC Supply
Attn: Accounts Payable
And Attn: Mr. Joe Black, President

Ladies/Gentlemen:
After repeated attempts to collect on our invoice #6656 in the amount of $1,856.04, we have received no response from your company. This letter is to notify you that this account will be turned over to our attorney, Ms. Susan Miller, to begin legal proceedings in five (5) days. This is not an action we like to pursue, but your lack of payment effort leaves us no choice.
Sincerely,

John Smith
Controller

In most instances you will not get any reaction to this last warning. However, on occasion company officials actually will seek to avoid this final step.

There is always some chance that the officials in charge have not seen or opened the previous communications and so are not aware of this late stage.

A Postdated Check Is Only a Promise to Pay

Most credit professionals, knowing that passing a bad check is a serious offense, will try to secure a check even with a future date from a customer. I have heard of requests for a series of checks dated one month apart that together total the outstanding amount. However, enforcement of postdated checks carries more psychological than legal weight. In most jurisdictions, a postdated check constitutes only "a promise to pay," and if it isn't good when you deposit it, it becomes just another collection problem. You can demand a check but receiving one written with a future date may not be prosecutable, unlike a check that fails to clear on the date made out.

Typically when you make a sale or complete a service that your customer pays for with a check, it is considered a cash sale. Beware of the customer who asks you to accept a check with a date written a few weeks or a month into the future. Since a job isn't completely paid for until the check for payment has cleared, the sale is actually made on credit rather than on a cash basis. Only extend this courtesy to a customer you know and whom you would otherwise give credit to. If the check then bounces, you have a collection problem on your hands. A current check exchanged for value is a clear effort at fraud; a postdated check is more obscure.

▶▶ TEST DRIVE

You have a few customers simply not paying at all. You are faced with a real collection process. To deal with such cases, ask yourself the following questions:

- ➲ Have you called the customer personally?
- ➲ Do you send demand letters via registered mail?
- ➲ Have you sent a final notice to the business owner before turning over the account to a collection agency?

4

Aggressive Collections

Understanding FDCPA

The rules on collecting from a consumer are vastly different from those on collecting from a business. Just as consumers are protected under the Equal Credit Opportunity Act (see Chapter 5), the federal government regulates credit agency collections from individual debtors through the Fair Debt Collection Practices Act (FDCPA). Individual consumers are also protected by state statutes.

Although some businesses that operate separate credit functions are governed by FDCPA regulations, if you are the original creditor attempting to collect a delinquent account, you are not subject to the terms of this law. Nevertheless, it is a good idea to understand its boundaries since collection agencies in fact act on your behalf to secure payments you are owed. The federal government has established parameters to prevent abusive collection activities, and even a company not barred explicitly from harassment practices would do well to set policies that follow these guidelines.

The Collection Call

FDCPA enables a collection agency to do its job so long as it doesn't engage in abusive practices toward a debtor. Collection-agency personnel are unknown third parties, some of whom use harassing and intimidating tactics. The employees are often paid on commission, which makes them eager—perhaps overeager—to collect a debt.

Property Owners Are Exempt as Well

When property owners hire outside managers to take care of tenants, these managers can usually collect rents as agents of the owners, which thereby exempts them from FDCPA regulations. In some states, they can also act on behalf of owners in small claims court when collection leads to enforcement or eviction. Landlord-tenant laws are distinct from collection laws and are discussed in greater depth in Chapter 18.

There are specific rules about when and how often a collector can call. They cannot call before 8 A.M. or after 9 P.M., and they cannot make multiple calls to the same debtor over a single day or multiple days in a row. This policy makes sense for you to follow as well; you should either talk to your delinquent customer or leave a message. Numerous phone calls only agitate a recipient, who will not respond any differently to you after a matter of hours.

You might be angry your bill is unpaid, and when you attempt to collect, the person who owes you might become evasive. That doesn't mean you should behave poorly in response. Intimidation will not generate cash if financial problems exist.

The Tone of the Call

Following a script might be appropriate to keep to the task and make the necessary points. Many collection agencies use a script because their callers are required to follow a certain protocol, such as identifying themselves as debt collectors and using their own names. Obscene language, racial or ethnic slurs, and intimidation (such as threatening to seize assets or to have a debtor arrested) are prohibited.

Proceeding constructively offers an opportunity to gather information on your customer's financial status (such as changes in income and job situation or suffering recent setbacks), which might facilitate your debt recovery. Provoking an overly distressed debtor without learning anything new merely wastes your time and effort.

Try a Little Kindness

This book focuses primarily on business-to-business collections because fewer companies carry direct consumer credit these days; consumers now have other financing alternatives. But if you are faced with a consumer's unpaid bill that has reached the aggressive collection stage, try using a little kindness with your customer.

Most people have experienced being on the receiving end of a collection call at least once, and it isn't any fun. Perhaps you missed a payment due to simple error, yet the situation is embarrassing to explain. Or if you are experiencing a temporary cash-flow problem, you feel the pressure personally.

You can still demand payment of an individual, but if you convey some level of understanding, your approach might breed success. Ask your customer to make a partial payment with a credit card. You are one individual talking to another, and your call does not have to be abusive even if there is no regulation against it. When the time comes that you believe stronger action is required, turn the matter over to a professional collection agency.

Do Not Violate the Applicable Law

Do not threaten your delinquent customer with legal action if you do not intend to carry it out. Do not threaten to have your customer arrested or to garnish his wages. Nor should you attempt to collect more than you are owed by adding fees not spelled out in your credit agreement. Do not misrepresent who you are. Why risk losing the right to collect what is owed you because in creating a false impression you have given your debtor a defense? When you go into full collection mode in-house, it is advisable to train your staff to follow FDCPA guidelines.

Calling Third Parties

Also be aware of the provisions of FDCPA law that protect privacy. For instance, you can only discuss a debt with your actual customer or her official representative, such as an attorney. As a general rule, you as the direct creditor must contact the debtor's lawyer if she has hired one to represent her, rather than deal directly with the party.

You cannot call a debtor at his place of work once he objects to this behavior, nor can you call a debtor's friends, neighbors, or relatives and leave any message other than simply to call you back. If your customer has disconnected his phone, you may attempt to track down his new number, within reason. If you are the direct creditor, do not advertise your collection practices to anyone who is not the actual debtor, even if they might be your customers.

Dealing with Cosigners

You are allowed to call a cosigner for an overdue payment (or for information) just as you would call the original debtor. Demanding payment through frequent calls to a cosigner might actually produce results, since a person in such a position seeks to protect her own credit rating and has an interest in resolving the matter by making payment. You do have the right to enforce collection action against a cosigner if you are not paid.

Remember that the cosigner might be unaware the debtor hasn't been making payments and that you might have other business with this individual. Keep the cosigner informed, but don't act as if she has tried to skip out on a bill. If she is a parent or relative of your customer, she could be in a position to generate some payments for you.

What to Do When You Are Told to Cease

There comes a time, when a debtor is wholly unhelpful, that the debt collection becomes little more than an ongoing argument. If at this point your customer breaks off conversation with you, you must respect that decision. This can happen if he hires a lawyer, whereupon you'll have to turn your attention to the attorney.

If a debtor informs a collection agency in writing that she wishes no further contact, the request must be respected by the agency. The agency will probably refer the case back to you to begin legal proceedings.

When a debtor files for bankruptcy under any chapter, all collection action must stop, whether by you as the direct creditor or your agent. All contact and proceedings must now proceed through the court (or its trustee), which then handles any future payments to creditors.

Collection Agencies May Be Sued

If you are the original creditor and you violate FDCPA laws, not much can be done to take official action against you. However, a debtor can initiate action against a collection agency for harassment or for violating privacy regulations of FDCPA. Does this mean that debtors are protected by law from meeting obligations? Not at all.

If a debtor does not pay but has the ability to do so, you can file a judgment that will enable you eventually to collect the money, less any fees. The federal law simply tempers overaggressive collection agencies.

Staying Polite and Providing Customer Service While Collecting

After a certain point you are dealing with someone you no longer think of as a customer. So why should you be concerned about a debtor's perception of your collection conduct? Because your interaction with a consumer who owes you money will be taken very personally, how you conduct yourself will be noted and possibly repeated to third parties. The reputation of your business as viewed by existing and potential customers is at stake.

In attempting to collect in-house from your customer, you are dealing with a personal relationship, perhaps with someone you know or a long-term customer of your business. Your behavior might be instrumental in salvaging a future relationship. Adopt a "good cop/bad cop" strategy in which you function as the good cop and leave it to the collection agency to serve as the "bad" one if necessary. But first letting your customer know you are trying to keep the case out of the hands of your collection agency (which would affect her credit rating) gives you leverage.

Making a Decision to Turn Over an Account

The parameters on when to turn an account over to a collection agency vary depending on whether you are dealing with consumers or businesses. A company that doesn't pay its bills can end up closing the doors or filing for bankruptcy. Unlike a business, consumers don't cease to exist simply because they can't pay their bills. In fact, unless they take the drastic action of filing for bankruptcy, the debt they owe you today shows on their credit report for years to come. On the other hand, without putting greater pressure on your debtor, you are unlikely ever to be paid.

Not Everybody Plays by the Rules

One of my business clients held a gasoline credit card in her own name that she used for business travel. Her company paid this bill until it began to have serious cash-flow problems. When my client did not pay it either, the bill was turned over to a collection agency fairly quickly. All the abusive behavior barred by FDCPA was considered fair game by this agency. When after hearing about the bill collector's harassing phone calls I had a chance to talk to the young man, I was amazed. His rude and demeaning behavior included inappropriate conversation with the attorney involved. In addition to the original cardholder, the five of us connected with the case were left with such a negative lasting impression that we determined never to do business again with the small chain of convenience stores that had issued the credit card. To this day I drive by these stores and never go in. The company not only lost our business, it didn't collect any money. And I continue to spread the word to acquaintances about the offending company.

Here are some guidelines on when to call an agency to collect a consumer debt:

1. The account is ninety days past due.
2. Two (or more) promises of payment have not been met.
3. The telephone is disconnected. (These days you need more than one phone number.)
4. The customer admits that he "can't" pay and will not discuss future payments.
5. The customer "suddenly" disputes the merchandise or service. (He is preparing a defense.)

When you have met with no success in collecting, it is time to take a new tactic.

Try Small Claims Court

Direct creditors of nonpaying customers, whether consumers or businesses, are entitled to file a claim in a local court often referred to as "small claims." Each state has an upper limit to what you can collect in small claims court, which is usually in the $3,000–$5,000 range. This might cover what is owed you.

Strictly Business

I know very few business owners who haven't gone unpaid by customers with whom they have had personal, nonbusiness friendships. Sometimes the credit terms in these cases were too loose and invited trouble. (And not everyone is who she seems to be.) There are times when a customer has expected too much from a relationship with a business owner.

In the case of one client, the last payment of $28,000 for completed work on a large construction project went uncollected for over a year. The amount due represented most of the profit. As my client's calls to the property owner became insistent, the friendship cooled and fingers started to point. The situation allowed no room for compromise, with the result that the bill has yet to be paid more than a year later. My client lost money, a customer, and a friend. Be careful before placing yourself in such a complicated situation. Be businesslike with every customer or client you deal with, whether personal friend or not.

Since the rules and limits are the same for consumer and business credit claims, the state-by-state details are listed in the next chapter. Court personnel in small claims court are usually very helpful, so you can file without an attorney. Refer to the rules of your state in Chapter 17, "Collecting from a Business."

Understand That Any Cash Is Better than No Cash

The percentage of recovered debt kept by a collection agency might give you pause in turning to outside collection. You sold the unpaid goods or services and have absorbed those actual costs plus the cost of carrying the debt. Now having to pay further costs to collect the money seems too much. Nevertheless, face the fact that you are going to lose money on the original deal; the only question is how much. If you take no action, you will lose the entire sum. Whatever you recover through the process of outside collection is found money.

▶▶ TEST DRIVE

When you are collecting from a consumer customer, make sure your conduct falls within the parameters of the Fair Debt Collection Practices Act (FDCPA). Remember that you are dealing with real people in a difficult situation. Ask yourself the following:

- Have you read over the rules of the FDCPA?
- Do you follow the federal law's general guidelines?
- Are you aware that in the course of collecting a debt you are sometimes talking to uninvolved individuals?
- Do you know when it is time to turn an unpaid account over to a collection agency?

FDCPA Does Not Apply

As has been discussed, the rules for providing business-to-business credit differ from those for consumer credit. The federal government is not as protective in matters of equality, privacy, and collection abuse that involve a business entity as it is of the individual consumer. In cases of competing claims for the assets of a business debtor, for instance, there is legal recourse for a single direct creditor. As a business creditor, however, you first need to understand the strategy of your debtors.

Although under federal law bill collectors can call a consumer only during certain hours, they can call a business anytime they want. Collectors cannot discuss the personal debt of an individual with a third party, but when a company owes money, they can speak to anyone who answers the business phone. But even though you can exercise a wide range of (noncriminal) behavior in debt collection from a company, even from its principal debtors, you should practice some self-imposed limits. Try to remain polite and businesslike because only a few of the employees you interact with are likely to be responsible for the debt; abusing staff members who simply work for the company is bad public relations. Besides, they will just make your job more complicated if you anger them.

Lawyers Are Expensive

I once had a client refuse to pay my fees or make any promise of payment. After a few months of argument, I would have settled for a portion, but she would not negotiate.

When my attorney wrote a letter threatening legal action, my client's response was to file a lawsuit against me. Each side dug in its heels for a few more months, demanding records and answers to written questions. The case was scheduled for arbitration—an informal proceeding intended for small amounts. Two days before the court date, my client's lawyer suggested we settle without further payment to each other. I agreed and received no more money, only a legal bill, as did my former client; the lawyers were the only ones paid. I'm still angry, as I am sure the woman is. This is the type of case in which nobody wins. There are times, however, when you are left with no other choices.

If You Have a Guarantee, Mention It

If the credit application with your nonpaying customer includes a clause in which an individual guarantees the company's debt, now is the time to mention this. Let the principal know you will pursue aggressively the money owed your company. As long as any part of the debt remains unpaid, you will seek full legal redress to collect from the responsible parties.

If you have a history of successful debt collection, mention this fact and that eventually you will force payment from someone. Convey that you are not issuing an idle threat and that, on the contrary, you will not walk away from money you have earned and are entitled to.

You are seeking communication in order to obtain information about if and when you will be paid; you need the cooperation of employees.

Do Not Inflate What Is Owed

Federal trade laws as well as those applicable in most states do in fact prevent you from adding extra charges to a business debt in excess of your stated (in your business customer agreement) late penalty and interest charges. Perhaps you assume that if your customer's amount grows quickly, you will be paid more quickly. This is not only unlikely, but you could be in violation of the law. Your company attorney or accountant should be able to give you guidance in this regard. Aside from compliance with existing law, understand that only a collection agency makes money from the collection process.

However, you can inform your debtor that once you take legal action, additional legal fees and court costs will run up the amount. These can add as much as thirty percent, a claim you are likely to win in court proceedings and can enforce in a judgment.

Calls Are Now Serious Business

By this time in your collection process, you should be exchanging calls with the principal of the business account. Serious action is being considered, too important for leaving phone messages. Try calling first thing in the morning or just after the business has closed for the day. See if you can get the personal e-mail address or cell-phone number of the owner. Use a home number if you have it. This is the final step before you give up part of your earned proceeds (and likely all of your profit) to a third party, so the time has come to explain the lawsuit ahead if your debtor does not pay in full or negotiate an acceptable settlement.

Secure Promises to Pay

Your questions to the debtor should be specific and direct: "How much can you send us and when can we expect that check?" You might want to request overnight mail or Electric Funds Transfer, if you are set up to receive this. You are looking for cash in hand and do not have time to listen to stories or negotiate deals. Any offer at this point must come with a check, cash, money order, or credit card number. Offer to send someone by the place of business to pick up the funds. A promise needs to be sealed with a cash transaction.

Document All of Your Demands

You need to document fully every letter, phone call, and visit with the debtor. Note when, how, and with whom you have made contact, and transcribe any conversations. Use a scheduling program that reminds you of your next steps and follow up on these precisely as promised. Be relentless in your collection procedure. Mention that "this is the fourth letter" or "we have spoken before," and record all explanations made and promises broken.

Electronic File Management

If your company handles more than a few credit accounts, you need to install a data management system. Your increased efficiency (how soon you make phone calls and do follow-ups) and greater accuracy with documents will result in real cost savings for your business. Off-the-shelf software programs for converting paper documents to electronic images and managing a contact program are available at a reasonable price; examples include such programs as ACT or Sage CRM (which allows you to look

See for Yourself

One of my manufacturing company's distributors was always late making payments, using the excuse that he still had on his shelves the material we had manufactured for his customer. The companies that distributed our protective clothing had to keep large quantities in stock for when their customers would require these. We accommodated this standard procedure in our industry by granting our distributors more liberal terms for buying on credit from us.

Since we did most of our business with the distributor on the phone (the company was in a neighboring state ninety-five miles away), I took him at his word—that is, until his account became particularly high and we received no payments for over ninety days. I was about to turn the account over to a collection agency but in a final attempt to collect in-house decided to drive to Ohio to pay the company a visit.

I was greeted warmly but cautiously. I assumed a friendly demeanor and in the course of conversation mentioned that I could take some inventory back for credit. I wanted to assess for myself the distributor's inventory problems.

"Let's see how much extra material you have, and I'll take some of it back with me," I offered, expecting to receive some cash as well. The more we could lower the balance due us, the better.

"Well, I'm not sure what we have."

According to the distributor's excuses, the company should have had thousands of dollars of our product on their shelves, but there was virtually nothing there. We were both embarrassed. I left with a check and the conviction that if I wanted to collect all our money, I would have to close this account and send it to collection—which I did. The payment for our product had come and gone.

into the actual Account module to get up-to-date information). Your initial costs will be repaid in months by your ability to collect payments more efficiently.

Personal Visits Are Allowed and Might Work

There is no reason you cannot make a personal visit to any company that owes you money. People usually have a hard time looking someone in the face and saying they won't pay. Your strategy is to make it as hard for your business customer as possible. Don't try to schedule an appointment;

rather, find out when your customer is usually at work and make it your business to be there. Your intention here is not to provoke a confrontation but to appeal to the business owner's sense of fairness—and to see for yourself what is going on at the place of business. You might even walk away with some money.

Take copies of the open invoices with you, and be prepared to show a statement of the account with all charges and credits up to this point. You want to be able to answer any questions on the spot and prove the accuracy of the amount currently owed. Some customers will pay when they have run out of excuses.

Don't Threaten Action You Do Not Intent to Take

Even though a business-to-business credit transaction is not regulated by FDCPA, you are still barred from making idle or illegal threats. Do not threaten any of your customers with arrest for not paying their bill. Do not say that you have sued someone or that you are sending over the constable to confiscate their possessions. There are legal steps you should take, but making harassing threats is not allowed in any business transaction.

Can You Take It to Small Claims Court?

The first issue to consider is the size of your claim. Each state sets a maximum amount you can sue for in small claims court, regardless of the amount owed you. If you win the top amount allowed by state law, your case is settled in full. But pursuing a small claim costs so much less than full litigation that a compromise might be worth it.

In most states the procedure in small claims court is fairly easy. The district offices that serve metropolitan areas can help in showing you how the paperwork must be filled out and then served on the debtor. Some states require formal service of the complaint (that is, delivering it in person) and others allow service via certified mail.

Although attorneys are allowed in some small claims courts, they are not required. You are given the opportunity to explain your side of the story to a magistrate or judge and offer your evidence. The defendant has the same right. A decision can be handed down immediately from the bench and later confirmed in writing.

Material evidence wins in small claims court. The more documentation you can provide about a debt, the more likely you are to win. The debtor cannot simply say your work was unacceptable or a bill has already been paid but has to prove her case with records of her own (such as via cancelled checks).

In some states the decision in small claims court is final, with no possibility for appeal; in others, either one side or each side is given up to forty-five days to file an appeal and have the case reviewed or reheard. In the latter case, the final determination is not always rapid. A debtor intent on avoiding a claim can take the matter to state court.

Collecting What You Owe

The court will order a judgment in your favor for the money you have been awarded plus court costs. But you still have to collect the actual money from the defendant. You can usually use a sheriff to help and can serve your papers on a bank to collect money or on a business or home to take possessions. The enforced collection of money is not an easy process, but once you win a judgment from small claims court, it is expedited.

A State-by-State Review of Small Claims Court

The laws regulating the small claims process vary by state. If you are considering going through small claims court to collect a debt, first check the applicable laws in your state to determine whether the effort is worth your while.

State:	**ALABAMA**	*Limit on Suit:* $3,000
Where to file:	In the county where defendant resides. A company can be sued in the counties where it does business.	
Attorneys:	Allowed.	
Appeals:	Either party may appeal within fourteen days.	
Other information:	Once a defendant has been served, must file a written answer within fourteen days or loses by default.	

State: **ALASKA**   *Limit on Suit*: $10,000

Where to file: The nearest court to defendant's residence or the district where a company does business.

Attorneys: Allowed.

Appeals: Only required for collection agencies.

Other information: Written answer required by defendant within twenty days or default judgment is entered.

State: **ARIZONA**   *Limit on Suit*: $2,500

Where to file: Court near defendant's residence or where the transaction took place.

Attorneys: Attorneys only with mutual written agreement.

Appeals: Cases of $2,500–$5,000 may be transferred.

Other information: Written answer required by defendant within twenty days. Collection agencies not permitted.

State: **ARKANSAS**   *Limit on Suit*: $5,000

Where to file: County where defendant resides or transaction took place.

Attorneys: Not allowed.

Appeals: Appeals are allowed within thirty days.

Other information: Written answer required by defendant within twenty days. Collection agencies not permitted.

State: **CALIFORNIA**   *Limit on Suit*: $7,500

Where to file: District where defendant lives or transaction took place.

Attorneys: Not permitted.

Appeals: Appeals allowed within thirty days on counterclaims.

Other information: Collection agencies not permitted. Court advisors may be available.

State: **COLORADO**   *Limit on Suit*: $7,500

Where to file: County where defendant resides or transaction took place.

Attorneys:	Attorneys can appear only if representing their own interests, in which case the other side is allowed an attorney also.
Appeals:	Appeals permitted to district court within fifteen days.
Other information:	Collection agencies not permitted.

State:	**CONNECTICUT**	*Limit on Suit*:	$5,000
Where to file:	County where defendant resides or does business.		
Attorneys:	Allowed; required for companies.		
Appeals:	No appeals.		
Other information:	Case may be moved to superior court when a counterclaim exists.		

State:	**DELAWARE**	*Limit on Suit*:	$15,000
Where to file:	Anywhere in state.		
Attorneys:	Allowed.		
Appeals:	Appeal for new trial allowed within fifteen days.		
Other information:	Parties may be able to demand a jury trial.		

State:	**DISTRICT OF COLUMBIA**	*Limit on Suit*:	$5,000
Where to file:	County where defendant lives or where transaction took place.		
Attorneys:	Attorneys are required for companies and permitted by others.		
Appeals:	Appeal permitted within fifteen days.		
Other information:	May require mandatory mediation.		

State:	**FLORIDA**	*Limit on Suit*:	$5,000
Where to file:	County where defendant lives or business transaction took place.		
Attorneys:	Attorney allowed.		
Appeals:	Appeals permitted within ten days of decision.		
Other information:	A jury trial may be demanded by either party.		

State:	**GEORGIA**	*Limit on Suit:* $15,000
Where to file:	County where defendant resides.	
Attorneys:	Attorneys permitted.	
Other information:	Complaint must be answered by defendant within thirty days to prevent default.	

State:	**HAWAII**	*Limit on Suit:* $3,500
Where to file:	Judicial district where defendant lives or where transaction occurred.	
Attorneys:	Attorneys are allowed.	
Appeals:	There are no appeals.	
Other information:	Jury trials may be heard in higher court.	

State:	**IDAHO**	*Limit on Suit:* $4,000
Where to file:	County where defendant resides or where transaction occurred.	
Attorneys:	Attorneys not allowed.	
Appeals:	Appeals for a new trial permitted within thirty days.	
Other information:	No jury trials. No collection agencies allowed.	

State:	**ILLINOIS**	*Limit on Suit* $10,000
Where to file:	County of defendant's residence or business transaction.	
Attorneys:	Attorneys permitted.	
Appeals:	Appeals allowed within thirty days.	
Other information:	Jury trial may be requested.	

State:	**INDIANA**	*Limit on Suit:* $6,000
Where to file:	County where defendant resides or business is transacted.	
Attorneys:	Attorneys allowed.	
Appeals:	May appeal to higher court.	
Other information:	Defendant may request jury trial.	

State: **IOWA**   *Limit on Suit:* $5,000

Where to file: County where the defendant resides or business transaction occurred.

Attorneys: Attorneys are allowed.

Appeals: Oral requests may be made at the end of the hearing for an appeal or a written notice filed by defendant within twenty days.

Other information: Written answers must be filed by defendant within twenty days to prevent default. Court retains jurisdiction on collection.

State: **KANSAS**   *Limit on Suit:* $4,000

Where to file: County where defendant resides or where business was transacted.

Attorneys: Allowed by both parties.

Appeals: Appeals permitted within ten days notice.

Other information: Plaintiffs are limited to certain number of suits per year.

State: **KENTUCKY**   *Limit on Suit:* $1,500

Where to file: Judicial district where defendant lives or does business.

Attorneys: Attorneys allowed.

Appeals: Appeals permitted within ten days.

Other information: Collection agents not permitted. No person may file more than twenty-five claims in a district court.

State: **LOUISIANA**   *Limit on Suit:* $3,000

Where to file: Defendant's parish.

Attorneys: Attorneys are allowed.

Appeals: Appeals for a new trial can be made within fifteen days.

Other information   *Default judgment stands if answer is not filed within fifteen days.*

State:	**MAINE**	*Limit on Suit*: $4,500
Where to file:	District where defendant lives or business transaction took place.	
Attorneys:	No attorneys.	
Appeals:	Appeals allowed within ten days.	
Other information:	Case may be referred to mediation.	

State:	**MARYLAND**	*Limit on Suit*: $5,000
Where to file:	County where defendant lives or county where transaction took place.	
Attorneys:	Attorneys are allowed.	
Appeals:	Appeals are allowed within thirty days.	
Other information:	Either side may demand a jury trial and move the action to a higher court.	

State:	**MASSACHUSETTS**	*Limit on Suit*: $2,000
Where to file:	District where plaintiff or defendant live or do business.	
Attorneys:	Lawyers allowed.	
Appeals:	Appeals from defendant allowed within ten days.	
Other information:	May request move to higher court.	

State:	**MICHIGAN**	Limit on Suit: $3,000
Where to file:	District where defendant resides or where breach or injury occurred.	
Attorneys:	Attorneys not allowed.	
Appeals:	If trial was before district court magistrate, yes within seven days; otherwise no.	

State:	**MINNESOTA**	*Limit on Suit*: $7,500
Where to file:	County where defendant lives.	
Attorneys:	No attorneys permitted.	
Appeals:	No appeals permitted	

State: **MISSISSIPPI**   Limit on Suit: $2,500
Where to file: Where defendant resides; for nonresident
                            defendants, where breach or injury occurred.
Attorneys: Attorneys allowed.
Appeals: Allowed by either side within ten days for a new trial.

State: **MISSOURI**   *Limit on Suit*: $3,000
Where to file: District where defendant lives or transaction took place.
Attorneys: Attorneys allowed.
Appeals: Appeals may be made within ten days.

State: **MONTANA**   *Limit on Suit*: $3,000
Where to file: Any judicial district.
Attorneys: Attorneys not allowed except by mutual consent.
Appeals: Appeals may be made within thirty days.
Other information: Defendant may request move to District Court.

State: **NEBRASKA**   *Limit on Suit*: $2,700
Where to file: Defendant's resident county.
Attorneys: No attorneys allowed.
Appeals: Appeals permitted within thirty days.
Other information: May be moved to higher court.

State: **NEVADA**   *Limit on Suit*: $5,000
Where to file: City of defendant's residence.
Attorneys: Attorneys allowed.
Appeals: Appeals allowed within thirty days.
Other information: May be transferred to higher court if there is a
                            counterclaim.

State: **NEW HAMPSHIRE**   Limit on Suit: $5,000
Where to file: Where plaintiff or defendant resides; for nonresident
                            defendants, where breach or injury occurred.
Attorneys: Attorneys allowed.
Appeals: Allowed by either side within thirty days for review
                            of law, not facts.

State:	**NEW JERSEY**	*Limit on Suit*: $3,000

Where to file: County where defendant resides or corporation is headquartered.

Attorneys: Attorneys allowed.

Appeals: Appeals may be taken within forty-five days.

Other information: May request transfer to higher court.

State:	**NEW MEXICO**	*Limit on Suit*: $10,000

Where to file: County where defendant lives or company does business.

Attorneys: Attorneys allowed.

Appeals: Appeals may be made within fifteen days.

State:	**NEW YORK**	*Limit on Suit*: $5,000
		($3,000 depending on own or city)

Where to file: Defendant's resident county. To sue in New York City, plaintiff or defendant must live or work there.

Attorneys: Attorneys allowed.

Appeals: Appeals may be made within thirty days.

Other information: May utilize electronic filing.

State:	**NORTH CAROLINA**	*Limit on Suit*: $5,000

Where to file: Defendant's home county.

Attorneys: Attorneys allowed.

Appeals: Appeals within ten days.

Other information: May request move to higher court.

State:	**NORTH DAKOTA**	*Limit on Suit*: $5,000

Where to file: Defendant's home county.

Attorneys: Attorneys allowed and may be provided for low-income individuals.

Appeals: Appeals allowed for thirty days.

State:	**OHIO**	*Limit on Suit*: $3,000

Where to file: County where defendant lives or company transacts business.

| *Attorneys*: | Attorneys allowed. |
| *Appeals*: | Fifteen days to appeal. |

State:	**OKLAHOMA**	*Limit on Suit*:	$6,000
Where to file:	County where defendant lives or transaction occurred.
Attorneys:	Attorneys allowed.
Appeals:	Appeals must be made within thirty days.

State:	**OREGON**	*Limit on Suit*:	$5,000
Where to file:	County of defendant's residence or where business transaction took place.
Attorneys:	Attorneys not allowed.
Appeals:	Defendant may file an appeal within ten days.

State:	**PENNSYLVANIA**	*Limit on Suit*:	$8,000
Where to file:	Where defendant lives or works and can be served and where transaction took place.
Attorneys:	Attorneys allowed.
Appeals:	Thirty days to appeal.

State:	**RHODE ISLAND**	*Limit on Suit*:	$2,500
Where to file:	District where either party can be served.
Attorneys:	Attorneys are allowed.
Appeals:	No appeal unless a counterclaim is filed.

State:	**SOUTH CAROLINA**	*Limit on Suit*:	$7,500
Where to file:	County where defendant has residence.
Attorneys:	Attorneys allowed.
Appeals:	No appeals.

State:	**SOUTH DAKOTA**	*Limit on Suit*:	$8,000
Where to file:	Defendant's home county.
Attorneys:	Attorneys allowed.
Appeals:	Appeals within thirty days.

State: **TENNESSEE**   *Limit on Suit:* $15,000–$25,000
                                                (depending on county)
Where to file: Plaintiff or defendant county of residence.
Attorneys: Attorneys allowed.
Appeals: Appeals within fifteen days.
Other information: Answers required to prevent default judgment.

State: **TEXAS**   *Limit on Suit:* $5,000
Where to file: County where defendant lives.
Attorneys: Attorneys permitted.
Appeals: Ten-day period for appeal.

State: **UTAH**   *Limit on Suit:* $7,500
Where to file: County where defendant lives.
Attorneys: Attorneys permitted.
Appeals: No appeal period.

State: **VERMONT**   *Limit on Suit:* $3,500
Where to file: District where defendant or plaintiff lives.
Attorneys: Attorneys are permitted.
Appeals: Appeals may be filed within thirty days.

State: **VIRGINIA**   *Limit on Suit:* $2,000
Where to file: Where defendant lives, is employed or where trans-
                       action took place.
Attorneys: Attorneys not permitted.
Appeals: Ten-day period to appeal.
Other information: May request transfer to higher court.

State: **WASHINGTON**   *Limit on Suit:* $4,000
Where to file: Residence of defendant.
Attorneys: Attorneys not allowed.
Appeals: May appeal within fifteen days.

State: **WEST VIRGINIA**   *Limit on Suit*: $5,000
Where to file: Where defendant lives or transaction took place.
Attorneys: Attorneys allowed.
Appeals: Twenty days to appeal.

State: **WISCONSIN**   *Limit on Suit*: $5,000
Where to file: County of defendant's residence or where transaction occurred.
Attorneys: Attorneys allowed.
Appeals: Appeals allowed under some circumstances.

State: **WYOMING**   *Limit on Suit*: $5,000
Where to file: County where defendant resides or transaction occurred.
Attorneys: Attorneys allowed.
Appeals: Ten-day appeal period.

▶▶ TEST DRIVE

When you have reached the stage of aggressive collection from a business, prepare for future court action. The easiest court to use is small claims. Are you first trying all the means at your disposal before moving on to a collection agency or small claims court?

- ➲ Do you keep all transaction documents in a customer account?
- ➲ Have you directly called the principal of the business that owes you money?
- ➲ Have you considered a personal visit to check on the circumstances of the nonpaying company?
- ➲ Have you only threatened legal action when you are ready to take it?
- ➲ Have you tried filing in small claims court?

The Terms Are in the Lease

Often businesses find themselves in the position of casual landlords, renting out space in excess of their own operations. Some companies invest in real estate as a business strategy, while others buy commercial property to protect or enhance their operation. Collecting money owed by a tenant is a fairly complex area, and you need to know what you can and cannot do.

A lease is a contract between tenant and landlord that spells out the terms and conditions of a rental agreement. It cannot be changed while the term is running except with the agreement of both parties. A lease may run for a specified period of time (for example, one year), or it may be established on a month-to-month basis, which means that either side may terminate with a thirty-day notice. In most cases, a lease that runs over its existing term is considered on a month-to-month basis, meaning that the tenant continues to pay unless and until a new term is negotiated and a thirty-day termination notice is all that is required. Although a lease may be an oral agreement, both tenant and landlord would be foolish to make so informal an arrangement. One party is providing space, and the other is relying on having the space in which to reside or to run a business—the stakes for each are too high.

The Financial Terms Should Be Clearly Detailed

A lease describes the space that is being rented, the term of the agreement, the monthly payment, the date on which that payment is due, and the penalty for late payment. The signature of your tenant means that he has agreed to make these payments on a timely basis. Just because there should be no disagreement about the financial terms does not give assurance that your rent will be paid on time. There are times when a problem arises entirely due to money: a tenant loses her job, or a business isn't doing well. But there are also situations in which a tenant lodges a complaint due to the condition of the property. Assuming that you (the landlord) are given proper notice, the receipt of your rent may depend on how quickly and how well you handle the situation at hand.

Personal Guarantees on a Commercial Lease

Most closely held companies are asked to sign a personal guarantee on a business lease, unless the company has been in business for a long time and perhaps at the same location. Start-ups have a high mortality rate, and commercial landlords know this. Restaurants can come and go in less than a year. Depending on the work done to a rental space and who pays for this, there can be substantial money involved in finding a new tenant. Renting property can be a high-risk business. Those who are successful at it get as much of a security deposit as possible, which can be in the form of a personal guarantee.

Check Credit Before Renting

Later in the chapter we will discuss the differences between a residential tenant and a commercial tenant. In dealing with either case, you must take care to check out the tenant's credit rating. If you are renting to an individual, you should require a full application that includes his source of income and the contact information of previous landlords. Pull a full credit report on all named tenants and then call at least one of the landlords listed on the application. You want to know what sort of tenant each applicant has been.

With a company seeking a commercial lease, you need to know something about the business operation. Does it have sufficient revenue and profit to pay your rent easily? A new business is always a risk so you might ask for a few months of security. Ask about the finances of the business owner as well.

Residential Leases

A number of financial and operational items are covered in a residential lease. Make sure you clearly specify your tenants' obligations in renting space from you. Include clauses on the following subjects:

- Name of landlord
- Name of all tenants who will sign the lease
- Starting and ending date of lease

- Security deposit
- Key deposit
- Insurance requirements
- Assignment or sublease by tenant
- Responsibility for damage
- Use of premises
- Landlord's right to mortgage
- Landlord's right to enter
- Utility service
- Lease violations (this includes failure to pay as well as other cause for termination)
- Landlord's right to sue

Office-supply stores carry preprinted legal forms, and landlord associations provide lease forms. If you routinely lease property, have an attorney draw up or read over any legally binding documents you use.

Be a Consistent Landlord

Act consistently toward your tenants so they know what to expect from you. If you require rent due on the fifth of the month, consider it delinquent if you receive it even a day late, and notify your tenant to that effect. If you intend to begin an eviction process, sending an official notice of late payment starts the clock ticking.

Commercial Leases

A commercial lease is more comprehensive than a residential lease and should be written by an attorney. It should address issues of payment, renewal, cost sharing, maintenance, and even hours of operation. This last means that you must ensure that your property is accessible during required hours to provide cross traffic to tenant stores.

You must establish a fixed rent due on a determined date and include a penalty provision for late payment. In addition, many leases include a "common area maintenance" (CAM) charge, which enables you to pass on common costs such as a new roof or resurfacing of a parking lot.

Section 8 Tenants Are Low-Credit Risks

Some landlords willingly offer units for rent under the federal government's Section 8 program, a federally funded program (HUD) usually managed by local Housing Authorities, which provides government-subsidized housing vouchers. Other landlords are cynical about the program. You are permitted to decide whom to accept as Section 8 tenants, using the same criteria you would for any tenant. The rent is paid by a government agency, and the benefit to you as the landlord is that it is always paid regularly and on time. Being able to rely with certainty on receiving a regular monthly check is advantageous.

Built-in Renewals

Often it is in the interest of both tenant and landlord to include a second and even a third renewal term in a commercial lease. The initial lease might be for three years with an option for three more (allowing for a fixed percentage increase in the rent) and perhaps another three-year term. This gives your tenant stability to grow a business and ensures you a reliable tenant.

The Escalation Clause

An escalation clause means that if a tenant breaks a lease, the rental balance is "escalated" and due at that time. All commercial leases should include such a clause, since a tenant who vacates early proves costly. You will have to work to find a new tenant. Your agreement to a longer term of occupancy should not be disadvantaged by a tenant who decides to move on. There are times when tenants can "buy out" the balance of their leases.

Handling a Dispute

Whether your rental property is residential or commercial, as a landlord you have specific obligations regarding its maintenance and safety. You should schedule regular inspection of and repairs to your property, both to keep your investment intact and your tenant satisfied.

Upkeep of the mechanical operation of the building (plumbing, electric, gas service, etc.) is always your responsibility, as is maintenance of the roof and outside common areas. The conditions inside a unit are in part your tenant's responsibility. But it is in your interest to keep everything working and the rent money coming.

Gather a repair crew of people you can rely on to fix problems. A small plumbing problem might seem a mere nuisance, but your resulting water bill can skyrocket. If the damage was caused by a tenant, notify him immediately that he is responsible for payment.

Section 8 Will Schedule Inspections

If you are a Section 8 landlord, expect annual visits from an inspector who will notify you of any needed repairs. The government subsidizer will cease paying your rent if you don't tend to their list. A regular tenant as well can withhold rent to resolve a complaint. Become accustomed to responding to the concerns of your tenants.

Giving Notice to a Past-Due Tenant

You cannot simply throw a tenant out who doesn't pay the rent. There are rules to the eviction process.

Your first step is to terminate the tenancy. This requires giving notice, in writing, that a tenant's failure to pay rent has violated the terms of the lease. You can terminate the lease for cause through a notice such as the following:

NOTICE TO TERMINATE A LEASE

You are hereby required within ten (10) days from this date _____ to vacate, remove your belongings, and give up possession of the premises now used by you.

This eviction notice is the result of rent payment delinquency for which we will not continue to carry any arrears. Your responsibility to meet this obligation is covered by the lease you signed on _____. You are now in noncompliance.

Should you fail to pay within the allotted time, legal proceedings will be instituted against you to recover possession and to recover rents, damages, legal, and court costs.

Please contact this office immediately.

Rules vary across states but the first step in terminating a tenancy is serving a "notice to pay rent or quit." You are likely to give ten days for a cure before proceeding to civil court to file a judgment. Make sure that you distribute the termination notice to all applicable legal tenants.

Negotiating a Settlement

What do you do when your tenant decides to vacate your property (whether residential or commercial) because she no longer needs, wants, or can afford the rental space? The following circumstances allow termination of a lease:

⮑ Anyone called to active military duty may terminate a lease signed prior to that call. This requires a thirty-day notice.

⮑ A tenant over the age of sixty-two who must move to a care facility may also terminate an existing lease.

If your lease allows your tenant to assign or sublease the rental property, he could find a replacement as an alternative to breaking a lease. Such a solution is worth your approval as a way of avoiding the complexities of the eviction process.

The procedure, which involves seeking a judgment for money due you, followed by an action to repossess the property, is difficult enough that you might consider instead negotiating with your tenant. Options for settling include offering your tenant a rent deferral or payment plan. You could also agree to terminate an existing lease if your tenant agrees to leave voluntarily or to find a new tenant. Any solution that stops short of eviction will wind up saving you money and time.

Power Shortage

My own company operated for a number of years in a large industrial building that was old but well-wired. What I did not know was that the roof was leaking. The landlord, who occupied the top five floors of the building, knew of the problem but did not fix it. Eventually the entire building was affected and the electric boxes in our space shorted out. After having our system fixed myself, I began to withhold rent. We argued through our lawyers for six months before the landlord paid my expenses to leave. Four years remained on our lease, but we could no longer operate a company in that space, the physical conditions were that bad. I ignored the first signs of trouble because I knew how complicated it would be to move. The problems and the damage to my equipment made it even worse when the time came to do so.

Handling an Eviction

Once you as the landlord receive a court-ordered judgment to collect money due you, you then seek an action to officially terminate the tenancy. At this point the court order is turned over to a sheriff to execute. State laws differ as to the types of termination notice required and how this notice and subsequent eviction papers must be served. In some states you can complete the process in less than forty-five days, while in others this may take ninety days or more. A tenant who wants to delay eviction can do so by either filing a claim of her own or appealing to the court due to extenuating circumstances. Eviction proceedings can be held up by an error in your legal process or by a tenant's a defense, on a number of grounds.

You Cannot Lock Out a Tenant

After filing an action against your tenant to "pay rent or quit," your property is vulnerable to abuse. A tenant on his way out is not apt to be very careful about his surroundings. Even so, you cannot enter his premises without permission or lock him out. You must wait for a court decision and its enforcement authority. This is why it is in your interest to negotiate a settlement with your tenant that turns the property back over to you.

Termination on Sale

If you sublet space that you in turn rent from an owner, you might be bound by a clause in your lease that terminates your agreement upon sale of the property. The new owner will not be bound by the terms you have made with your existing tenants. Once you receive notice that the sale of the property has been finalized, all tenants must vacate the space without the need to give approval.

▶▶ TEST DRIVE

The terms of credit are structured by a landlord-tenant relationship but follow basic rules. Make sure that you are aware of the following:

⮕ Your rental terms are written into a lease.
⮕ Rental agreements differ depending on whether the property is residential or commercial.
⮕ You must handle a tenant complaint promptly or your rent might be justifiably withheld.
⮕ Negotiation with a tenant who has broken a lease is preferable to litigation.
⮕ The eviction process is neither easy nor quick and should be a last resort.

Check Out Agencies Before You Need One

The time comes when you realize your customer has no intention of making any further payments due you. Your communications, compromises, and in-house demands to collect have gone unheeded; your customer is clearly defaulting on his obligation to your business. The next step is to gather your documentation and turn the account over to a collection agency. It is better for you to move forward and leave the collection process to professionals.

Most collection agencies specialize in either consumer or business collection. Some agencies handle exclusively on-line business collection or work with a specific type of business or industry, such as medical collections. Because the policies and rules differ, it makes sense for agencies to separate consumer from business collections. In the case of collection of medical and doctors' bills, issues of insurance coverage are a factor. Different industries present specific challenges in the collection process. Agencies do best in handling cases they are experienced with, so you should research the type of agency you need in advance.

Further, not all agencies are equal in terms of professionalism and effectiveness. Collection is a complicated business. Debtors can be uncooperative, so the work is stressful. Agency fees are a percentage of the amount collected, so when a bill is never paid, there is no fee. Consider what it must be like to be on the phone all day convincing recalcitrant debtors to pay their bills. The job doesn't sound like much fun, does it? Hiring and training good bill collectors is an art. Many agencies, particularly the consumer ones, suffer from high turnover. Commercial bill collection is typically run more professionally.

Technology Has Improved the Business

Collection agencies manage their work more easily these days using computer technology. Contact management software enables debtor information to come up on screen quickly and accessibly. Moreover, a substantial part of the collection business consists in "skip tracing," which entails tracking down an individual or business that has moved and doesn't want to be found. Internet searches make this a much easier process than previously. Cell-phone numbers can be obtained, as can new addresses. It is

Look at Their Documents

When you interview an agency prior to engaging it, ask to see the letters it mails out to debtors. These should be a series of communications beginning with making initial contact through the threat of legal action. Do these look professional, polite, and comprehensive? Does the agency notify you by mail or phone when it makes contact with a debtor, or does it send a single monthly report listing all your debtor accounts? You don't want to turn over an account to an agency and never receive any updates. Many agencies are reluctant to return an uncollected account to you for further legal action, since it makes them look incompetent.

almost impossible to be wholly anonymous in the electronic information age. With a debtor's social security number, conducting a background search is cheap and virtually instantaneous.

Start Your Search with More than One Candidate

After comparing several agencies, select the one that meets the needs of your business based on the frequency and types of actions you will be turning over. Consider whether you have a large number of small claims or a few with a high dollar amount. The criteria you use should go beyond the cost to you (a percentage of payments collected).

Some agencies will sell you a comprehensive program that includes credit-management tools, such as providing past-due notices you can include in your statements. If a customer pays you after such a nudge for payment, you owe little to the agency for the forms. This service might be of value if you have customers who tend to become slow and careless about making payments.

What to Check Before Hiring an Agency

Inquire into the reputation of the agency, in regard to both its business ethics and the way it works with debtors. In terms of ethics, you are accepting the company's word as to what it has collected and when. Although it is likely to include receipt vouchers in its reports to you, your customer could have paid the agency without it in turn informing you. Having no contact with your original customer, you are relying on

Ask about Errors and Omissions Policies

Under FDCPA regulations, your business cannot be sued for violating collection laws but a collection agency can be. Savvy debtors, especially disgruntled ones, know which technical violations enable them to take action against a collection agency. A collection agency that protects itself with an "errors and omissions" policy shows astute business sense and also that it is conscientious about following the rules. Such a business is less likely to get into financial trouble over complaints and fines.

the agency to remit everything it has collected (less its percentage) on a timely basis. Ask the agency about its own financial condition and how long it has been in business. You don't want it to be using your money as its working capital. Smaller agencies have been known to go out of business without having paid their clients the monies collected on their behalf. Remember that most of the money an agency collects belongs to you and its other customers.

Ask for References

When you choose an agency (or any professional services firm, for that matter), it is a good idea to ask for a list of satisfied customers. Even allowing that there are probably some not-so-satisfied customers around, you can still glean information from interviews with referrals. Ask questions about the agency's level of success, the accuracy and timeliness of its reporting, and anything the customer may have learned about its methods of collecting. Be sure to ask other customers if they have experience with another agency and how it compares.

Your Name Is Connected with the Agency

The most professional way to run a collection agency is to hire qualified people, train them well, and pay them reasonably. Not all agencies work this way. Some hire part-time and casual workers and give them minimal oversight. Often such collectors assume that bullying tactics and intimidation of a debtor work. They are usually wrong, sometimes step over the line, and can infect your good name as a result. The recipient of such a call is likely to remember that "the collector from Bob's Jewelry

Store was rude to me." You have already lost some money; don't lose your good name as well.

Try One That Reports Credit as Well

A number of credit bureaus do some collection work as well as reporting. A letter from a credit bureau commands attention because a debtor realizes his nonpayment will soon become a part of his personal or business credit record. Consequently, he might negotiate promised payments to a credit bureau in return for a clean report. This additional leverage can be one of the strengths of using one of the consumer reporting bureaus (Dun and Bradstreet, for example) as a collection service.

Consider Looking for an Accredited Business Collection Agency

Some business-to-business collection agencies are members of the Commercial Collection Agency Association (CCAA). This organization is part of the Commercial Law League of America, which includes law practices specializing in collections and bankruptcy. To be a member of this group, a collection agency must meet the following criteria:

- Be licensed in its own jurisdiction.
- Be established for five years or more.
- Maintain a minimum bond of $300,000 to protect its customers.
- Maintain a separate trust account for monies belonging to direct creditors.
- Subscribe to a code of ethics.
- Attend advanced educational forums and meetings.

Although there are good agencies that do not belong to this association, its standards offer a useful guideline for measuring agencies. Ask an agency you are considering about these issues. Or you might contact CCAA and ask for a referral to a local collection agency.

What Do Agencies Generally Charge?

Agency fees are set on a contingency basis. Normally the debts must be over a certain size, or there is no profit in collecting for anyone. The fees are based on size and volume of accounts.

Fees can range from ten percent to fifty percent and often depend on the age of the debt, since the older this is, the harder it is to collect. Sometimes fees include a charge for transferring an account to a lawyer to begin legal proceedings, though extra lawsuit fees are often an add-on.

The typical fee is between twenty-five and thirty-five percent commission on the collected amount. The real way to determine your actual cost is to ask specifically for the agency's usual recovery rate. An agency with a low fee and a poor recovery rate will return less to you than one with a higher fee but a good recovery percentage. Also realize that the older an account, the higher your percentage charged to collect will be. Find out if there are any other costs that will be billed to you. Expect new costs if or when the account is referred to an attorney.

Do Not Hire an Agency That Poses as a Law Firm

A business can call itself by any name not being used by another company and that it has registered in its state. Some collection agencies use straightforward names that refer to their recovery of funds (such as ABC Recovery Associates). Then there are those that try to sound like law firms,

Trust Accounts Are Important

When an agency collects money for you, its fee (or earnings) is the percentage you have agreed on. They hold the balance of the collected money for your benefit. This money should not be placed in a general operating account and commingled with the agency's regular funds. A professional agency should manage a separate account (called a "trust account") in which all collected funds are kept until paid to the original creditor. This keeps the funds safe from any claims or misuse. Find out whether your agency maintains this type of account.

Spotting the Impostors

Recently I worked with a client who ended up in a Chapter 11 reorganization. In the weeks preceding the declaration of bankruptcy, I took all the collection calls. These were quite abusive at times, but because they were made to a business rather than an individual, there was no violation of law. At least four of the callers identified themselves as attorneys when a little investigation proved that they were not. I called back the numbers and asked some pointed questions. One of the callers worked for a major phone directory. We probably could have documented their violations and prosecuted them, but it wasn't worth the time. What these companies were doing was bad ethics and bad policy.

often designating themselves as "a professional corporation" on their letterhead, another deceptive ploy. And claiming to be a law firm, they then contact debtors and threaten to file a lawsuit immediately, among other onerous actions. This is a poor way to collect money; it is usually not effective, and it violates FDCPA law. You do not want your customer subjected to this kind of deception in your name.

Try Out Several Agencies at One Time

There is no good reason to sign a long-term contract with a collection agency. Retain an ability to change to another company whenever you wish. Discounts are often offered for volume, but these should not require a contract. Therefore, you are free to use more than one agency at any time. Doing so is a good way to discover which agency has the best success rate, which will determine the return to you.

Give each agency a few accounts and then wait to see the results each achieves. However, one important thing to remember: You cannot give the same account to more than one agency. That is against the law, and it likely would slow down the collection process by sowing confusion.

What Can an Agency Actually Do?

A collection agency can work with a debtor to try to reduce the size of the obligation until it is paid in full. An agency has no enforcement authority under law and cannot seize any assets or paychecks until legal action has been pursued successfully. It can report a bad debt to all of the credit bureaus, even if the original creditor has not reported this information to any agencies. Since this has a serious effect on a debtor's credit rating, an agency wielding such a threat might motivate a debtor to pay. A professional collector knows how to use its reporting ability as a negotiating tool.

Some Agencies Buy the Debt

Some collection agencies will purchase your old debt at a big discount. They will buy an entire portfolio for pennies on the dollar. On most of these debts, an agency will not collect anything; on others, an agency can collect enough to make an overall profit. Once an agency owns a debt, they can file suit against the debtor if they wish. Only very sophisticated direct creditors, such as bank card companies or other large card issuers, have the ability to sell off their bad debt in this manner.

When Is It Time to Turn Over the Account?

Every company has its own criteria for when it's time to turn an account over to a collection agency. When the following conditions become the pattern, you need to stop spending your time on in-house collection efforts.

- Your customer continues to complain without justification, using an excuse not to pay.
- Your customer denies she owes the payment amount despite seeing copies of the invoice.
- Your customer does not respond to the final notice.
- Customer mail is returned and phones are disconnected (in which case, the time has come for skip tracing).

▶▶ TEST DRIVE

It is always frustrating to have to chase after money you have earned, and eventually in-house collection becomes time-consuming. There comes a time to hire a collection agency. Before doing so, ask yourself the following questions:

- ⮑ Have you checked out a few different agencies before you hire one?
- ⮑ Is the collection agency a licensed business in your jurisdiction?
- ⮑ How often does the agency report on collection efforts and by what means?
- ⮑ Does the agency segregate collected funds in a client trust account?
- ⮑ Does the agency track its average recovery rate?

Get Something Filed Before It's Too Late

There are several good reasons, primarily financial ones, to hire a collection agency rather than an attorney. Hiring an agency generally costs less and sometimes can be just as effective. The agency works on its cases every day and results might come sooner. But there are situations in which you need to bypass this process and go directly to a lawyer's office. The legal process can take longer, but you will establish your rights.

Consider this situation: You know your customer is on the ropes and not paying anyone, including you. If this is an individual, you can check her current credit report and see how many other credit accounts have already gone into collection. In the case of a business, often the signs are that it has been laying off employees, there is little inventory in its store, or few customers are evident in its place of business. It simply will not have sufficient cash flow available for a long time—maybe never—to pay your debt. Does that mean you are out of luck?

Not necessarily. The question to ask is this: Are there any assets (not already encumbered beyond their value) that you might be able to attach a lien to or liquidate to satisfy your claim? If the answer is yes, then have your lawyer start the process allowing you to take further action. You can only take a secured interest in funds or property if you have won a court judgment. The sooner you file, the farther up in line you go.

We have already examined the action you can take on your own in small claims court. If you win these, you have the right to enforce a collection on that decision. But in some states the loser (in this case, the defendant) has the right of appeal, so there could be another round. The wheels of justice indeed grind slowly. A cagey debtor can avoid enforced collection for years.

The Reason to Have an Attorney Do the Filing

If you yourself are filing an appeal from small claims court, you are likely to need an attorney to handle the paperwork and any of an upper court's requirements. Or you might elect to file in a higher state court if the dollar amount you are seeking exceeds the limit you can recover in a lower court. If there is a dispute about the amount owed, a further examination of the facts is necessary. Your lawyer will be able to request

---

"If You Don't Pay Me, I Will Sue!"

Many business owners imagine a lawsuit as the ultimate threat. If a payment doesn't come in a few days, you will go to a lawyer and force your customer to pay. That might happen eventually, but the process is likely to take from six months to a year or longer if you have a debtor looking to fight. Be realistic about what you expect from your lawyer and from the pace of justice. Sometimes a serious letter from a lawyer threatening a lawsuit can motivate a debtor, but if not, you are in for a long haul. Weigh this prospect when your customer is negotiating with you for a compromise.

---

additional documents and to depose the debtor. The case will turn on the evidence presented in court, which your attorney can elicit.

When you file an action (known as a complaint) in state court, the defendant is served with papers formally notifying her that an action is pending. She is given up to thirty days to answer (depending on state law), and the action is scheduled for trial. In some states, lawsuits under a certain amount can be listed for arbitration, in which case a hearing before a panel of attorneys is conducted (and usually heard more quickly) rather than a full trial launched.

How Long Before the Action Is Decided?

However, even a case that is arbitrated instead of proceeding to full trial usually takes at least ninety days to be heard. Either side can probably obtain a forty-five-day to sixty-day delay upon request. (The members of the bar customarily allow each other this courtesy.) A debtor seeking to delay an action can easily string out a proceeding for six months, which can be a frustrating process for an unsuspecting creditor.

An Ounce of Prevention

If your business deals with contracts and collections on a regular basis, work with your attorney to review your procedures. Are your contracts clear, and do the terms conform with state requirements? What you don't specify can leave you legally liable.

A lawyer can review your credit applications to determine whether your language on personal guarantees and confessions of judgment will hold up under court challenge. She can also evaluate your credit practices for their effectiveness. Having a business lawyer handle all your accounts ensures that a delinquent account is monitored.

Lawyers Like Ongoing Business

Bringing in an attorney as a business advisor empowers your collection department. An attorney can call for a lien search or advise you when a customer has refused to pay some charges. Your team has a valuable new player.

Judgments and Liens

The judgment rendered in your favor through a lawsuit affords you an equitable remedy. A filed judgment places a lien on any real property owned by the defendant. Although this doesn't put actual cash in your pocket, it does mean that as a result of any financial transaction involving your customer's property, such as a sale or refinance, your lien must be paid. Your money is safe, if not in the mail.

Keep in mind, however, that such a judgment is awarded at the end of a trial or appeal. You start the lawsuit by filing a complaint against your debtor, which is answered by the defendant. Evidence is gathered, and a trial is scheduled. In the majority of cases involving money, your attorney will recommend that you settle before trial rather than continue the fight through time-consuming (and expensive) litigation. Even with success in

Lawyers Cooperate with Each Other

Lawyers are major players in the collection arena. An attorney might try to persuade you to sue your debtor or your debtor's lawyer threaten you with tough legal action. The reality is that few collection cases go to trial; most are settled by negotiations between lawyers. Business owners who realize this and use it to their benefit win more times than not. Find a good collection attorney who will negotiate forcefully on your behalf.

Homeowners May Be Motivated by a Mechanic's Lien

Homeowners want clear title to their property (aside from the mortgage debt they've assumed). Official notice of a mechanic's lien placed on the property gets their attention. Often it is easier for property owners to secure a small second mortgage or line of credit than to finance a property to which a lien has been attached. Most contractors are familiar with this enforcement tactic. You should have an attorney lined up to file such an action if necessary.

---

winning a judgment, however, the likelihood is that you will collect less than you expected, particularly after legal fees are deducted.

A Lien

A lien serves as a financial obligation on real property that must be settled if the property is refinanced or transferred. Conduct a title search to determine whether your lien has any value. If a lien is placed on property mortgaged beyond its current value, you will have to wait for future appreciation to collect from any sale.

A Mechanic's Lien

This is an encumbrance (or hold) on a piece of real property that in the case of a payment dispute is placed on behalf of the contractor whose labor and materials have improved the property. As a result of the lien, the owner's title suffers an "interference" that must be resolved before clear title can be restored.

Filing a mechanic's lien is a less cumbersome process than pursuing a lawsuit over collection. There are state limits on the period of time after work has been completed that this lien can be filed. Check the law in your state for specific requirements. Some states also allow auto mechanics to attach a lien to a car they have worked on without recompense. If you are able to attach a lien without challenge, eventually your money will be paid.

The Cost of Litigation—Who Wins?

If you are pursuing a legal case beyond small claims court, you will need a lawyer in spite of the cost. (Although a lawyer can advise you if a case is worth pursuing in the first place.) An attorney is necessary for handling court deadlines, filings, and arguing motions before a judge. Often lawyers charge a fee based on a percentage of payment recovery, though you will have to pay court filing fees up front. Although a lawyer's costs are higher than those of a collection agency, the amount of money recovered by a lawyer is likely to be higher than what an agency returns.

When You Have a Confession of Judgment

Earlier we discussed obtaining a confession of judgment, an additional level of protection you can require of a business owner seeking credit. An owner signing such a clause agrees that failure to pay what is owed you triggers the filing of a judgment without requiring a preliminary lawsuit. This saves the legal costs and time involved in first filing a complaint to establish liability. Even so, a defendant by claiming extraordinary circumstances has the right to file an action to avoid this judgment. Most of the time, however, you will win your judgment and with it the lien you need to take the next step. Just remember that the next step—execution of the judgment—also does not happen automatically.

Suing Under a Personal Guarantee

To pursue company owners who signed your credit application with a personal guarantee, you will need a lawyer to collect. A signed guarantee means that the principal personally agrees to pay a debt if the company fails to meet its obligations. Payment to you does not happen automatically. First you must file a lawsuit against the individual and win a judgment. That will hand you the lien you need to force a collection. You only have a claim against the guarantor's individually owned assets. If the guarantee is not signed jointly by a married couple, you will have difficulty collecting on any assets held in common.

Collecting Takes Time

When I owned a manufacturing company, a vendor in my industry was awarded a substantial, long-term contract to supply gloves to a large industrial company. Although the vendor shipped thousands of dollars' worth of product, it received payments slowly; every other check was short. Within six months, the vendor was owed so much money that it ceased shipping and filed a lawsuit. The company that had received the goods, a Fortune 500 company, put up only a minimal defense. The supplier won a judgment but by now had incurred legal costs compounding the money owed them. But it took the vendor another six months to collect the judgment because there were no local banks to serve (deliver) the appropriate documents and take money from the debtor's account. Attaching a lien to an industrial plant entailed starting a foreclosure action. A judgment is a piece of paper that requires execution to turn it into money.

Judgments Are Not Money—
They Must Be Collected

The easiest way to collect a judgment is to serve it on the bank of the debtor, drawing proceeds directly from the debtor's account. Knowing where your customer banks gives you a real advantage. Make sure to copy all checks you receive as payment on an account so that you have the name of the customer's bank and the account number.

Liens that are placed on real estate do not become liquid until the property is sold or refinanced. A mortgage company requires that all judgments and liens on real property be satisfied before closing.

Rules about how a judgment must be served and what may be seized to satisfy the judgment are governed by state. In many locales, a sheriff serving a writ of execution on a residence or place of business will notify the debtor that his personal property must be sold to satisfy the debt. After a certain period you are entitled to a public sale of the debtor's property and to keep what you are owed. You are also able to serve customers who owe money to your debtor, thereby staking a claim for what you are due.

Some States Prohibit Garnishment

Not all states allow wages to be garnished. In Florida, you cannot take this action against a head of household. In Pennsylvania, South Carolina, North Carolina, and Texas, you cannot garnish wages for the collection of any private debt. (All states allow income garnishment for the collection of child-support payments and unpaid taxes.) You cannot garnish a person's pension. Federal employees and military personnel have to be served through a more cumbersome process that involves their agency headquarters rather than a local office. In some cases local court officials are not able to garnish wages. All of these actions mediated by a court, from filing the original lawsuit through winning a judgment to forced collection, require legal guidance.

You May Be Able to Garnish Wages

In the case of an individual debtor who is employed, in some states you can serve her employer with a garnishment of wages. Protections covered by federal law do not allow garnishment unless the debtor's wages are above the poverty line, in which case you can take no more than twenty-five percent of the available wage. (Twenty-five percent is the upper limit on any income garnishment with the exception of child support, which can be garnished up to fifty percent of payments.) Some states allow only fifteen percent of wages to be garnished.

To enforce a garnishment, you provide the sheriff or other local official with a copy of your judgment and the address where the debtor works. Service is completed by delivery to the debtor's employer, at which point the money is paid to the sheriff's office and then turned over to you. Although federal law prohibits an employer from terminating anyone due to wage garnishment, many people choose to pay their debt voluntarily to prevent an employer's knowledge. An employee irresponsible with his own funds may not be entrusted with company property. You don't want your debtor to lose her job.

▶▶ TEST DRIVE

The final success of any collection process depends on how much money you recover. This often requires the services of an attorney. Do you know when it is advisable to pursue collection through an attorney rather than through a collection agency? Ask yourself the following questions:

➱ Is your debtor on the brink of bankruptcy? (If so, the situation requires swift and effective legal action, which is discussed in the next chapter.)

➱ Do you know what is involved in filing a lien against a debtor?

➱ Will you collect more than it will cost you in legal fees?

➱ Do you understand how to execute a judgment so that it results in actual payments?

Are You Secured in Any Assets?

There are times when a debtor, whether company or individual, is stretched so financially thin that filing for bankruptcy seems the only answer. This action can be of benefit to you as the creditor, bringing order and supervision to the case. If there are assets to divide, the bankruptcy court will keep the distribution fair. Even so, you need to understand your rights.

The previous chapter discussed filing judgments and securing liens, including mechanic's liens. In the case of your debtor's bankruptcy, the standing of your judgment or lien depends on its timing. This is why you want to ask for one sooner rather than later. If you file a judgment or lien at least ninety days before your debtor files for bankruptcy, you are considered a secured, rather than an unsecured, creditor—assuming there is existing collateral. In the eyes of the law, taking last-minute action against an insolvent business entity or person is unfair to other creditors. During the ninety-day period before the bankruptcy filing, the debtor is considered insolvent.

By the same token, the debtor cannot move cash during that ninety-day period by paying some creditors and not others. He cannot sell assets at below-market value. Nor can he transfer assets to himself or to a member of his family during the twelve months prior to any filing. The rules are set up to create an even playing field. All creditors are entitled to receive some of the proceeds from any assets owned by a bankrupt debtor. Bankruptcy can be a constructive process that gives a business a chance to continue (after restructuring).

Three Types of Bankruptcy

Three types of bankruptcy are declared most frequently, each affecting a creditor differently. Here are guidelines:

Chapter 7—The debtor's assets are liquidated, and a trustee distributes any proceeds to creditors after legal and administrative debts are paid. Under the new bankruptcy law passed in 2005, many debtors are required to file under Chapter 13 and to make some payback, which in personal cases seldom leaves any assets. Business liquidations can eventually leave assets to divide.

Chapter 11—Referred to as a "Debtor in Possession," a business in Chapter 11 bankruptcy continues to operate under supervision of a trustee's office while it generates a plan to pay back a portion of the debt. The plan is submitted to creditors for their vote. This process is meant to be completed in less than 120 days, but it often takes six months or more. The debtor files monthly operating reports that creditors review and then circulates among them a plan along with a full disclosure of operations. The vote determines whether the business has a future.

Chapter 13—In what is referred to as the "Wage Earners Plan," the debtor sends a fixed portion of her earned income to a Chapter 13 trustee each month. The amount is then distributed among creditors in proportion to their claims. The changes in law since 2005 provide for more money available to creditors over a longer period of time as a result of higher and longer payments from the debtor, although most creditors receive only a portion of their claims.

A Recent Purchase May Be Reclaimed

In the most recent version of the bankruptcy laws, there are provisions for the return of a debtor's merchandise bought within a certain period before the filing. The reasoning is that the debtor might have bought items in anticipation of the bankruptcy filing, in which case the equitable interest belongs to the creditor. If you have made a shipment of goods to a customer in the weeks or even the few months before a bankruptcy filing, check with your attorney. You might be able to reclaim your goods rather than be out the unpaid money. Too many companies after learning that a customer has filed for bankruptcy give up their claims, assuming their unpaid goods are lost. This is not necessarily the case, whether in a Chapter 7 or a Chapter 11 filing.

> ### You May Have to Return Money
>
> There is a flip side to the bankruptcy law allowing the return of a debtor's purchased goods. If you were paid on an old debt (not including payments from normal business transactions) within ninety days of a filing, you may be forced to return the money. Since the ninety-day period prior to bankruptcy is the time of presumed insolvency, such a transfer of money might be considered preferentially favoring one creditor over others.
>
> Your customer would have to list the debt payment on his filing petition, at which point the court would order the return of the money. Such an action is initiated by the debtor; you as a creditor do not have to search your records to report to the court. Watch out for a business customer on the eve of bankruptcy who issues a flurry of payments to you to induce you to ship more goods. You might wind up deeper in his debt than you already are. When a debtor wants to trade past-due money for new goods, be careful.

Chapter 7—
Get Your Portion of the Distribution

Chapter 7 bankruptcy, whether personal or business, consists in the complete liquidation of a debtor's assets by a trustee acting under court supervision. An individual is allowed to keep a certain amount of assets, the value of which depends on the allowable state or federal exemption (typically around $16,000 per person). In some states residential property is also exempt. A business is totally liquidated, and assets from buildings, inventory, and accounts are collected by the trustee.

Upon liquidation, all money is kept in an escrow account by the trustee to be distributed to all creditors according to their standing and proportion of share. If you are such a creditor, pay attention to the situation so if you are entitled to a return, you receive it. Again, since 2005 this is less likely in personal cases. The exception would be if there are unsettled legal or insurance claims. If the trustee determines that these are property of the estate, the money is collected for the benefit of creditors.

What Does a Creditor Have to Do?

If you have a secured interest in any property of a debtor, have your attorney immediately notify the court and the trustee. If you are the only interest holder, you might be able to take possession of the asset in satisfaction of your claim. You can file for a "relief from stay," which allows you to repossess your property. If you hold a mortgage or a loan on equipment, repossession can be a simple matter.

If yours is an unsecured claim, check the bankruptcy filing to make sure your claim is listed and the amount is correct. If not, you can file a "proof of claim" that will be honored during distribution unless the debtor objects. When a company is ending its life in a Chapter 7 liquidation, few owners are careful about what is still owed. Their records are often in turmoil. Your records as a creditor are likely more reliable. Your goal is to see at least some return on the amount owed you.

Chapter 13— As a Creditor, Get Monthly Payments

As in a Chapter 7 plan, claims in a Chapter 13 bankruptcy are listed in the debtor's original filing, and you will be notified by the court. Verify the accuracy of your debt listing; if it isn't what you think it should be, file a "proof of claim" with both the court and the trustee.

Payments work differently in a Chapter 13 bankruptcy than in a Chapter 7 plan. The Chapter 7 liquidation consists of a one-time liquidation payment to creditors. In a Chapter 13 plan, the debtor is required to contribute a portion of her income each month as a payback on her debt. The money is sent to the trustee's office and from there disbursed proportionally to all creditors. A Chapter 13 payment plan can last from three to five years. Depending on the debt and the income of the debtor, you might receive in time a good portion of what you are due, or you might see just pennies on the dollar. Some Chapter 13 plans go to completion, but don't be surprised if the payments suddenly stop. The program requires prolonged discipline, and many starting with good intentions don't make it to the end. If the bankruptcy case is dismissed, you are then free to pursue your debtor for the full amount.

Chapter 11—
Be a Member of the Committee When Possible

A Chapter 11 bankruptcy is a complicated business strategy to save the life of a company and, it is hoped, to pay back some of its debts. If you are a creditor in a large corporate bankruptcy, forget about seeing any meaningful return or, most likely, any money at all. The enormous legal fees and other administrative costs will take all the cash the company can generate for years. Your business is a relative small fish, so pay little attention to such a cases—unless you are considering continuing your business relationship. Then you want to know how the corporation is faring.

If you are a fair-sized creditor in a small Chapter 11 filing, however, it can be to your benefit to pay attention and even to serve on the creditors' committee. The ten largest creditors are usually the ones appointed, but some of them won't want to serve. If you have not been asked to serve, contact the trustee office in your district and express interest in becoming a member of the committee. You are likely to be appointed.

The benefit of being on the creditors' committee is that you have a front-row seat for the proceedings. Since the committee is permitted to hire an attorney to represent it, such an experienced legal advisor can

You Want the Business to Succeed

If one of your business customers owes you a lot of money and then without warning files for protection under bankruptcy law, you might well be angry. There are certainly instances in which business owners have misappropriated company money or simply not done their job. And there are far more cases of trouble for which no one was at fault. Does that mean you want revenge?

The fact is that if the company can be stabilized and turned around, everyone will be better off. The business will remain a customer and be able to pay off an old debt. If the business is to continue, it will have to make a deal with creditors to pay off some of what they are owed. This is a way for you as a creditor to recover some of your debt. So even though you might feel cheated, you want the business to go forward. Although the past can't be undone, the future might be corrected.

Working Together to Turn Things Around

I was approved by a bankruptcy court to work as a financial advisor on fifteen Chapter 11 reorganizations. My job was to manage the internal financial operation of the debtors. These were not easy companies to operate because everyone was overly stressed and money was tight. Yet all but one successfully underwent reorganization and paid back money to creditors. In one case, the return was almost sixty percent. Reorganization failures in such situations are often caused by poor communication and lack of cooperation between debtor and creditors. As an outsider, I was often able to convince both sides of their mutual interests. Bear in mind that if one of your business customers confronts a Chapter 11 bankruptcy challenge, it could be in your interest to help the company go forward.

assure that the "debtor in possession" provides all information required for creditors to monitor how the company is progressing. When a business is in Chapter 11, it needs to take action to correct the bad practices that brought it to this point. More of the same only depletes the estate further and keeps creditors from receiving any return at all. The committee, although by no means in charge, can request a meeting with the debtor to check on progress as the bankruptcy plan is being formulated.

The Plan of Reorganization

At the end of 120 days, the Chapter 11 debtor begins the process of filing a plan to repay a portion of its debt, which will usually extend over a period of five years. The creditors' committee can be a strong voice in determining how the plan is written since it recommends passage to the remaining creditors who have a vote.

To pass a plan requires calculating a complicated formula based on the number of votes plus the value of the claims. The question up for discussion is whether the creditors would receive more money under the plan than they would in a liquidation. As a direct creditor, you have a vested interest in seeing this plan work. Forgetting the cost and aggravation to you, if you do not allow this debtor to continue in business, you will not receive any money back. And keep in mind the possibility of future profits from new orders. After the business reorganization is over, you might be able to recover more of its debt to you.

Objecting to Discharge

If you have any reason to think the debt owed you resulted from fraud or misrepresentation, you have the right to object to the bankruptcy court's discharge of that debt. Take your documentation to an experienced creditor's attorney to file the appropriate motions in court. You might be able to retain your claim after other claims are discharged. Many credit card companies are taking this tack and winning, charging that nonessential (luxury) items were purchased within ninety days of a company's bankruptcy filing and cash advances drawn. Check with your lawyer to see if you have such a case.

Should You Do Business Again with the Same Customer?

This is a very interesting question with a complex set of answers. If a customer brings cash into your business, why wouldn't you take her money? At first thought, most everyone says he would. But, particularly in business-to-business transactions involving a credit failure, the creditor feels cheated and takes it personally. And for a closely held company, it is personal. The financial loss if you are the owner is yours. You might like the debtor to feel pain, and not want to see her again. But there are a few considerations to keep in mind while you are making your own decision.

First, a sale is a sale, and when it brings in cash, you should think of it purely in business terms. If the deal is profitable, it is beneficial to your company, and new profits help to replace the money lost.

In the second place, few debtors are really as carefree about their financial situation as you might believe. Whatever they might say publicly, privately they are feeling guilty. Offer some sympathy and see how much it is appreciated. There are always a few people trying to get away with not paying their debts, but they do not represent the majority. Most customers will be very grateful for your support and work to keep it.

Should You Give Credit a Second Time?

Here is where the answer gets tricky. Once individuals or businesses have failed to pay you, should you ever give them credit again? As far as consumers are concerned, they cannot file a second bankruptcy again for ten years, so any new debt will not be discharged through bankruptcy. Of course, it may not necessarily be paid, because that depends on the individual.

The situation with a business still operating is more complicated. Few companies can go forward if they must pay cash in advance for everything. Their borrowing ability is nonexistent, and internally generated cash may accumulate too slowly for the company to get back on track.

The decision in the case of a business of whether to give credit again is a judgment call. You should be quite familiar with the particular situation in your considerations. Granting full credit is a big risk for you. Asking a business customer for a deposit and requesting the balance due within a reasonable time is fair. Set the company's credit limit low and let it grow with success. Consider charging on a COD basis so that the money must be paid when the goods are delivered. If you have faith in your customer, negotiate a solution that works for both of you.

▶▶ **TEST DRIVE**

There are times when a debtor stops trying to pay anyone and files for bankruptcy in one of its several forms. As a direct creditor, do you know what to do when this happens? Make sure you do the following:

➲ Determine whether you have a secured interest in the business's assets.

➲ Ask your lawyer whether you can reclaim your unpaid goods.

➲ When there is a distribution or payment through the bankruptcy court, be sure your name is on the list of creditors.

➲ If any company fraud is involved, object to the discharge of its debts by the bankruptcy court.

➲ Consider your future business prospects with a reorganized business.

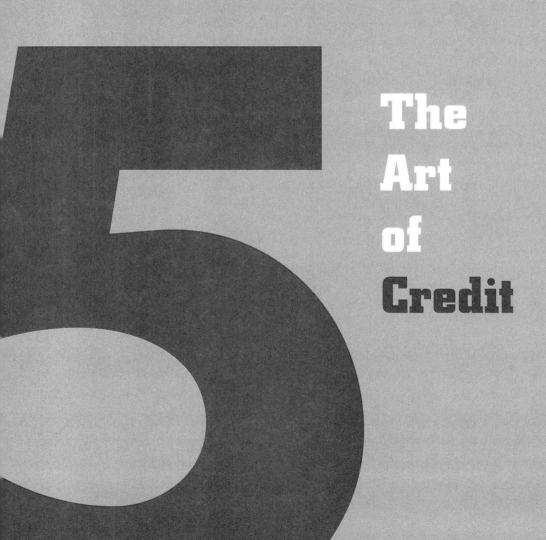

5

The
Art
of
Credit

Why Some Creditors Never Make Demands

Money is a form of exchange between buyer and seller or service supplier and client. It seems quite logical that such a transaction would take place in an impersonal way. And as a matter of fact, the majority do work that way. But there is an element of personal dynamics in money deals that impacts this otherwise dispassionate exchange.

In business-to-business commerce, the major credit mistake most companies make is in not trying aggressively to collect the money due them. The drive of a company is directed toward winning an order. A good amount of business effort is expended in developing relationships with customers. Many companies put their most skilled personnel and all their financial resources into creating, marketing, and selling a product or service that will be in demand. The sale is enhanced by adding value and service. Since the goal in business is to make a profit on revenue, it is necessary to create sufficient customer demand at a fair price. Business sells into a competitive environment.

There are occasions when a deal does not go as smoothly or as easily as the seller would like. Time frames or expectations aren't met. It can be difficult in retrospect to reconstruct just what it would have taken to make the deal seem more fair to the buyer. This is the time when making a phone call or mailing a demand for payment would reopen the conversation about what went wrong with the deal.

But the call isn't made, and the serious letter is left unsent. In such a situation, the business owner wants to avoid a confrontation—interestingly, not one over money, but instead over value and quality. And as a result, this lack of follow-up comes with a serious financial cost, one that can cause serious problems for a company.

Business owners and office managers might hear a familiar ring in the following exchange. If one of these parties sounds like you, consider why.

"Shouldn't we call Joe at ABC Supply? His bill is over sixty days."

"He'll send a check soon; he always does."

"This time is longer than usual, and I don't think he was happy with the last shipment."

"Don't bother him—we'll get paid."

Lawyers, Accountants, and Other Professionals

I have been in enough offices of companies having money trouble to know there are very few business owners who do not owe money to their lawyers, accountants, and other business service professionals. Some of my clients have not paid for tax returns completed several years ago or lawsuits that have been defended for months. Yet, when I look through clients' mail and statements, I virtually never find a letter of demand from a lawyer or accountant. This has always surprised me, but having had conversations with these types of creditors, I know they have a serious professional ego involved and are unwilling to hear that their services were less than excellent. When you bill for time only, then product outcome is not the central issue. In fact, when I have written letters on behalf of my clients to some of these same professionals with claims of substandard work, the majority of the recipients have just gone away. They do not like to discuss their expertise or admit that at times their work isn't up to standards. Intangible work is often hard to defend, and where there are quality questions involved, the discussion can become uncomfortably personal. My own strategy is to seek an advance and bill against it as I complete work. I always collect vigorously but with a willingness to compromise on the fee if necessary. As a lifelong entrepreneur, I understand why the business owner wants to quantify expenses. Most businesses that produce a product or a service are only paid when the work turns out well. Professionals expect to be paid regardless of outcome. These different criteria are often at odds, and so sometimes no money changes hands.

Being a business owner takes a reasonable level of confidence and—to be honest—a strong ego. Frequently, the money involved is as much a tool for keeping score as an exchange of value. Far too many entrepreneurs are driven by the amount of gross revenue rather than by the profit at the end after results are collected. Positive cash flow is a function of real profit, which always entails collecting receivables. Bad debts, when they are realized on the books, become an offset of sales. They negate all the work (and the money) that went into making the deal and doing the job. For some owners, it is easier to keep an old debt on the books than to take the final step of writing it off. They keep hoping the customer will pay the bill and end the issue. And if a partial payment is finally sent, they retain the balance on account despite knowing it is totally uncollectible.

Entrepreneurs Are Rarely Financial People

Most new business owners come from a specific discipline (field of expertise) or a sales and marketing background. Even though making money might be one of the motivators in starting their own companies, finance is seldom their area of expertise. This lack of knowledge tends to make entrepreneurs uncomfortable in financial discussions with accountants, bankers, and even the people who owe them money. And because they want the approval of their clientele, they often leave it to others in the company to collect money owed, even if they seldom authorize others to be as hard-nosed as they should be. Resolving what is, in essence, a financial dispute (cost vs. value) is not an arena many entrepreneurs want to operate in. Their real love is the deal making and often the work itself.

Customers Who Don't Pay Even When They Are Able

There are a variety of reasons why customers, either businesses or consumers, fail to pay their bills. Some jobs involve fundamental disputes or misunderstandings, and a withholding of money is the only way to resolve matters. And sometimes businesses and individuals are having such serious financial problems that they are unable to pay at the time— or perhaps ever.

In between these two poles lie attitudes toward money and financial strategies that affect the steady accumulation and slow disbursement of funds. In the case of individual consumers, the culture at large and collective value system come into play. The dramatic increase in bankruptcy in the last decade indicates that people have less sense of responsibility with regard to their debt than did previous generations. Bills go unpaid while spending continues apace. The credit grantor is considered an impersonal entity who can afford to carry the debt; from a customer's point of view, a company's debt is just part of the expense of doing business.

The only way to change this perception is to develop personal relationships with your customers and convince them that they need to keep up their payments to you because they care about your respect. Make sure they understand you are working hard to earn a living just as they

What's Your Motivation?

A mid-Atlantic regional distributor I sold to held major contracts with two of the big auto companies. The distributor supplied eight plants, and the purchase contract was worth millions. But cash flow was an ongoing nightmare because the distributor didn't receive its money until at least ninety days after shipment, and its invoices were routinely unpaid. This didn't seem like an accident. The distributor couldn't pay me or any of his suppliers on time, and we weren't happy. At times the distributor was really caught in the middle.

The larger the distributor grew, the greater the cash pressure became. At a national show, I had a chance to discuss this situation with the two principals. It was more satisfying to them (and their business egos) to be big fish in the supply business even if they were always the ones under pressure. The prestige and quest itself were the motivators; the money was secondary. They always believed the payoff would be coming soon. On paper, the business looked good—unfortunately, its bank account never did. The company was around for almost twenty years, but the final few were very hard.

Know which prize in the game of business drives you.

are. Money is power—and there are those who like to play power games involving money. Develop good instincts for your customers' sense of responsibility and work through any personal, nonbusiness issues.

The Nonpaying Corporation Is Different

Large companies with good cash flow that don't pay their bills on time are not as infrequent as you would think. They often set up their accounting system to pay in ninety or one hundred and twenty days because they can get away with it. And if enough of their vendors do not complain, their behavior becomes policy. You could modify your own payment track with a similar policy, issuing payments only on the 10th and 25th. This would give you more time to pay by a matter of days at least.

Depending on how a large company manages its cash flow, the use of good short-term investment vehicles means that the money they don't pay to vendors is money they can make a return on. If you are one of those vendors, you are likely paying interest to fund your own cash flow while the corporations you sell to are making money on theirs. Ask yourself: Can you make money under these circumstances? And do you really want to operate in the face of such policy? Perhaps you could raise prices to account for the financing cost—or if not, your business may not be worth the effort.

Tips on Having Discussions about Money

What we are discussing in this book concerns the trade of cash for goods and services in running a business. The money that changes hands is a commodity transaction. This activity is not personal and should not be treated like it is. The business conversations you have must be objective; these will be the most effective.

Whether dealing with consumers or businesses, with those who owe you money or those whom you owe money to, you need to stay professional and understand that you are communicating on behalf of an entity—your company—and not yourself. Your customers are not transacting with "you" but rather making business decisions they believe are necessary or wise—even when they really aren't. Keep the discussion focused on the objective facts.

How can you do this? Referring to the term "your account balance" instead of to what "you owe us" is one technique. Ask "Can we find a resolution of the outstanding balance?" rather than "When are you going to pay me?" You are discussing a business transaction, not a personal promise. Although this situation does involve honesty and ethics, it is not up to you to have a serious conversation about such topics with those who owe you money, nor is your business the place for that.

Never Talk about Need

Some company owners use a collection ploy of telling a customer how much they "need" the money, presumably thinking that will bring sympathy and cash. Usually this simply adds to the power a nonpaying customer is able to wield (assuming he can pay), which means for some not paying just makes the game more interesting. You don't want to play that power game; you earned the money for your goods or service and are entitled to collect it. The time to discuss how critical cash flow is to your company is when you are building your business relationship with a customer and negotiating original terms.

Know Whom You Are Dealing with First

Businesses don't pay bills; people do. The credit history of a company is as important as the financial strength of an individual consumer. But just as important is the character of your customer, whether company owners, controllers, or a consumer. Although your customer application asks for formal information, you might want to find out about the people you are dealing with. Ask questions within your industry or in your community. These days you can do an Internet search on individuals and learn whatever is in the public record, including pending legal issues. Don't be impressed by the trappings of wealth in others; be extensive in your knowledge of whom you are dealing with.

If You Have Any Questions, Arrange to Meet in Person

If you are working on a large deal or a long-term supply agreement with a customer, your credit decisions are important. Most of the time you can make these on the basis of information on a customer's application and from other reports. But if you have any remaining questions, ask them face-to-face. You might seek better insight into a customer's plans or commitment to a new venture or perhaps it's important to determine the honesty and sincerity of the individual. Most of us with business experience can gauge character. If the going gets tough, you want to know whose interest a customer has at heart.

Discounting to Make a Friend

Another way in which business owners often put themselves at a disadvantage financially is by making a sale at a low price because a customer has prevailed on them to provide a discount. You know what your costs are and how important the profits and cash flow are to your future. If there is no compelling business reason to lower a price (that is, your business is neither slow nor overstocked), resist the urge to please a customer by meeting this request.

There are proper times to conduct sales, and when you do, be sure to remove your credit risk from the deal. "All sales in cash" and "no returns on sale merchandise" are good policies to enforce. If you are not commanding a reasonable price, you cannot afford to add collection time to the deal in addition.

▶▶ TEST DRIVE

When it comes to issues of money and debt, people's attitudes and behavior vary markedly. Are you considering the following issues in developing a collection strategy?

- Are you making strong demands to be paid?
- Do you understand a customer's reluctance to meet obligations even when she is financially able to do so?
- Are you comfortable and effective discussing the money a customer owes you?
- In terms of handling a debt responsibly, do you check out an individual customer as closely as a company?
- Are you getting the price you deserve?

Always Communicate with Your Creditors

The credit cycle runs full circle. You start a business by seeking credit, grow a business by granting it, and sustain one by handling your own credit issues. There are times when you will be late paying your bills; it's a part of the life cycle of a business. It can happen because sales have been off or because other customers haven't paid you. By the time you experience this event, you should treat your creditors as you want to be treated as a creditor. This means paying them as fairly as you can—don't let a creditor force you to take action that will not benefit your company in the long term.

As a creditor, you have a trigger point for handling debtors: The time to turn an account over to collection is when you cannot get in touch with your debtor. When you are in the position of debtor in a business transaction, keep in mind that providing any answer to your creditor is better than no answer. So always take the phone calls directed at you or return messages that have been left. Remember how angry your customer's suspicious silence left you when you were owed money.

Now that the shoe is on the other foot, you realize how tough it is to tell a creditor you can't pay her. She wants to know why, and it is your responsibility to give an answer. Be as honest as possible and try to rebuild the creditor's confidence in you.

You incurred a debt with the expectation that you would be able to pay when the time came. What happened in the interim? If it was an unexpected problem, share the information. If a major event has happened, your creditor may already know. She won't like to hear of your inability to pay, but hearing an explanation will help her to understand and decide if she can work with you until the situation changes.

If, however, you made a decision to allocate available cash to other vendors, you face a more difficult problem. You can't quite admit that you took action that disadvantaged this creditor over another. What you can do is apologize for the dilemma and offer some sense of when and how it will be solved. Don't be defensive about it; you are in fact the one at fault. Day-to-day business decisions are never easy, and resources must be directed where they are needed. Even so, you as the person in charge need to take responsibility for not being able to pay a creditor.

> ### Be Cautious with Competitive Information
>
> If you are talking with a company that sells to others in your industry, be circumspect about how much specific information you share. People, whether male or female, have a tendency to gossip. If you are having problems with a customer, the last thing you want is for your competitors to hear about it. Next thing you know, they will use that information to gain entry into your market. Be more general in your explanation and hope your sincerity is enough to be convincing.

Do Not Promise What You Cannot Pay

"Tell them they'll have a check by the end of the week."

Have you ever told your office manager to say this to a vendor when there is no way it can be true? The words come out without thought because the end of the week is still a few days away; maybe something will break before then, or at least you hope that will happen. The vendor who is calling (assuming this is only the first or second time he's heard it) will be satisfied until the following week when the check does not arrive. Then the process will begin all over again. You would feel the same dismay on the other end.

Soon your vendor will demand more specific information, like how much money is being sent, what your check number is, and when exactly the check will be in the mail. Your word will no longer be believed and his anger will increase. That is just how you would feel if the positions were reversed.

Instead of creating all this drama, take the call and be honest:

"Bob, I can send you $500 on the tenth, and I will call in another two weeks to let you know when the next check will go out."

Bob may want $1,000, but if you promise that amount to him and then can't send it, you will make matters worse. What if he is planning his own cash flow based on your promise? Now, he's the one in the middle. If the amount you have to send is $500, be honest and tell him.

It is easier to tell people what they want to hear than to be direct and let them know the truth. There are times when your honesty will be

| Inside Track | Owning Up to Your Mistakes |

When I was in charge of my manufacturing company, I tried very hard to keep raw material in balance with orders and production needs. It didn't always happen, and some of the mistakes were greater than others. The first time I authorized the flameproof treating of fabric that we stored at a plant in Ohio, I did not know I had to specify exact roll numbers. This information determined how much total material I was releasing. I realized the mistake when a forty-foot trailer arrived to deliver at least a year's supply, perhaps more.

I immediately called the treating company and explained my dilemma. The bottom line was that I wasn't going to be able to pay for the goods any time soon. I offered to send a check every two weeks for nine months, which was grudgingly accepted. I never missed a payment. The mistake had been mine, and I was grateful for a solution. Over the next twenty years of business, this vendor never forgot my effort.

valued—and there are times when the matter of money owed will make any communication difficult. But at all times don't add a layer of dishonesty to complicate the situation. Your ongoing business relationship with the vendor is worth more than the temporary relief of having him give you a week off before he starts collecting again.

Make an Honest Offer and Stick to It

Paying off a $10,000 debt over the next twelve months will likely go more slowly than any of your creditors would like. But those with any credit sophistication know that any forced collection takes time and that a voluntary agreement is always preferable. Examine your cash flow and make an offer that is realistic with what you can actually handle. The only thing more difficult than trying to turn a short-term obligation into virtually a long-term loan is convincing your creditor to go along, only to not make the payments. Offer an amount you know you can get your hands on one way or another and meet every payment promise you make. Your effort will be remembered. A creditor would rather be paid in full even more slowly if it means not having to take further action to collect.

Don't Be Frightened by Threats

By now you know better than to be one of those creditors who tries threats and intimidation to collect your debts. You have learned that such behavior does not really increase your success and that the image of your business suffers by these sorts of transactions. And once you've had the opportunity to be on the receiving end of rude behavior, you are quite ready to forswear these tactics.

"If I don't have the check by Friday, I am going to sue you."

"Do you realize how long that will take?"

"I'll make your life miserable."

"It hasn't been so easy these days—I'm trying to straighten out my finances as quickly as I can."

"Tell it to the judge!"

Often an uneducated creditor will make all the threats she thinks she can in the hope that you the debtor will respond by sending money. Now that you are familiar with the collection process, you know how much time and effort a creditor must expend to actually collect. If you can avoid being intimidated by your angry creditor and take the high ground, your calm is likely to defuse the situation. Surely you understand the creditor's frustration.

"My lawyer is ready to file suit on Friday if I don't receive a check from you by then."

"But I've told you several times there is no extra money this week. I'm not going to make a promise I can't keep. I am working on paying you. Why do you want to add lawyer's fees?"

"If I sue you, you'll have to pay."

"You'd find that isn't necessarily the case. But the point is that I intend to pay you without any legal action."

"Okay, but call me next week."

You can prevent a confrontation by the creditor over money you owe from escalating if you don't respond in kind. His threats are meant seriously, but the collection process he would have to undertake is long and involved.

How to Deal with Taxing Authorities

The most frightening of all collection efforts for a company being dunned come from the IRS or state and local taxing bodies. The fact is that these have far more enforcement authority than a business creditor. Once an assessment is made, the IRS and some state tax bodies can levy your bank account directly to withdraw the funds you owe.

Even so, this can't happen until numerous notices are sent you asking for payment, the final ones coming by registered mail. Ignoring these letters is a poor way to handle the situation. If you call as soon as you are notified, you will be surprised at how accommodating revenue officers can be.

Nonpayment Penalties Are Steep

If you don't pay your federal withholding tax for your employees, the penalties can be very high—the added fee is five percent per month that remains unpaid, up to twenty-five percent in total. And, if you do not file the tax return by the due date, another five percent penalty per month can be added. Interest is on top of that.

Trust fund taxes (such as employee taxes) are those you withhold for the benefit of the taxing body. These include the sales tax you collect from customers. As the collector of these funds, you are not allowed to use them for any other business purpose. That is why the penalty is so steep.

Making an Arrangement to Pay

Sitting down face-to-face with a tax collector is intimidating, but remember that this person is only doing her job. And she would rather have an offer from you than enforce the powers she has. My experience is that you can get on a twenty-four-month payment plan. (And making the first payment at the meeting would be a good idea.)

Make Yourself Judgment Proof

Perhaps one of your large customers has failed and left you holding debt that will never be paid. Costs have gone up (energy, for one), you have been losing money, and it looks like it will be impossible to turn the business around. Or the plan to save your business will involve a good amount of time and pain. Either scenario puts you at risk to lose personal assets based on personal guarantees to banks and vendors.

It's time to call in a lawyer and plan a defense, responding to any filings you receive. As soon as you can, make sure you have few or no possessions titled in your own name. You can't take such an action less than six to twelve months before creditors seek your assets. But if you are personally uncollectible, fewer people can pursue you, and those who do are likely to settle for a portion of the amount owed.

You didn't plan to find yourself in this situation, but if circumstances bring you here, there is little sense in turning yourself into a human sacrifice. Tough times do happen to honest people.

If you need more than twenty-four months to pay, ask for it; that is better than agreeing to an amount you cannot pay. Your request might be passed on to another person with more authority.

When Money Is Tight, Prioritize

One of the sure things about business is how unsure, even erratic, cash flow can be at times. It could be a temporary situation that comes unexpectedly or a regular seasonal event. Many contractors deal with this on a regular basis as do retail businesses dependent on holiday sales.

Your bills, meanwhile, continue, such as your overhead expenses. The job of scheduling payments will likely become very difficult, and you will have to give necessary payments priority.

Inside Track   Misplaced Priorities

One of my former clients, a manufacturing company in business almost twenty years, has always had a slow first quarter. Sales are off thirty percent from normal volume the rest of the year. He always avoids making tough decisions, so that by the time of the second quarter, his company is spending increasing time fighting off creditors. Each year the situation has gotten tougher, to the point that the company itself is threatened. The past few years, the toughest unpaid creditor has been the IRS. Payroll remains too high during the slow time, with the result that withholding tax and FICA are not paid. After penalties are assessed, this debt grows by fifty percent in six months. As cash flow increases, a deal is cut and extra tax payments are made. The next year, the process starts all over again. Each year the IRS becomes less lenient, and payments to them become higher. Soon the company will reach the point at which their debt will strangle them. The shame is that the net tax due isn't where the burden is; the penalty and interest are the problems. If tax payment had been a priority, penalties and interest would not have grown so critically.

Paying taxes, rent, and utilities is critical; once you get behind with any of these, it can be impossible to catch up. Even though bank payments are very important to pay, try talking to your banker to secure a temporary deferral in principal payments. Notify anyone expecting a regular payment who is not receiving it. It's far easier to extract concessions from creditors in advance of a tough period than after you have become a past-due account.

Key Vendors May Accept Partial Payments

After handling those items critical to keeping the doors open, make some effort to pay for your material or products even if you can't pay bills in full. Don't make the mistake of directing funds to the people you know instead of to the people you need. Out of your available financial resources, pay something to all your vendors. Those who continue to ship will become more valuable, so keep that in mind.

▶▶ TEST DRIVE

Credit granting is not a unilateral business act. All companies are users as well as grantors of credit. Do you know how to handle the situation when you are the debtor? Ask yourself the following questions:

- ⊃ Do you communicate well with creditors during difficult financial times for your business?
- ⊃ Are you careful not to make any specific promises to pay when you aren't able to meet these?
- ⊃ Is it your policy to make an effort to retire obligations as quickly as is feasible?
- ⊃ Are you respectful of a creditor's frustration with nonpayment even while understanding all the steps involved in the collection process?
- ⊃ Do you take the time to set payment priorities when money is tight?

Using a Factor

There will be more complexities in your relationships with customers than you realize when you start your business. Making a sale can take months, and delivering or completing the product adds to the passage of time, during which period your customer's cash flow can change. Handling the credit issue with outside credit vendors can help your business function smoothly.

Consider this scenario: You make a deal with a customer, complete the shipment, and issue an invoice. Then you sell the account to a factor. Ownership of the debt or receivable becomes the property of the factor, which sends you the proceeds less its fee. You benefit by instant payment for your sale, but your cost is the discount (fee) you allow the factor. The factor makes its money by buying debt at less than face value and collecting the gross amount.

For example, if you make a $5,000 sale for which your factor charges a seven percent fee, it will send you a check for $4,650 ($5,000 less $350). If your customer pays the factor in thirty days, it profits well from the deal. The cost of money might be a fraction of one percent. If the account becomes overdue, the factor will add a service charge and interest to its profits. But it will also absorb any loss if the account does not pay.

The rate charged by most factors is normally based on the credit rating of the customer; the higher the risk of the customer, the higher the factor's fee to you. Most factors reserve the right to refuse any additional orders from a client in default. Your responsibility is to monitor an ongoing project so you don't reach the end only to find out you can't get the factor to fund it.

The Credit Decision Still Must Be Made

When you have a customer who is being funded by a factor, you are not completely out of the game. Very likely your funding source will set a credit limit on your customer, which you need to know about. In almost all cases when an account is over sixty days old, the factor will deny new credit and might place a dollar limit on the total outstanding credit allowed. Monitor this information via your internal system lest

Develop an Alliance

If you think a leasing type of arrangement would work for your business, consider opening a relationship with one or perhaps two leasing companies. Make them aware of your products and customer base and find out their typical credit requirements and financing fees. This information will tell you which customers are likely to qualify and what their estimated monthly payment would be.

The auto industry has flourished for years on the basis of leasing arrangements. The dealer actually sells a car to a leasing company and then is out of the deal before the auto is delivered. Remember that this is usually a fully secured deal, meaning there is a tangible asset as collateral. Leasing companies will write agreements for all types of deals, including software and other computer products. I knew a restaurant owner who financed his kitchen through a leasing deal.

an invoice for merchandise shipped or work completed is sent back to you unpaid. This does not mean your customer does not have to or will not pay, only that the transaction is outside of your factor's existing underwriting.

If you still believe your customer is a good risk (perhaps because you understand her present circumstances), you could resume the relationship on a direct basis and no longer have to pay the cost of the factoring.

Try a Leasing Company

Another outside funding source you can offer your customers is a leasing arrangement. Your customer makes a purchase from you, and you fund the deal through a leasing company. The customer applies to the leasing company for the financing and has to meet its credit requirements. Business leases always require a personal guarantee, but the terms tend to be liberal. Once the deal is approved, the leasing company completes the purchase with you and pays you. All future payment transactions are between your customer and the leasing company. This is a one-time transaction, and once it has been approved, the money coming to you is secure.

Securing Deposits and Retainers Before You Work

When a customer orders a customized product or books work in advance that requires a cost commitment from you, make sure you ask for a deposit. This signifies that the deal is serious and that you are not taking on a financial risk. The more you can fund your work with your customer's money, the less likely you have the credit issue of waiting for your money.

Keep in mind, however, that the funds you hold for unfinished work or unpaid inventory are not yours. They are required at a later time to pay the expense of the job. Don't be fooled into using the positive cash flow to fund overhead so that you don't have the resources to handle the real costs of the job.

Retainers

The professional equivalent of a deposit is a retainer, which lawyers, accountants, architects, and designers often require before they begin a job. When your work is intellectual, with little work product (except results) to deliver and absolutely nothing to repossess, payment streams may be slow. You might be reluctant to ask for payment, particularly if you are a service provider attempting to solve a problem for a client not happy to be involved in the first place. This is not an easy collection to make from a client. Unless there is excellent communication, your billings

---

Use Your Accounting System to Monitor Deposits

When cash comes in as a deposit, do not post it in your accounting system as sales income. You must designate the money in the bank through a liability account titled "customer deposits." Then as you incur or pay the actual costs of the deal, you can move the cash into your revenue account.

When you are holding a substantial amount of customer money, take a snapshot of your current cash position by deducting your deposit money (less your gross profit) from your "cash in bank." Your accounts receivable also are fairly liquid, of course, and since these represent money actually owed for completed work, the expense is strictly embedded (meaning the material and labor have already been expensed).

---

beyond the retainer could be at risk, in which case your retainer should be high. Be specific about how you credit your client's advance to ongoing charges, so your client knows when to expect his credit balance to turn into an invoice due.

Floor Planning and Installment Loans

If you are a reseller of big-ticket items, you can finance your inventory with a type of loan called "floor planning." This means that your financing is secured by your inventory, and your loan is paid down as the product is sold. You might also be able to offer direct financing to your customers by way of the same lender you use. Find a bank that is a big player in retail banking (meaning that it has a large consumer base) and offer to promote its services along with your sales. Your ability to offer seamless financing might raise your sales and be of value to your bank. You will be out of the credit transaction once you make a referral.

Promote the "Monthly Cost" along with the Price

Having such a finance referral deal with your lender allows you to advertise a low monthly cost to customers as a sales incentive. Many people pay off their major purchases over time, which is the basis on which the big-box stores drive traffic. In order to compete while keeping your credit risk low, making an alliance with a lender can provide financing to grow your company through sales.

Debit Cards, Credit Cards, and Electronic Funds Transfer

The best sale for any business is a cash sale. With the delivery of your product or service the transaction is complete. You receive your money, and from a financial perspective (in contrast to a customer-service perspective, which continues in order to produce future sales), the deal is done. Any claims down the road might result in a customer credit, but for the present you are operating a cash-flow company.

To get started, arrange with a card-processing company to accept the various types of cash transfer transactions. The two factors to consider are cash versus availability.

1. **The cost to use**—Some cards charge from two to three percent to the vendor, while others have a higher fee. This amount is automatically deducted from your bank account. The value of the sale is reduced by the amount you pay for access to the cash. Compare this to the interest rate you might pay on a loan or the service charge from a vendor.

2. **How soon the money will be in your account**—An electronic transfer can show in your account in a matter of hours, whereas credit and debit cards take from twenty-four to twenty-eight hours.

Your Credit Will Be Checked

Not every company secures the rights to take credit instruments. Your own credit ratings will be taken into consideration, for reasons of fraud protection. There is a history of companies in trouble that run up charges on fake cards in order to raise quick cash. Once the charges hit the holder, they are reversed and the business uses new cards to replace the cash. This is against the law but not an unknown tactic for a cash-strapped company.

The first place to call to secure a credit card processing service is your own bank. The larger institutions have their own in-house providers, which they consider a good fee-based addition to their banking. Because in buying additional services you are a more valued customer, the bank sales force in turn might allow you access to credit card (debits and EFT) processing. Newer companies might need such a bank alliance.

In-House Processing

The newest technology in banking services is to have a check-clearing reader at your own place of business. In the same way a teller runs a check that reads the magnetic strip, you complete your deposit without going to the bank. You key in the amount and run the check itself through a data reader on your desk, which transmits the transaction to your bank. This is a real use of electronic funds transfer.

Not Just for Consumers

You can use the COD technique with any size customer. When I was in business, I once sent a shipment to a General Motors plant COD. Some of my friends thought I was crazy, and I must admit I wasn't sure it would work. The GM accounting department told me it couldn't process a check that way, but over the past year they hadn't been very good at paying bills in less than seventy-five days. My company made heat mitts to order, which was labor intensive and more aggravation than it was worth. I was able to arrange for an UPS COD delivery, and in a few days United Parcel sent me my check.

Surprisingly enough I retained the GM account after making this demand, for at least a year or so, and once I agreed to ship on open account, my bills were paid promptly. I am sure I wasn't this corporation's favorite vendor, but I had bills to pay.

COD: Cash on Delivery

A customer places an order, but delivery isn't scheduled for a while. She doesn't want to pay in advance, and you aren't quite secure enough to permit credit terms upon completion of the transaction. Perhaps you are shipping goods by a package-delivery service or by a common carrier rather than through your own service. You can require that a check be paid before the final delivery is made.

When you produce the packing list and bill of lading for the shipment, make a note that payment must be picked up before the goods are released. The small package carriers can feed this (frequent) request directly into their system and generate a tag for the box. A large trucking company can also process such a request, although handling it is a bit more cumbersome. Give your own drivers specific instructions.

If this is a new customer in an unknown area for whom you have little information, request a certified check. If you deliver and the check bounces, you could have a serious dilemma on your hands. The delivery personnel will follow your instructions.

There Is a Cost for Using This Method—Pass It On

All companies will charge you to do a COD delivery, and you need to add this cost to your invoice. If the first delivery attempt fails because the check is not there or there is no one to sign for it, the need for a second delivery will increase the cost (which might be hard to add in).

Progress Payments

When you are involved in a long-term project, you need to work out a deal wherein you will be paid along the way. Spell out the terms of this agreement (usually through meeting benchmarks) in your original contract. A construction job will issue stage payments less a retainer (ten percent of which is held until the end). The contractor submits the bill, and once an inspection is complete, money is released.

No matter what type of work you do, you can design a progress payment plan. Tangible work or product might seem easier to bill, but even a consulting job can be set up to fund along the way. I have seen attorneys doing bankruptcies require monthly payment deposits to assure their fee will be paid in the end. And their clients have complied.

The Funders May Pay the Bill

In cases where your client has used a bank or lending institution to finance a complete deal, the lender could be the bottom-line decision maker as to whether you get paid. The bank or lender might need only a sign-off, or it might need a walk-through inspection. If you make sure your agreed-to targets are met, your money will be on its way. The lender will be anxious to remit the proceeds so it can begin to collect.

Credit Insurance to Rely On

There is a form of insurance known as "credit risk insurance" that protects you from the insolvency or past-due default of your client. Only a few underwriters specialize in this type of coverage. They will perform in-depth credit evaluations before considering the accounts you wish to insure, and they approve on the basis of credit limits as well. So this is not a program to use in lieu of a credit policy of your own. Rather, you will be a partner in loss prevention. Don't expect to write a policy in anticipation of a large potential loss because if there is any risk you know of, the insuring company will have access to the same information.

The Terms of the Policy

This is highly customized insurance; almost every policy is custom-designed on some level. You will have a deductible or "risk retention" on your portfolio, which may range from ten to twenty percent, in addition to the exposure limit on individual clients. You might also have an overall limit of exposure, though that shouldn't be an issue because it is unlikely all of your clients will default at the same time. And it is possible to carry excess insurance, in terms of a second policy that backs up the first. You want to cover all your direct and overhead costs.

Finding the Right Insurer

Since there are very few of these types of companies, you will not find much competition. Make sure you find a company that has experience and focus in this area and that is licensed to do business in your state. Find one that has the support staff to monitor your company, keeping you in compliance and covered. The cost is really not that high, working out to a fraction of one percent of your receivables.

▶▶ TEST DRIVE

There are a number of creative ways to minimize your risk in the world of credit. Are you using one or more? Consider the following:

- ➲ Would selling your accounts to a factor work in your industry?
- ➲ Can you ask your client for a deposit or retainer in advance?
- ➲ Are you able to take credit cards and process electronic checks?
- ➲ Do you generate progress payments on longer-term jobs?
- ➲ Are you eligible for credit insurance?

Profit Isn't Real until the Money Is Received

The amount of total sales is the number on which new business owners place the most importance; gross revenue is ego-driven. An owner can't wait to develop a million-dollar business. But the only number that really matters is profit—what is left at the end of the day after the bills are paid. You aren't working primarily to pay others. Rather, the idea is to build equity.

Let's imagine that your company is contacted by a new customer looking for the product or service you provide. He wants an estimate or quote for a job, so you work hard determining what your actual costs will be plus what is a fair markup or profit. This is the beginning of the transaction.

The next part of the process is to sell the order and close the deal. Your job is done only in part at this point because you must complete the work and satisfy the needs and expectations of your customer. When the job is done, you submit an invoice for all or part of the work, depending on what contractual arrangements have been made. If the bill isn't paid in a timely fashion, the erosion of your profit begins. However, few companies even track this cost—the cost of funds. If your current interest rate on your loans is eight percent, a bill not paid for ninety days costs you two percent just to fund. And the loss of cash flow has a cumulative effect because when you have extra money, you can take discounts or purchase good deals that save you money. When all your cash is in the hands of your customers, you are at their mercy and your deals are not completed.

The reality is that if your customer is one of the big retailers, you could still face returns months after you ship. And the money might be at risk for even longer. Some of the giant resellers believe that what they don't sell for months can be returned; the risk is yours, not theirs. Once your material has been paid for, you have leverage. If you have not received the cash, however, you might never see all of it. Therefore, your goal is to complete the transaction by receiving the final payment.

Keeping an Account Open Costs Money

An open credit account means not only lost cash and lost opportunity, but an ongoing administrative cost as well. Consider the real costs of issuing and sending statements every month as well as the time involved

The Publishing Industry

As a lifelong entrepreneur as well as writer, I have never understood the economics of the publishing industry. It is unevenly beneficial to the bookstores, which return unsold books as long as a few years after they are shipped. Although the sale is not officially referred to as consignment, the publisher's transaction surely resembles this. Publishers factor this shrinkage in their costs. Authors are often shocked at how this reads on a royalty statement. Three years after a book is sold, some are still being returned. Any profit for the publisher that seemed once possible is gone. The only reason this arrangement works in the industry is for the chance of a major return on a big seller.

in making phone calls and sending letters. Attention required to keep in touch with your nonpaying client draws time away from other duties, which adds to your overhead expense. And when you have already booked the income from the sale, this cost continues to come off your bottom line. You aren't being paid, and you are losing money as well.

Make Sure Your Books Reflect the Reality

A company that carries uncollectible debts on its books for long isn't facing the real circumstances of its business. Many entrepreneurs are reluctant to take the debt write-off because this reduces their assets and lowers their net worth. But the fact is that unpaid invoices have no value if they will not turn into cash. And, if they have to be deeply discounted to collect, that will end up on a balance sheet write-off as well. You need to know what your cash flow is, and a big element in that calculation results from the collection of outstanding receivables. You must have an accurate number of the accounts that are performing.

A Cash Statement Reflects Only Cash Received

Although not usually the better way to keep a company's books, a "cash statement" accounting system reflects as the income of the company only money received. Unpaid customer invoices do not show as income. The downside of this type of system is that the only expenses shown are ones that have actually been paid. If you aren't being paid and you are not paying your bills, this fact may not show up until too late.

In the "accrual basis" type of accounting system, all revenue earned is recorded as income. When you pay sales tax on an accrual basis, you could be paying on income you have never received. You can compensate for both accounting methods by deducting expenses incurred whether or not they are ever paid. This gives you profit-and-loss information based on the assumption that all transactions will be completed, monies owed you will be collected, and debts owed by you will be paid. When these are not the case, adjustments have to be made.

Bad Debts Can Undermine a Good Business

Richard is someone who can sell ice to the Eskimos—he is charming and convincing. Making a deal is his strength; handling the after-care is not. The bottom line is that his contracting company collected only seventy-eight percent of its invoices. After every few months collection efforts would stop while everyone focused on the new business coming in the door. After five years of this, the company had to shut its doors. The owner found himself deep in personal debt after years of hard work.

When the profits show up on your income statement but not in your pocket, you are at risk. The solvency of a company is based on cash flow received in a timely way. When receivables remain on the balance sheet but do not turn into cash, your debt increases as assets decrease. Eventually the business can drift into insolvency and obligations not be met.

Bad Debts Are Written Off Sales

You can remember the principle of how to write off a bad debt without having to understand accounting standards. At the end of the year, normally a business reviews unpaid accounts and determines those likely to be uncollectible. Those accounts are charged off (credited to) the books and the accounts receivable reduced by that amount. This same number is written off the sales side, reducing your total income and your gross and net profit. The result is an immediate change in your bottom line that can undermine the success you've had the entire year. So if you don't collect the debt, you take a loss.

Do Not Borrow Against Bad Receivables

When customers don't pay as expected, you can't manage the need of the company to make payroll and overhead as well as handle your vendor obligations. Many business owners then look to other sources of cash, such as drawing on a line of credit or trying to secure a new loan. Even when you do not receive a customer payment; your debt to the lender is still due. Always exercise caution before taking on debt to replace lost cash. You should understand your balance sheet well enough to recognize danger signs.

Your Credit Provides You with Options

Some of the expenses of your company are short-term, such as buying inventory to use in a manufacturing process, material for a contracting job, or products you will be reselling fairly soon. You use the cash provided at the end of a job to pay vendor bills. And some of your expenses provide a long-term return. The equipment and technology that make your operation more profitable, for example, return positive cash flow over months and perhaps years. You have to be able to finance both needs, and this requires a variety of credit relationships.

What you learn in any long-term business operation is that each credit relationship is unique, based on the needs of the grantor at the time it makes its decision and the flexibility of the grantor's policy with regard to payback. You need these differing types of credit facilities and so must develop relationships with options.

Typically, short-term credit is provided by vendors, and long-term credit provided by lenders. Mid-term credit can be available from either; you decide which to call on based on accessibility and cost. Some banks require a serious amount of paperwork for smaller loans, which adds to the cost, but having a line of credit in place to draw on when you need it is always a good plan. Before an actual credit need arises, check out the possibilities of having a line of credit available to draw down when you need to cover your cash flow. Be sophisticated about using vendor credit, taking time to pay suppliers when you need to, but refraining from causing a supplier any inconvenience.

Leasing and Extended Vendor Credit Are Also Options

As you have learned from the discussions of credit recovery, when you have recourse to reclaiming your goods you have better leverage. The financing entities (like leasing companies) that keep title to property can be more flexible than a typical vendor. Your company pays for the use of your purchase as you would if you were renting it, and at the end of the lease period, you have a nominal purchase option (often as low as a dollar).

The other credit option you might be able to receive is dating from your vendor. Instead of a net thirty days, as you would expect, you have net ninety days or payments even over a longer period. If your credit relationship has been good, ask for what you need in order to meet expectations. Many vendors would rather bill at the agreed-to terms than have their standard terms missed.

Credit and Trust Are Twin Values—Use Both

Credit really is an issue of trust. Ethical behavior in a business transaction, from quote to sell to completion to payment, is a win for both buyer and seller. Shortcuts or misrepresentations anywhere along this chain put the financial outcome in jeopardy. A quote exceeded when the sale is billed, a shipment incomplete or of lesser quality, a job not done properly—these are issues that call into question the trust between a business and its customer. When that bond is broken, the smooth flow of cash can go with it.

As a customer, you expect your vendors to keep their commitments to you throughout a transaction cycle. When this isn't the case, you might retaliate by delaying or withholding payments. The justification here is that you are equalizing your inconvenience. Your customers practice the same type of self-interest.

And at the end of that chain, your vendor is more likely to pay attention to your requests and your special interests when it can count on you to pay what you owe on a timely basis or to let them know of any delay. Unreturned calls or missed promises move you to the back of the line on all levels when it comes to shipment as well as customer service. A desirable client to you is a desirable client to your vendor: one who is loyal, honest, and pays her bills as well as she can.

Lessons Learned

Running my own manufacturing company was a good way for me to develop a business value system. In my early years, I was a real rookie at deal making, and at times I was not quite sure what my distributor was looking for from me. One in particular explained that he wanted me to use lower price (and value) raw materials in some of my products while marking them up the same amount as the higher-quality goods. He offered slightly more profit for my company, but his margin increased far more than mine.

I didn't want to lose the business, so I agreed and produced one order. We shipped to his customer who rejected the goods and refused payment. I had no use for the items and steadfastly refused to take them back. I didn't give in, but I didn't get paid. We both lost a customer and some money, which should not have been a surprise. This was an experience I only had to have once.

If You Have Done the Work, You Are Entitled to the Money

When you make a sale and supply the products or services that are expected and deemed acceptable, the contract has been fulfilled. You have the right, both legally and ethically, to be paid for the value of that work. This must be your position from the original date of the invoice you submit for payment. Do not back down from your rightful claim. Meet with your client face-to-face and answer his questions, offering a solution. You will know what to expect then.

Be organized enough to provide additional information and documentation but be steadfast as well in your right to be paid. This is your income, not a gift from your customer. Timely and complete payment is not a favor but the completion of the business transaction. If you set the right value on your product or service and deliver it in a professional way, payment should take place seamlessly.

▶▶ TEST DRIVE

Your goal is a financially sound company. This means that you sell a sufficient amount of product or services priced at a profitable level and that you collect the money in full. Are you aware of the following?

➲ Profit on paper is not profit in the bank.
➲ Bad debts represent a reduction to sales and a risk to the future of the company.
➲ Credit is a tool that gives a company many options.
➲ Credit behavior is a reflection of business ethics.
➲ Customers have an obligation to pay, and a company needs to remind them periodically.

Epilogue

Possessing a marketable concept, a special skill, or a particular area of expertise, you have started a business. Rather than expend your efforts on someone else's company, you have decided to go out on your own. The spirit of entrepreneurship is driven by independence and creativity, and now opportunity awaits you. But the tasks and challenges can also be daunting, requiring constant attention to detail and extensive financial knowledge. And as this book has shown, the day-to-day issues that arise in the thorny area of business credit and payment collection frequently determine whether a company succeeds or even survives.

You need various types of credit for your company, necessitating a business relationship with vendors as well as with a range of lenders. Your company grows not only from the use of human resources but also from outside capital. Bank loans, for instance, provide capital for the purchase of assets. You might want to purchase materials to use in your product and to pay for these over time, as they are turned back into cash through resale of goods. Step one in learning the credit process has been to find out how you can position your company to secure the credit it needs.

You likely have found differences among potential suppliers and bankers in deciding how much credit to grant your company, requiring an application process ranging from easy to unreasonably difficult. You have learned to use the process common to commercial lending as a model in granting credit in turn, strengthening both your level of customer service and your tools of financial management.

You want your customers to find your company user friendly and, at the same time, professional and effective. If you have designated personnel (or a department) for handling your credit decisions and monitoring collections, you make sure they are well-trained in procedures, kept informed, and supported. You grant customer credit in order to generate new business or bigger sales, knowing not to undermine your effort with poor customer service.

The unfortunate day may come when you have to enforce collection procedures against nonpaying customers. Between walking away from a collection account, on the one hand, and refusing to compromise by accepting a settlement, on the other, you have learned in these chapters the appropriate steps to collect the money owed you.

You are now well-prepared to take the financial side of your business seriously. Whether dealing with an error in an order, a miscommunication in a job, a misprint in billing, or an unreliable customer, you perceive that disruption of your earned cash flow makes your work tougher and your future less stable. At this point you know why the process of receiving and granting business credit requires a consistent set of policies and sound decision making, just as collection demands implementing effective and professional business practices. Managing issues of credit and collection—though perhaps not as much fun as focusing on sales and marketing—is indeed of paramount importance in the success of your business.

APPENDIXES

Annual Percentage Rate (APR)

The yearly interest fee charged by the credit grantor for the use of funds.

assets

Any tangible possession, personal or business, which is owned wholly or partially. The value is usually placed at market price for purposes of collateral.

authorized account user

Individuals who are permitted to use an account without being responsible for payments.

bankruptcy

A federal proceeding that stops all collection activity while dispersal of assets is placed under court supervision.

bankruptcy discharge

The act of court ending bankruptcy proceedings and the discharging of all debts.

bankruptcy dismissal

The order of court that ends the protection from creditors and allows all debt collection to resume.

charge card

A credit facility that requires payment in full in each thirty-day cycle.

charge-off

Creditor writes off a debt as uncollectible and typically reports this action to credit reporting agencies.

C.O.D.

Cash (or Collect) on Delivery, meaning that payment is required when product is delivered.

collateral

The assets of a company or an individual that are pledged to secure a loan. If the loan goes into default, the lender has the right to foreclose on or repossess the collateral.

confession of judgment

This is a clause in a credit note that allows the grantor to record a lien in the county records against all of the assets of a debtor without having to bring a suit. A confession is usually executed only when there is a default on payment by the debtor.

collection account

This denotes a business or consumer account that has been turned over by the original creditor to an agency for collection action.

consolidation loan

A loan intended to be used to pay off all or most of a consumer's debts, leaving the consumer with a single, smaller monthly payment.

cosigner

Any signatory to a note beyond the primary signer. A cosigner becomes fully obligated to all the responsibilities of the note until it is paid.

credit

The promise to pay later for goods or services received today.

credit grantor

Person or business that is selling goods or services on the basis of a future payment.

credit limit

The maximum amount allowed charged on an account or credit card.

credit repair

Using techniques to delete negative items on a credit report or correct misinformation. May also advise consumers on how to raise their credit score.

credit report

The data collected by several primary companies that detail the extent of a consumer's outstanding credit and how payments have been made in prior periods. Used to extend credit and sometimes to check potential employees.

credit score

Designed by the Fair Isaac company, this is a number from 350–850 that is used to rate the credit of individuals. The elements weighed are length of credit, history of repayment, and extensive use of credit. Scores in the range of 650–750 are considered favorable.

debit card

A card linked directly to the consumer's bank account that transfers money when purchases are made.

debt

The amount of money owed to others on a formal or informal basis, which has a definite repayment schedule.

Equal Credit Opportunity Act

The federal law requiring all creditors to make credit available to persons without discrimination in regard to race, age, sex, marital status, national origin, or source of income from assistance programs.

garnishment

Judgment credit allowing seizure of some or all of a debtor's assets, including wages, to satisfy outstanding debt.

grace period

A specified period before the due date on an account during which interest or finance charges are not applied.

guaranty

This is an agreement by a third party to pay a specific portion of or all of the debt of the borrower if not made in a timely fashion by the primary credit holder.

insolvency

A financial condition in which liabilities exceed assets and the business or individual is unable to meet obligations.

interest

The charge for borrowing or credit usually expressed as a percentage of the unpaid balance.

judgment

The determination or decision of the court with regard to a suit or action filed. This becomes a part of the public record.

lien

A legal claim on property held as security for a debt or claim. A lien must be satisfied (paid) to be released.

mechanic's lien

A hold or claim on property for the benefit of someone whose work or material improves the condition of the property.

personal guarantee

The agreement by an individual to pay the loan or debt of a business entity.

repossession

Forced or voluntary surrender of material or merchandise to satisfy an action for failure to pay.

revolving account

One that requires a specific monthly payment each month as well as an interest charge. The amount due often goes down as the balance diminishes.

secured credit card

The card holder must put on deposit with the card granter an amount equal to the credit limit on the card. This is a no-risk account for the grantor.

unsecured card

A credit card that has no link to any collateral. The interest rate is based on the level of risk the card holder represents.

APPENDIXES

Alabama Statutes of Limitation

Contracts under seal: 10 years (A.C. 6-2-33)

Contracts not under seal; actions on account stated and for detention of personal property or conversion: 6 years (A.C. 6-2-34)

Sale of goods under the UCC: 4 years (A.C. 7 -2-725)

Open accounts: 3 years (A.C. 6-2-37)

Actions to recover charges by a common carrier and negligence actions; 2 years (A.C. 6-2-38)

Actions based on fraud: 2 years (A.C. 6-2-3)

Maximum Interest: Legal 6%; Judgment 12%

Alaska Statutes of Limitations

Action on a sealed instrument: 10 years (A.S. 09.10.40)

Action to recover real property: 10 years (A.S. 09.10.30)

Action upon written contract: 3 years (A.S. 09.10.55) Note: prior to 8/7/97 the statute of limitations for written contracts was 6 years.

Action upon contract for sale: 4 years (A.S. 45.02.725) However, limitations by agreements may be reduced, but not less than 1 year (A.S. 45.02.725).

Maximum Interest: Legal 10.5%; Judgment 10.5% or by contract

Arizona Statutes of Limitation

Written contracts: 6 years, runs from date creditor could have sued account.

Oral debts, stated or opens accounts: 3 years.

Actions for fraud or mistake: 3 years from the date of the discovery of the fraud or mistake.

Actions involving fiduciary bonds, out-of-state instruments and foreign judgments: 4 years. Note: Arizona applies its own statute of limitations to foreign judgments rather than that of the state that originally rendered the judgment, whether the judgment is being domesticated under the Uniform Enforcement of Foreign Judgments Act or pursuant to a separate action on the foreign judgment.

An Arizona judgment must be renewed within 5 years of the date of the judgment.

Maximum Interest: Legal 10%; Judgment 10% or contractual

Arkansas Statutes of Limitation

Written contracts: 5 years. Note: Partial payment or written acknowledgement of default stopped this statute of limitations. (A.C.A. 16-56-111)

Contracts not in writing: 3 years (A.C.A. 16-56-105)

Breach of any contract for the sale of goods covered by the UCC: 4 years (A.C.A. 4-2-725)

Medical debts: 2 years from date services were performed or provided or from the date of the most recent partial payment for the services, whichever is later. (A.C.A. §16-56-106)

Negligence actions: 3 years after the cause of action. (A.C.A. § 16-56-105)

Maximum Interest: Legal 6% or 5 points above federal discount rate; Judgment 10%

California Statutes of Limitation

Written agreements: 4 years, calculated from the date of breach.

Oral agreements: 2 years.

The statute of limitation is stopped only if the debtor makes a payment on the account after the expiration of the applicable limitations period.

Maximum Interest: Legal 10%; Judgment 10%

Colorado Statutes of Limitation

Domestic and foreign judgments: 6 years and renewable each 6 years. Note: If for child support, maintenance or arrears the judgment (lien) stays in effect for the life the judgment without the necessity of renewal every 6 years.

All contract actions, including personal contracts and actions under the UCC: 3 years (C.R.S. 13-80-101), except as otherwise provided in 13-80-103.5; All claims under the Uniform Consumer Credit Code, except sections 5-5-201(5); All actions to recover, detain or convert goods or chattels, except as otherwise provided in section 13 -80-103.5.

Liquidated debt and unliquidated determinable amount of money due; Enforcement of instrument securing the payment of or evidencing any debt; Action to recover the possession of secured personal property; Arrears of rent: 6 years (C.R.S. 13-80-103.5)

Maximum Interest: Legal 8%; Judgment 8% or contract rate

Connecticut Statutes of Limitation

Written contact, or on a simple or implied contract: 6 years (CGS 52-576)

Oral contract, including any agreement wherein the party being charged has not signed a note or memorandum: 3 years (CGS § 52-581)

Maximum Interest: Legal 8%; Judgment 10%

Delaware Statutes of Limitation

General contracts: 3 years

Sales under the UCC: 4 years

Notes 6 years

Miscellaneous documents under seal: No limitation.

Maximum Interest: Legal federal discount rate + 5%; Judgment same

District of Columbia Statutes of Limitation

Contract, open account or credit card account: 3 years from the date of last payment or last charge. Note: An oral promise to pay restarts the 3 years.

Contracts under seal: 12 years.

UCC Sales of Goods: 4 years.

Maximum Interest: Legal 6%; Judgment 70% of current IRS note

Florida Statutes of Limitation

Contract or written instrument and for mortgage foreclosure: 5 years. F.S. 95.11.

Libel, slander, or unpaid wages: 2 years.

Judgments: 20 years total and to be a lien on any real property, it has to be re-recorded for a second time at 10 years.

The limitations period begins from the date the last element of the cause of action occurred (95.051). Note: The limitation period is tolled (stopped) for any period during which the debtor is absent from the state and each time a voluntary payment is made on a debt arising from a written instrument.

Almost all other actions fall under the 4-year catchall limitations period (F.S. 95.11(3)(p)).

Maximum Interest: Legal 10%; Judgment 10% or contract rate

Georgia Statutes of Limitation

Breach of any contract for sale: 4 years (OCGA 11-2-725). Note: Parties may reduce limitation to not less than one year, but not extend it. A cause of action accrues when the breach occurs, regardless of the aggrieved party's lack of knowledge of the breach.

Contract, including breach of warranty or indemnity: 4 years (OCGA 11-22A-506) Note: The parties may reduce the period to one year.

Written contract: 6 years from when it becomes due and payable and the 6-year period runs from the date of last payment. (OCGA 9-3-24)

Open account; implied promise or undertaking: 4 years (OCGA 9-3-25). Note: Payment, unaccompanied by a writing acknowledging the debt, does not stop the statute. Therefore, the statutory period runs from the date of default, not the date of last payment.

Bonds or other instruments under seal, 20 years (OCGA 9-3-23) Note: No instrument is considered under seal unless it is stated in the body of the instrument.

Maximum Interest: Legal 7%; Judgment 12%; Commercial 18%

Hawaii Statutes of Limitation

Breach of contract for sale under the UCC: 4 years.

Contract, obligation or liability: 6 years.

Judgments: 10 years, renewable if an extension is sought during the 10 years.

Note: The time limitation stopped during the time of a person's absence from the state or during the time that an action is stayed by injunction of any court.

Maximum Interest: Legal 10%; Judgment 10%

Idaho Statutes of Limitation

Breach of contract for sale under the UCC: 4 years.

Written contract or liability: 5 years.

Contract or liability that is not written: 4 years. Note: The time period begins as of the date of the last item, typically a payment or a charge under a credit card agreement. A written acknowledgement or new promise signed by the debtor is sufficient evidence to cause the relevant statute of limitations to begin running anew. Any payment of principal or interest is equivalent to a new promise in writing to pay the residue of the debt.

Judgments: 5 years but may be renewed for another 5-year period. Note: An independent action on a judgment of any court of the United States must be brought within 6 years.

The time limitation for the commencement of any action is tolled during the time of a person's absence from the state or during the time that an action is stayed by injunction or by statutory prohibition action.

Maximum Interest: Legal 12%; Judgment 10.875% plus base rate

Illinois Statutes of Limitation

Breach of contract for sale under the UCC: 4 years.

Open account or unwritten contract: 5 years. Note: Except, as provided in 810 ILCS 5/2-725 (UCC), actions based on a written contract must be filed within 10 years, but if a payment or new written promise to pay is made during the 10-year period, then the action may be commenced within 10 years after the date of the payment or promise to pay.

Domestic judgments: 20 years, but can be renewed during that 20-year period.

Foreign judgments are the same time as allowed by the laws of the foreign jurisdiction.

Tolling: A person's absence from the state or during the time that an action is stayed by injunction, court order or by statutory prohibition tolls the time limit.

Non-Sufficient Fund (NSF or Payment of Negotiable Instruments) checks: 3 years of the dishonor of the draft or 10 years after the date of the draft, whichever expired first: 810 ILCS 5/3-118

Maximum Interest: Legal 8%; Judgment 7%

Indiana Statutes of Limitation

Breach of contract for sale under UCC: 4 years.

Unwritten accounts or contracts and promissory notes or written contracts for payment of money executed after August 31, 1982: 6 years.

Written contracts unrelated to the payment of money: 10 years.

Written acknowledgment or new promise signed by the debtor, or any voluntary payment on a debt, is sufficient evidence to cause the relevant statute of limitations to begin running anew.

Judgments: 10 years unless renewed.

Maximum Interest: Legal 8%; Judgment 8%

Iowa Statutes of Limitation

Open account: 5 years from last charge, payment, or admission of debt in writing. Unwritten contracts: 5 years from breach.

Written contracts: 10 years from breach.

Demand Note: 10 years from date of note.

Judgments: 20 years. However, an action brought on a judgment after nine years but not more than ten years can be brought to renew the judgment.

Note: Deficiency judgments on most residential foreclosures, and judgments on mortgage notes become essentially worthless two years from date of judgment.

Maximum Interest: Legal 5%; Judgment 10%

Kansas Statutes of Limitation

Written agreement, contract or promise: 5 years.

Expressed or implied but not written contracts, obligations or liabilities: 3 years.

Relief on the grounds of fraud: 2 years.

Maximum Interest: Legal 10%; Judgment 12%

Kentucky Statutes of Limitation

Recovery of real property: 15 years (KRS 413.0 10).

Judgment, contract or bond: 15 years (KRS 413.110).

Breach of sales contract: 4 years (KRS 355.2-725).

Contract not in writing: 5 years (KRS413.120). Note: Action for liability created by statute when no there is no time fixed by statute: 5 years (KRS413.120).

Action on check, draft or bill of exchange: 5 years (KRS 413.120).

Action for fraud or mistake: 5 years (KRS 413.120).

Actions not provided for by statute: 10 years (KRS 413.160).

Maximum Interest: Legal 8%; Judgment 10%

Louisiana Statutes of Limitation

Contracts: 10 years.

Open accounts: 3 years.

Lawsuits, which are filed but not pursued, become null three years after the last action taken.

Judgment: 10 years, and if not renewed within the ten years become a nullity.

Maximum Interest: Legal 9.75%; Judgment 9.75%

Maine Statutes of Limitation

Generally all civil actions must be commenced within 6 years after the cause of action accrues. (14 M.R.S.A. 752)

The primary exception is for liabilities under seal, promissory notes signed in the presence of an attesting witness, or on the bills, notes or other evidences of debt issued by a bank, in which case, the limitation is 20 years after the cause of action accrues. (14 M.R.S.A. 751)

Judgments are presumed paid after 20 years. (14 M.R.S.A. 864)

Maximum Interest: Legal 8%; Judgment 15% (less than 30,000)

Maryland Statutes of Limitation

Civil action: 3 years from the date it accrues, unless:

Breach of contract under any sale of goods and services under the UCC: 4 years after the cause of action, even if the aggrieved party is unaware of the breach.

Promissory notes or instruments under seal, bonds, judgments, recognizance, contracts under seal, or other specialties: 12 years.

Financing statement: 12 years, unless a continuation statement is filed by a secured party six (6) months prior to end of twelve (12) year period. (Maryland, Commercial Law article Sec. 2-725; Courts & Judicial Proceedings Article Sec. 5-101-02, 9-403).

Note: The 3-year statute of limitations begins again if creditors can document that a debtor has reaffirmed a debt by a good faith basis by a written agreement, orally, or by payment.

Maximum Interest: Legal 6%; Judgment 10% or contract rate

Massachusetts Statutes of Limitation

Debt instruments issued by banks, Contract under seal: 20 years.

Judgments: 20 Years.

Oral or Written Contracts: 6 Years.

Consumer Protection Actions: 4 Years.

Recovery of Property: 3 Years.

Probate Claims: 1 Year from date of death.

Claims on mortgage notes following foreclosure or on claims junior to a foreclosed mortgage: 2 Years.

Maximum Interest: Legal 6%; Judgment 12%; Contract 12%

Michigan Statutes of Limitation

Breach of Contract: 6 years (MCL 600.5807(8)).

Breach of Contract for Sale of goods under the UCC: 4 years: including deficiency actions following repossession and sale of goods subject to a security interest (MCL 440.2725(1)).

Judgments: 10 years, but are renewable by action for another 10 years, MCL.600.5809(3).

Note: Another state's limitation period may apply check statutes carefully.

Maximum Interest: Legal 5%; Judgment 7%

Minnesota Statutes of Limitation

Breach of contract for sale under the UCC: 4 years (MSA 336.2.).

Note: Except where the Uniform Commercial Code otherwise prescribes, actions based on a contract or other obligation, express or implied, must be brought within 6 years after the cause of action occurred (Chapter 541).

Tolling: New written acknowledgment or payment tolls the statute of limitations for the debt.

Judgments: 10 years.

Maximum Interest: Legal 6%; Judgment 5%

Mississippi Statutes of Limitation

Contracts and Promissory Notes: 3 years (MCA 75-3-118, 75-2-725, and 15-1-49).

Open Accounts: 3 years from the date at which time the items on the account became due and payable, (MCA 15-1-29 & MCA 15-1-31).

Judgment liens on real estate: 7 years, but can be renewed by filing suit to renew judgment prior to expiration of 7th year (MCA 15-1-47).

Deficiency claims: 1 year from sale of collateral (MCA 15-1-23)

Enforcement of construction liens: 1 year from date lien is filed (MCA 85-7-141)

Maximum Interest: Legal 8%; Judgment contract rate or court discretion

Missouri Statutes of Limitation

Written agreement that contemplates the payment of money or property: 10 Years (Mo. Rev. Stat. §5l6.ll 0). Note: Under certain circumstances, the contractual statute of limitations may be reduced to 5 years.

Open accounts: 5 years (Mo. Rev. Stat. §5l6.l20).

Sale of goods under the UCC: 4 years. Note: The statute begins to run from the date when the breach occurred for contracts and from the time of the last item in the account on the debtor's side for actions on accounts.

Maximum Interest: Legal 9%; Judgment 9%

Montana Statutes of Limitation (MCA Title 27, Chapter 2)

Written contract, obligation or liability: 8 years.

Contract, account or promise that is not based on a written instrument: 5 years.

Montana obligation is to provide a certain level of support for a spouse, child or indigent parent: 2 years.

Obligation or liability, other than a contract, account or promise not based on a written instrument: 3 years.

Relief on the grounds of fraud or mistake: 2 years.

Note: A written acknowledgment signed by the debtor or any payment on a debt is sufficient evidence to cause the relevant statute of limitations to begin running anew.

Judgment or decree of any U.S. court: 10 years. Note: Judgments rendered in a court not of record: 6 years.

Maximum Interest: Legal 10%; Judgment 10% or contract rate

Nebraska Statutes of Limitation

Real estate or foreclosure mortgage actions; product liability; 10 years.

Foreign judgments, contract or promise in writing, express or implied: 5 years.

Unwritten contract, express or implied; Recovery of personal property; Relief on grounds of fraud; breach of contract for sale of goods; and open account: 4 years.

Liability created by federal statute with no other limitation: 3 years. Malpractice: 2 Years.

Note: Statute of Limitation can be interrupted by partial payment or written acknowledgment of debt. The statute starts to run anew from the date of the partial payment or written acknowledgment (Neb. Rev. Stat. §25-216)

Note: Actions on breach of contract for sale may be reduced to not less than 1 year.

Maximum Interest: Legal 12% or contract; Judgment 1% above U.S. Treasury Bond Rate

Nevada Statutes of limitation

Written contract: 6 years.

Verbal contract: 4 years.

Property damage: 3 years.

Personal injury: 2 years.

Maximum Interest: Legal 2% over prime; Judgment 2% over prime

New Hampshire Statutes of Limitation

Contracts and open accounts: 3 years (RSA 508:4).

Contracts for the sale of goods under UCC: 4 years (RSA 382-A: 2-725).

Notes, defined as negotiable instruments: 6 years (RSA 382-A: 3-118)

Judgments, recognizance, and contracts under seal: 20 years (RSA 508:5)

Notes secured by a mortgage: 20 years and applies even if the mortgage has been foreclosed (RSA 508:6).

Tolling: Payment on an account tolls the statute.

Note: Installment loans allow for separate measurement of the statutory period as each separate payment comes due, unless the loan has been accelerated.

Maximum Interest: Judgment 7.6%

New Jersey Statutes of Limitation

Conversion of an instrument for money: 3 years (N.J.S.A.12A: 3-118(g)).

Sale of goods under the UCC: 4 years (N.J.S.A. 12A; 2-725).

Real or personal property damage, recovery and contracts not under seal: 6 years (N.J.S.A. 2A: 14-1).

Demand Notes when no demand is made: 10 years. If demand made: 6 years from date of demand (12A: 3-118(b)).

Obligations under seal for the payment of money only, except bank, merchant, finance company or other financial institution: 16 years (N.J.S.A. 2A: 14-4) actions for unpaid rent if lease agreement is under seal (N.J.S.A. 2A: 14-4).

Real estate: 20 years (N.J.S.A. 2A: 14-7); Judgments: 20 years, renewable (2A: 14-5); Foreign judgments: 20 years (unless period in originating jurisdiction is less) (2A: 14-5).

Unaccepted drafts: 3 years from date of dishonor or 10 years from date of draft, whichever expires first (12A: 3- 118(c)).

Maximum Interest: Legal 6%; Judgment—not specified

New Mexico Statutes of Limitation

Contract in writing: 6 years (except any contract for the sale of personal property is 4 years or the last payment, whichever is later).

All other creditor-debtor transactions are 4 years after accrual of the right to sue.

Note 1: An action accrues on the first date on which the creditor can sue for a breach or for relief, generally from the last purchase or the last payment.

Note 2: If the limitations period has expired, an acknowledgment or payment starts the period running again.

Judgments: 14 years.

Maximum Interest: Judgment 8.76% or contract rate

New York Statutes of Limitation

N. Y. Civil Practice Law and Rules: Chapter Eight of the Consolidated Laws, Article 2—Limitations of Time:

211. Actions to be commenced within twenty years. (a) On a bond. (b) On a money judgment. (c) By state for real property. (d) By grantee of state for real property. (e) For support, alimony or maintenance.

212. Actions to be commenced within 10 years. (a) Possession necessary to recover real property. (b) Annulment of letters patent. (c) To redeem from a mortgage.

213. Actions to be commenced within 6 years: where not otherwise provided for; on contract; on sealed instrument; on bond or note, and mortgage upon real property; by state based on misappropriation of public property; based on mistake; by corporation against director, officer or stockholder; based on fraud.

213-a. Actions to be commenced within four years; residential rent overcharge.

213-b. Action by a victim of a criminal offense.

214. Actions to be commenced within 3 years: for nonpayment of money collected on execution; for penalty created by statute; to recover chattel; for injury to property; for personal injury; for malpractice other than medical or dental malpractice; to annul a marriage on the ground of fraud.

UCC, Section 2—725. Statute of Limitations in Contracts for Sale. (1) An action for breach of any contract for sale must be commenced within 4 years after the cause of action has accrued. By the original agreement the parties may reduce the period of limitation to not less than 1 year but may not extend it. (2) A cause of action accrues when the breach occurs, regardless of the aggrieved party's lack of knowledge of the breach. Contract for lease of goods: 4 years (N. Y. U.C.C. 2-A-506(1)).

S 203. Method of computing periods of limitation generally. (a) Accrual of cause of action and interposition of claim. The time within which an action must be commenced, except as otherwise expressly prescribed, shall be computed from the time the cause of action accrued to the time the claim is interposed.

Uniform Commercial Code—Index

New York State Consolidated Laws

Maximum Interest: Legal 16%; Judgment 9%

North Carolina Statute of Limitation

Express or implied contract, not under seal: 3 years.

Contract and sale of personal property under seal: 10 years.

Open account: 3 years, Note: Each payment renews the Statute of Limitations on all items purchased within the 3 years prior that payment. If no payment is made, the Statute runs from date of each individual charge. Contracts: From date of breach or default, unless waived or performance under the contract is continued.

Judgments: 10 years

Partial payment BEFORE the Statute of Limitations expires renews the Statute from date of payment.

Payment AFTER Statue of Limitations expires renews the Statute, ONLY if, at time of payment, circumstances infer the debtor recognized obligation to pay. Partial payment on open account restarts Statute of Limitations on purchases made within 3 years of payment date, if acknowledgment can be inferred, starts the statute anew as to the full obligation acknowledged, even if all of the charges were not made within the last 3 years.

Partial payment by one debtor does not renew the statute of limitations against any co-debtor unless that co-debtor agreed to, authorized or ratified the partial payment.

Partial payments DO NOT affect the 10-year limitation on enforcing or renewing judgments.

Bankruptcy, Death or Disability: Filing of a bankruptcy tolls the statute of limitations for the enforcement of contracts and judgments.

The death, minority, disability or incompetence of a debtor also tolls the limitation period until such time as a personal representative of the estate or a guardian of the incompetent or minor is appointed.

Maximum Interest: Legal 8%; Judgment 8%

North Dakota Statutes of Limitation

Breach of contract for sale under the UCC: 4 years.

All other actions based on a contract, obligation or liability, express or implied: 6 years.

Note: A new written acknowledgement or promise or voluntary payment on a debt revives the statute of limitations for the debt.

Judgments: 10 years.

Maximum Interest: Legal 6%; Judgment 12%

Ohio Statutes of Limitation

Written or oral account: 6 years (O.R.C. §2305.07).

Written contract: 15 years (O.R.C. §2305.06).

Oral contract: 6 years (O.R.C. §2305.07).

Note payable at a definite time: 6 years (O.R.C. § 1303 .16(A); (2)).

Demand Note: 6 years after the date on which demand is made or 10 years if no demand is made and neither principal nor interest has been paid over that time (O.R.C. §1303.16(B)).

Dishonored check or draft: 3 years after dishonor (O.R.C. §1303.16 (C)).

Maximum Interest: Legal 10%; Judgment 10%

Oklahoma Statutes of Limitation

Written Contract: 5 Years (O.S. § 95(1)).

Oral Contract: 3 Years (O.S. § 95(2))

Attachments: 5 Years (O.S. § 95(5))

Domestic Judgment: 5 Years (O.S. § 95(5))

Foreign Judgment: 3 Years (O.S. § 95(2)

Maximum Interest: Legal 6%; Judgment 4% over U.S. Treasury Bill not

Oregon Statutes of Limitation

Unlawful trade practices: 1 year (ORS 646.638(5).

Note: There is no statute of limitations for a cause of action brought as a counterclaim to an action by the seller. (ORS 646.638(6)).

Contract or liability: 6 years (ORS 12.080)

Judgment: 10 years (ORS 12.070).

Maximum Interest: Judgment 9% or contract rate

Pennsylvania Statute of Limitations

Contracts: 4 years (used to be six).

Contracts under seal: 20 years.

Sale of goods under UCC: 4 years.

Negotiable instruments: 6 years (13 PA C.S.A.§3118).

Maximum Interest: Legal 6%; Judgment 6%

Rhode Island Statutes of Limitation

Contracts and open accounts: 10 years (9-1-13(a)).

Breach of a sales agreement under the UCC: 4 years (6A-2-725(1)).

Contracts or liabilities under seal and judgments: 20 years (9-1-17).

Hospital liens: 1 year from payment (9-3-6).

Against insurer to enforce repairer's lien: 1 year from payment to insured (9-3-11).

Support obligations of common law father: 6 years (15-8-4).

Mechanic's lien: notice given is 1 year and 120 days (34-28-10. 10).

Maximum Interest: Legal 12%; Judgment 12%

South Carolina Statutes of Limitation

Breach of Contract: 3 years, (SCCLA 15-3-530).

Note: A partial payment or acknowledgment in writing tolls the Statute of Limitation (SCCLA 15-3-30).

Foreign or Domestic Judgments: 10 years (SCCLA 15-3-600).

Maximum Interest: Legal 8.75%; Judgment 12%

South Dakota Statutes of Limitation

Contract: 6 years (SDCL 15-2-13).

Domestic Judgments: 20 Years (SDCL 15-2-6).

Foreign Judgments: 10 Years (SDCL 15-2-8).

Claims of Fraud: 6 Years (SDCL 15-2-13).

Sealed Instrument: (except real estate): 20 Years (SDCL 15-2-6).

Actions not otherwise provided for: 10 Years (SDCL 15-2-8).

Open Accounts: 6 Years (SDCL 15-2-13).

Sale of Goods: 4 Years (SDCL57A-2-725).

Maximum Interest: Legal 12%; Judgment 10%

Tennessee Statutes of Limitation

Breach of contract: 6 years (T.C.A. 28-3-109).

Open accounts: 6 Years (T.C.A. 28-3-109).

Domestic or foreign judgments: 10 years (T.C.A. 28-3-110).

Maximum Interest: Legal 10%; Judgment 10% or contract rate

Texas Statutes of Limitation

The Texas Civil Practice & Remedies Code provides a 4-year limitations period for types of debt. The SoL begins after the day the cause of action accrues (Section 16.004 (a) (3)).

Maximum Interest: Legal 6% with agreement—up to 18% without agreement; Judgment 10%

Utah Statutes of Limitation

Any signed, written contract, obligation or liability: 6 years.

Unwritten contract, obligation or liability: 4 years.

Open account for goods, wares, merchandise, and services rendered or for the price of any article charged on a store account: 4 years.

Note: A written acknowledgment signed by the debtor revives the SoL.

Judgment or decree of any court or State of the United States: 8 years.

Maximum Interest: Legal 7.35%; Judgment – contract rate or federal rate

Vermont Statutes of Limitation

Contracts and goods on account: 6 years.

Witnessed promissory notes: 14 years

Maximum Interest: Legal 12%; Judgment 12%

Virginia Statutes of Limitation

Open account: 3 years from the last payment or last charge for goods or services rendered on the account.

Written contracts (non-UCC): 5 years.

Sale of goods under the UCC: 4 years.

Virginia Judgments: 10 years, and renewable (extended) to 20 years.

Foreign judgments: 10 years.

Maximum Interest: Legal 8%; Judgment 9% or contract rate

Washington Statutes of Limitation

Written contracts and accounts receivable: 6 years (RCW 4.16.040).

Oral contract: 3 years (RCW 4.16.080).

Recovery of property and judgments: 10 years (RCW 4.16.020).

Maximum Interest: Legal 12%; Judgment 12%

West Virginia Statutes of Limitation

Unwritten and implied contracts: 5 years (W. Va. Code 55-2-6 [1923]).

Note: If a debtor makes an acknowledgment by a new promise, or voluntarily makes a partial payment on a debt, under circumstances that warrant a clear inference that the debtor recognizes the whole debt, the statute of limitations is revived and begins to run from the date of the new promise (W. Va. Code §55-2-8)

Breach of a sale of goods, lease of goods, negotiable instruments and secured transactions under the UCC, is found Article 46 of the West Virginia Code.

Maximum Interest: Legal 6%; Judgment 10%

Wisconsin Statutes of Limitation

Contracts, professional services, or an open account based on a contract: 6 years.

Note: Payments made toward the obligation toll the statute and the time period will then run from the date of last payment or last charge by the debtor, whichever occurs later.

Maximum Interest: Legal 5%; Judgment 12%

Wyoming Statutes of Limitation

Any contract, agreement or promise in writing: 10 years (WS 1-3-105(a)(i)).

Unwritten contract, express or implied: 8 years (WS 1-3-105(a)(ii)).

Recovery of personal property: 4 years (WS 1-3-1 05 (a) (iv)).

Dishonor of draft (check): 3 years (WS 34.1-3-118 (c)).

Judgment: 21 years.

Note 1: Judgments cannot be revived after twenty-one years unless the party entitled to bring the action was a minor or subject to any other legal disability at the time the judgment became dormant, in this case action may be brought within 15 years after disability ceases, (WS 1-16-503).

Note 2: If no execution is issued within 5 years from date of judgment or last execution is issued, the judgment becomes dormant and ceases to operate as a lien on the estate of the debtor (WS 1-17-307).

Note 3: A dormant judgment may be revived in the same manner as prescribed for reviving actions before judgment or by action (WS 1-16-502).

Maximum Interest: Legal 7%; Judgment 10% or contract

Virgin Islands Statutes of Limitation

Civil action under a contract or liability, express or implied: 3 years.

Instruments under seal, judgments or decree of any court of the United States or of any state, commonwealth or territory within the United States: 20 Years (Title 5, Section 31, Virgin Islands Code).

APPENDIXES

Appendix One
Glossary

Appendix Two
**Applicable Laws and Statutes
of Limitations by State**

Appendix Three
Consumer Credit Laws to Know

As mentioned several times in this book, the legal restrictions on consumer credit and collections activities are significantly greater than those related to business-to-business credit. In order to help you better understand the legal requirements you must follow when extending consumer credit, we have included here the full text of the Fair Debt Collection Practices Act, and the most relevant sections of the Equal Credit Opportunity Act.

The Fair Debt Collection Practices Actw

§ 801. Short Title [15 USC 1601 note]

This title may be cited as the "Fair Debt Collection Practices Act."

§ 802. Congressional findings and declarations of purpose [15 USC 1692]

(a) There is abundant evidence of the use of abusive, deceptive, and unfair debt collection practices by many debt collectors. Abusive debt collection practices contribute to the number of personal bankruptcies, to marital instability, to the loss of jobs, and to invasions of individual privacy.

(b) Existing laws and procedures for redressing these injuries are inadequate to protect consumers.

(c) Means other than misrepresentation or other abusive debt collection practices are available for the effective collection of debts.

(d) Abusive debt collection practices are carried on to a substantial extent in interstate commerce and through means and instrumentalities of such commerce. Even where abusive debt collection practices are purely intrastate in character, they nevertheless directly affect interstate commerce.

(e) It is the purpose of this title to eliminate abusive debt collection practices by debt collectors, to insure that those debt collectors who refrain from using abusive debt collection practices are not competitively disadvantaged, and to promote consistent State action to protect consumers against debt collection abuses.

§ 803. Definitions [15 USC 1692a]

As used in this title—

(1) The term "Commission" means the Federal Trade Commission.

(2) The term "communication" means the conveying of information regarding a debt directly or indirectly to any person through any medium.

(3) The term "consumer" means any natural person obligated or allegedly obligated to pay any debt.

(4) The term "creditor" means any person who offers or extends credit creating a debt or to whom a debt is owed, but such term does not include any person to the extent that he receives an assignment or transfer of a debt in default solely for the purpose of facilitating collection of such debt for another.

(5) The term "debt" means any obligation or alleged obligation of a consumer to pay money arising out of a transaction in which the money, property, insurance or services which are the subject of the transaction are primarily for personal, family, or household purposes, whether or not such obligation has been reduced to judgment.

(6) The term "debt collector" means any person who uses any instrumentality of interstate commerce or the mails in any business the principal purpose of which is the collection of any debts, or who regularly collects or attempts to collect, directly or indirectly, debts owed or due or asserted to be owed or due another. Notwithstanding the exclusion provided by clause (F) of the last sentence of this paragraph, the term includes any creditor who, in the process of collecting his own debts, uses any name other than his own which would indicate that a third person is collecting or attempting to collect such debts. For the purpose of section 808(6), such term also includes any person who uses any instrumentality of interstate commerce or the mails in any business the principal purpose of which is the enforcement of security interests. The term does not include—

(A) any officer or employee of a creditor while, in the name of the creditor, collecting debts for such creditor;

(B) any person while acting as a debt collector for another person, both of whom are related by common ownership or affiliated by corporate control, if the person acting as a debt collector does so only for persons to whom it is so related or affiliated and if the principal business of such person is not the collection of debts;

(C) any officer or employee of the United States or any State to the extent that collecting or attempting to collect any debt is in the performance of his official duties;

(D) any person while serving or attempting to serve legal process on any other person in connection with the judicial enforcement of any debt.

(E) any nonprofit organization which, at the request of consumers, performs bona fide consumer credit counseling and assists consumers in the liquidation of their debts by receiving payments from such consumers and distributing such amounts to creditors; and

(F) any person collecting or attempting to collect any debt owed or due or asserted to be owed or due another to the extent such activity (i) is incidental to a bona fide fiduciary obligation or a bona fide escrow arrangement; (ii) concerns a debt which was originated by such person; (iii) concerns a debt which was not in default at the time it was obtained by such person; or (iv) concerns a debt obtained by such person as a secured party in a commercial credit transaction involving the creditor.

(7) The term "location information" means a consumer's place of abode and his telephone number at such place, or his place of employment.

(8) The term "State" means any State, territory, or possession of the United States, the District of Columbia, the Commonwealth of Puerto Rico, or any political subdivision of any of the foregoing.

§ 804. Acquisition of location information [15 USC 1692b]

Any debt collector communicating with any person other than the consumer for the purpose of acquiring location information about the consumer shall—

(1) identify himself, state that he is confirming or correcting location information concerning the consumer, and, only if expressly requested, identify his employer;

(2) not state that such consumer owes any debt;

(3) not communicate with any such person more than once unless requested to do so by such person or unless the debt collector reasonably believes that the earlier response of such person is erroneous or

incomplete and that such person now has correct or complete location information;

(4) not communicate by postcard;

(5) not use any language or symbol on any envelope or in the contents of any communication effected by the mails or telegram that indicates that the debt collector is in the debt collection business or that the communication relates to the collection of a debt; and

(6) after the debt collector knows the consumer is represented by an attorney with regard to the subject debt and has knowledge of, or can readily ascertain, such attorney's name and address, not communicate with any person other than that attorney, unless the attorney fails to respond within a reasonable period of time to the communication from the debt collector.

§ 805. Communication in connection with debt collection [15 USC 1692c]

(a) COMMUNICATION WITH THE CONSUMER GENERALLY. Without the prior consent of the consumer given directly to the debt collector or the express permission of a court of competent jurisdiction, a debt collector may not communicate with a consumer in connection with the collection of any debt—

(1) at any unusual time or place or a time or place known or which should be known to be inconvenient to the consumer. In the absence of knowledge of circumstances to the contrary, a debt collector shall assume that the convenient time for communicating with a consumer is after 8 o'clock antemeridian and before 9 o'clock postmeridian, local time at the consumer's location;

(2) if the debt collector knows the consumer is represented by an attorney with respect to such debt and has knowledge of, or can readily ascertain, such attorney's name and address, unless the attorney fails to respond within a reasonable period of time to a communication from the debt collector or unless the attorney consents to direct communication with the consumer; or

(3) at the consumer's place of employment if the debt collector knows or has reason to know that the consumer's employer prohibits the consumer from receiving such communication.

(b) COMMUNICATION WITH THIRD PARTIES. Except as provided in Section 804, without the prior consent of the consumer given directly to the debt collector, or the express permission of a court of competent jurisdiction, or as reasonably necessary to effectuate a postjudgment judicial remedy, a debt collector may not communicate, in connection with the collection of any debt, with any person other than a consumer, his attorney, a consumer reporting agency if otherwise permitted by law, the creditor, the attorney of the creditor, or the attorney of the debt collector.

(c) CEASING COMMUNICATION. If a consumer notifies a debt collector in writing that the consumer refuses to pay a debt or that the consumer wishes the debt collector to cease further communication with the consumer, the debt collector shall not communicate further with the consumer with respect to such debt, except—

(1) to advise the consumer that the debt collector's further efforts are being terminated.

(2) to notify the consumer that the debt collector or creditor may invoke specified remedies which are ordinarily invoked by such debt collector or creditor; or

(3) where applicable, to notify the consumer that the debt collector or creditor intends to invoke a specified remedy.

If such notice from the consumer is made by mail, notification shall be complete upon receipt.

(d) For the purpose of this section, the term "consumer" includes the consumer's spouse, parent (if the consumer is a minor), guardian, executor, or administrator.

§ 806. Harassment or abuse [15 USC 1692d]

A debt collector may not engage in any conduct the natural consequence of which is to harass, oppress, or abuse any person in connection with the collection of a debt. Without limiting the general application of the foregoing, the following conduct is a violation of this section:

(1) The use or threat of use of violence or other criminal means to harm the physical person, reputation, or property of any person.

(2) The use of obscene or profane language or language the natural consequence of which is to abuse the hearer or reader.

(3) The publication of a list of consumers who allegedly refuse to pay debts, except to a consumer reporting agency or to persons meeting the requirements of section 603(1) or 604(3) of this Act.

(4) The advertisement for sale of any debt to coerce payment of the debt.

(5) Causing a telephone to ring or engaging any person in telephone conversation repeatedly or continuously with intent to annoy, abuse, or harass any person at the called number.

(6) Except as provided in section 804, the placement of telephone calls without meaningful disclosure of the caller's identity.

§ 807. False or misleading representations [15 USC 1692e]

A debt collector may not use any false, deceptive, or misleading representation or means in connection with the collection of any debt. Without limiting the general application of the foregoing, the following conduct is a violation of this section:

(1) The false representation or implication that the debt collector is vouched for, bonded by, or affiliated with the United States or any State, including the use of any badge, uniform, or facsimile thereof.

(2) The false representation of—

(A) the character, amount, or legal status of any debt; or

(B) any services rendered or compensation which may be lawfully received by any debt collector for the collection of a debt.

(3) The false representation or implication that any individual is an attorney or that any communication is from an attorney.

(4) The representation or implication that nonpayment of any debt will result in the arrest or imprisonment of any person or the seizure, garnishment, attachment, or sale of any property or wages of any person unless such action is lawful and the debt collector or creditor intends to take such action.

(5) The threat to take any action that cannot legally be taken or that is not intended to be taken.

(6) The false representation or implication that a sale, referral, or other transfer of any interest in a debt shall cause the consumer to—

(A) lose any claim or defense to payment of the debt; or

(B) become subject to any practice prohibited by this title.

(7) The false representation or implication that the consumer committed any crime or other conduct in order to disgrace the consumer.

(8) Communicating or threatening to communicate to any person credit information which is known or which should be known to be false, including the failure to communicate that a disputed debt is disputed.

(9) The use or distribution of any written communication which simulates or is falsely represented to be a document authorized, issued, or approved by any court, official, or agency of the United States or any State, or which creates a false impression as to its source, authorization, or approval.

(10) The use of any false representation or deceptive means to collect or attempt to collect any debt or to obtain information concerning a consumer.

(11) The failure to disclose in the initial written communication with the consumer and, in addition, if the initial communication with the consumer is oral, in that initial oral communication, that the debt collector is attempting to collect a debt and that any information obtained will be used for that purpose, and the failure to disclose in subsequent communications that the communication is from a debt collector, except that this paragraph shall not apply to a formal pleading made in connection with a legal action.

(12) The false representation or implication that accounts have been turned over to innocent purchasers for value.

(13) The false representation or implication that documents are legal process.

(14) The use of any business, company, or organization name other than the true name of the debt collector's business, company, or organization.

(15) The false representation or implication that documents are not legal process forms or do not require action by the consumer.

(16) The false representation or implication that a debt collector operates or is employed by a consumer reporting agency as defined by section 603(f) of this Act.

§ 808. Unfair practices [15 USC 1692f]

A debt collector may not use unfair or unconscionable means to collect or attempt to collect any debt. Without limiting the general application of the foregoing, the following conduct is a violation of this section:

(1) The collection of any amount (including any interest, fee, charge, or expense incidental to the principal obligation) unless such amount is expressly authorized by the agreement creating the debt or permitted by law.

(2) The acceptance by a debt collector from any person of a check or other payment instrument postdated by more than five days unless such person is notified in writing of the debt collector's intent to deposit such check or instrument not more than ten nor less than three business days prior to such deposit.

(3) The solicitation by a debt collector of any postdated check or other postdated payment instrument for the purpose of threatening or instituting criminal prosecution.

(4) Depositing or threatening to deposit any postdated check or other postdated payment instrument prior to the date on such check or instrument.

(5) Causing charges to be made to any person for communications by concealment of the true purpose of the communication. Such charges include, but are not limited to, collect telephone calls and telegram fees.

(6) Taking or threatening to take any nonjudicial action to effect dispossession or disablement of property if—

(A) there is no present right to possession of the property claimed as collateral through an enforceable security interest;

(B) there is no present intention to take possession of the property; or

(C) the property is exempt by law from such dispossession or disablement.

(7) Communicating with a consumer regarding a debt by postcard.

(8) Using any language or symbol, other than the debt collector's address, on any envelope when communicating with a consumer by use of the mails or by telegram, except that a debt collector may use his business name if such name does not indicate that he is in the debt collection business.

§ 809. Validation of debts [15 USC 1692g]

(a) Within five days after the initial communication with a consumer in connection with the collection of any debt, a debt collector shall, unless the following information is contained in the initial communication or the consumer has paid the debt, send the consumer a written notice containing—

(1) the amount of the debt;

(2) the name of the creditor to whom the debt is owed;

(3) a statement that unless the consumer, within thirty days after receipt of the notice, disputes the validity of the debt, or any portion thereof, the debt will be assumed to be valid by the debt collector;

(4) a statement that if the consumer notifies the debt collector in writing within the thirty-day period that the debt, or any portion thereof, is disputed, the debt collector will obtain verification of the debt or a copy of a judgment against the consumer and a copy of such verification or judgment will be mailed to the consumer by the debt collector; and

(5) a statement that, upon the consumer's written request within the thirty-day period, the debt collector will provide the consumer with the name and address of the original creditor, if different from the current creditor.

(b) If the consumer notifies the debt collector in writing within the thirty-day period described in subsection (a) that the debt, or any portion thereof, is disputed, or that the consumer requests the name and address of the original creditor, the debt collector shall cease collection of the debt, or any disputed portion thereof, until the debt collector obtains verification of the debt or any copy of a judgment, or the name and address of the original creditor, and a copy of such verification or judgment, or name and address of the original creditor, is mailed to the consumer by the debt collector.

(c) The failure of a consumer to dispute the validity of a debt under this section may not be construed by any court as an admission of liability by the consumer.

§ 810. Multiple debts [15 USC 1692h]

If any consumer owes multiple debts and makes any single payment to any debt collector with respect to such debts, such debt collector may not apply such payment to any debt which is disputed by the consumer and, where applicable, shall apply such payment in accordance with the consumer's directions.

§ 811. Legal actions by debt collectors [15 USC 1692i]

(a) Any debt collector who brings any legal action on a debt against any consumer shall—

(1) in the case of an action to enforce an interest in real property securing the consumer's obligation, bring such action only in a judicial district or similar legal entity in which such real property is located; or

(2) in the case of an action not described in paragraph (1), bring such action only in the judicial district or similar legal entity—

(A) in which such consumer signed the contract sued upon; or

(B) in which such consumer resides at the commencement of the action.

(C) Nothing in this title shall be construed to authorize the bringing of legal actions by debt collectors.

§ 812. Furnishing certain deceptive forms [15 USC 1692j]

(a) It is unlawful to design, compile, and furnish any form knowing that such form would be used to create the false belief in a consumer that a person other than the creditor of such consumer is participating in the collection of or in an attempt to collect a debt such consumer allegedly owes such creditor, when in fact such person is not so participating.

(b) Any person who violates this section shall be liable to the same extent and in the same manner as a debt collector is liable under section 813 for failure to comply with a provision of this title.

§ 813. Civil liability [15 USC 1692k]

(a) Except as otherwise provided by this section, any debt collector who fails to comply with any provision of this title with respect to any person is liable to such person in an amount equal to the sum of—

(1) any actual damage sustained by such person as a result of such failure;

(2) (A) in the case of any action by an individual, such additional damages as the court may allow, but not exceeding $1,000; or (B) in the

case of a class action, (i) such amount for each named plaintiff as could be recovered under subparagraph (A), and (ii) such amount as the court may allow for all other class members, without regard to a minimum individual recovery, not to exceed the lesser of $500,000 or 1 per centum of the net worth of the debt collector; and

(3) in the case of any successful action to enforce the foregoing liability, the costs of the action, together with a reasonable attorney's fee as determined by the court. On a finding by the court that an action under this section was brought in bad faith and for the purpose of harassment, the court may award to the defendant attorney's fees reasonable in relation to the work expended and costs.

(b) In determining the amount of liability in any action under subsection (a), the court shall consider, among other relevant factors—

(1) in any individual action under subsection (a)(2)(A), the frequency and persistence of noncompliance by the debt collector, the nature of such noncompliance, and the extent to which such noncompliance was intentional; or

(2) in any class action under subsection (a)(2)(B), the frequency and persistence of noncompliance by the debt collector, the nature of such noncompliance, the resources of the debt collector, the number of persons adversely affected, and the extent to which the debt collector's noncompliance was intentional.

(c) A debt collector may not be held liable in any action brought under this title if the debt collector shows by a preponderance of evidence that the violation was not intentional and resulted from a bona fide error notwithstanding the maintenance of procedures reasonably adapted to avoid any such error.

(d) An action to enforce any liability created by this title may be brought in any appropriate United States district court without regard to the amount in controversy, or in any other court of competent jurisdiction, within one year from the date on which the violation occurs.

(e) No provision of this section imposing any liability shall apply to any act done or omitted in good faith in conformity with any advisory opinion of the Commission, notwithstanding that after such act or omission has occurred, such opinion is amended, rescinded, or determined by judicial or other authority to be invalid for any reason.

§ 814. Administrative enforcement [15 USC 1692l]

(a) Compliance with this title shall be enforced by the Commission, except to the extent that enforcement of the requirements imposed under this title is specifically committed to another agency under subsection (b). For purpose of the exercise by the Commission of its functions and powers under the Federal Trade Commission Act, a violation of this title shall be deemed an unfair or deceptive act or practice in violation of that Act. All of the functions and powers of the Commission under the Federal Trade Commission Act are available to the Commission to enforce compliance by any person with this title, irrespective of whether that person is engaged in commerce or meets any other jurisdictional tests in the Federal Trade Commission act, including the power to enforce the provisions of this title in the same manner as if the violation had been a violation of a Federal Trade Commission trade regulation rule.

(b) Compliance with any requirements imposed under this title shall be enforced under—

(1) section 8 of the Federal Deposit Insurance Act, in the case of—

(A) national banks, by the Comptroller of the Currency;

(B) member banks of the Federal Reserve System (other than national banks), by the Federal Reserve Board; and

(C) banks the deposits or accounts of which are insured by the Federal Deposit Insurance Corporation (other than members of the Federal Reserve System), by the Board of Directors of the Federal Deposit Insurance Corporation;

(2) section 5(d) of the Home Owners Loan Act of 1933, section 407 of the National Housing Act, and sections 6(i) and 17 of the Federal Home Loan Bank act, by the Federal Home Loan Bank Board (acting directing or through the Federal Savings and Loan Insurance Corporation), in the case of any institution subject to any of those provisions;

(3) the Federal Credit Union Act, by the Administrator of the National Credit Union Administration with respect to any Federal credit union;

(4) subtitle IV of Title 49, by the Interstate Commerce Commission with respect to any common carrier subject to such subtitle;

(5) the Federal Aviation Act of 1958, by the Secretary of Transportation with respect to any air carrier or any foreign air carrier subject to that Act; and

(6) the Packers and Stockyards Act, 1921 (except as provided in section 406 of that Act), by the Secretary of Agriculture with respect to any activities subject to that Act.

(c) For the purpose of the exercise by any agency referred to in subsection (b) of its powers under any Act referred to in that subsection, a violation of any requirement imposed under the title shall be deemed to be a violation of a requirement imposed under that Act. In addition to its powers under any provision of law specifically referred to in subsection (b), each of the agencies referred to in that subsection may exercise, for the purpose of enforcing compliance with any requirement imposed under this title any other authority conferred on it by law, except as provided in subsection (d).

(d) Neither the Commission nor any other agency referred to in subsection (b) may promulgate trade regulation rules or other regulations with respect to the collection of debts by debt collectors as defined in this title.

§ 815. Reports to Congress by the Commission [15 USC 1692m]

(a) Not later than one year after the effective date of this title and at one-year intervals thereafter, the Commission shall make reports to the Congress concerning the administration of its functions under this title, including such recommendations as the Commission deems necessary or appropriate. In addition, each report of the Commission shall include its assessment of the extent to which compliance with this title is being achieved and a summary of the enforcement actions taken by the Commission under section 814 of this title.

(b) In the exercise of its functions under this title, the Commission may obtain upon request the views of any other Federal agency which exercises enforcement functions under section 814 of this title.

§ 816. Relation to State laws [15 USC 1692n]

This title does not annul, alter, or affect, or exempt any person subject to the provisions of this title from complying with the laws of any State with respect to debt collection practices, except to the extent that those laws are inconsistent with any provision of this title, and then only to the extent of the inconsistency. For purposes of this section, a State law is not inconsistent with this title if the protection such law affords any consumer is greater than the protection provided by this title.

§ 817. Exemption for State regulation [15 USC 1692o]

The Commission shall be regulation exempt from the requirements of this title any class of debt collection practices within any State if the Commission determines that under the law of that State that class of debt collection practices is subject to requirements substantially similar to those imposed by this title, and that there is adequate provision for enforcement.

§ 818. Effective date [15 USC 1692 note]

This title takes effect upon the expiration of six months after the date of its enactment, but section 809 shall apply only with respect to debts for which the initial attempt to collect occurs after such effective date.

Approved September 20, 1977

END NOTES

1. So in original; however, should read "604(a)(3)."

LEGISLATIVE HISTORY:
Public Law 95-109 [H.R. 5294]
HOUSE REPORT No. 95-131 (Comm. On Banking, Finance, and Urban Affairs).
SENATE REPORT No. 95-382 (Comm. On Banking, Housing, and Urban Affairs).

CONGRESSIONAL RECORD, Vol. 123 (1977);
Apr. 4, considered and passed House.
Aug. 5, considered and passed Senate, amended.
Sept. 8, House agreed to Senate amendment.
WEEKLY COMPILATION OF PRESIDENTIAL DOCUMENTS, Vol. 13, No. 39;

Sept. 20, Presidential statement.

AMENDMENTS:

SECTION 621, SUBSECTIONS (b)(3), (b)(4) and (b)(5) were amended to transfer certain administrative enforcement responsibilities, pursuant to Pub. L. 95-473. § 3(b), Oct. 17, 1978, 92 Stat. 166; Pub.:L. 95-630, Title V § 501, November 10, 1978, 92 Stat. 3680; Pub. L. 98-443, § 9(h), Oct. 4, 1984, 98 Stat. 708.

SECTION 803, SUBSECTION (6), defining "debt collector," was amended to repeal the attorney at law exemption at former Section (6)(F) and to redesignate Section 803(6)(G) pursuant to Pub. L. 99-361, July 9, 1986, 100 Stat. 768. For legislative history, see H.R. 237, HOUSE REPORT No. 99-405 (Comm. On Banking, Finance and Urban Affairs). CONGRESSIONAL RECORD: Vol. 131 (1985); Dec. 2, considered and passed House Vol. 132 (1986); June 26, considered and passed Senate.

SECTION 807, SUBSECTION (11), was amended to affect when debt collectors must state (a) that they are attempting to collect a debt and (b) that information obtained will be used for that purpose, pursuant to Pub. L. 104-208 § 2305, 110 Stat. 3009 (Sept. 30, 1996).

Equal Credit Opportunity Act

Sec. 202.1 Authority, scope and purpose.

(a) Authority and scope. This regulation is issued by the Board of Governors of the Federal Reserve System pursuant to title VII (Equal Credit Opportunity Act) of the Consumer Credit Protection Act, as amended (15 USC 1601 et seq.). Except as otherwise provided herein, the regulation applies to all persons who are creditors, as defined in Sec. 202.2(l). Information collection requirements contained in this regulation have been approved by the Office of Management and Budget under the provisions of 44 USC 3501 et seq. and have been assigned OMB control number 7100-0201.

(b) Purpose. The purpose of this regulation is to promote the availability of credit to all creditworthy applicants without regard to race, color, religion, national origin, sex, marital status, or age (provided the applicant has the capacity to contract); to the fact that all or part of the applicant's income derives from a public assistance program; or to the fact that the applicant has in good faith exercised any right under the Consumer Credit Protection Act. The regulation prohibits creditor practices that discriminate on the basis of any of these factors. The regulation also requires creditors to notify applicants of action taken on their applications; to report credit history in the names of both spouses on an account; to retain records of credit applications; to collect information about the applicant's race and other personal characteristics in applications for certain dwelling-related loans; and to provide applicants with copies of appraisal reports used in connection with credit transactions.

Sec. 202.2 Definitions.

For the purposes of this regulation, unless the context indicates otherwise, the following definitions apply.

(a) Account means an extension of credit. When employed in relation to an account, the word use refers only to open-end credit.

(b) Act means the Equal Credit Opportunity Act (title VII of the Consumer Credit Protection Act)

(c) Adverse action.

(1) The term means:

(i) A refusal to grant credit in substantially the amount or on substantially the terms requested in an application unless the creditor makes a counteroffer (to grant credit in a different amount or on other terms) and the applicant uses or expressly accepts the credit offered;

(ii) A termination of an account or an unfavorable change in the terms of an account that does not affect all or a substantial portion of a class of the creditor's accounts; or

(iii) A refusal to increase the amount of credit available to an applicant who has made an application for an increase.

(2) The term does not include:

(i) A change in the terms of an account expressly agreed to by an applicant;

(ii) Any action or forbearance relating to an account taken in connection with inactivity, default, or delinquency as to that account;

(iii) A refusal or failure to authorize an account transaction at a point of sale or loan, except when the refusal is a termination or an unfavorable change in the terms of an account that does not affect all or a substantial portion of a class of the creditor's accounts, or when the refusal is a denial of an application for an increase in the amount of credit available under the account;

(iv) A refusal to extend credit because applicable law prohibits the creditor from extending the credit requested; or

(v) A refusal to extend credit because the creditor does not offer the type of credit or credit plan requested. (3) An action that falls within the definition of both paragraphs (c)(1) and (c)(2) of this section is governed by paragraph (c)(2) of this section.

(d) Age refers only to the age of natural persons and means the number of fully elapsed years from the date of an applicant's birth.

(e) Applicant means any person who requests or who has received an extension of credit from a creditor, and includes any person who is or may become contractually liable regarding an extension of credit. For purposes of Sec. 202.7(d), the term includes guarantors, sureties, endorsers and similar parties.

(f) Application means an oral or written request for an extension of credit that is made in accordance with procedures established by a creditor for the type of credit requested. The term does not include the use of an account or line of credit to obtain an amount of credit that is within a previously established credit limit. A completed application means an application in connection with which a creditor has received all the information that the creditor regularly obtains and considers in evaluating applications for the amount and type of credit requested (including, but not limited to, credit reports, any additional information requested from the applicant, and any approvals or reports by governmental agencies or other persons that are necessary to guarantee, insure, or provide security for the credit or collateral). The creditor shall exercise reasonable diligence in obtaining such information.

(g) Business credit refers to extensions of credit primarily for business or commercial (including agricultural) purposes, but excluding extensions of credit of the types described in Sec. 202.3 (a), (b), and (d).

(h) Consumer credit means credit extended to a natural person primarily for personal, family, or household purposes.

(i) Contractually liable means expressly obligated to repay all debts arising on an account by reason of an agreement to that effect.

(j) Credit means the right granted by a creditor to an applicant to defer payment of a debt, incur debt and defer its payment, or purchase property or services and defer payment therefore.

(k) Credit card means any card, plate, coupon book, or other single credit device that may be used from time to time to obtain money, property, or services on credit.

(l) Creditor means a person who, in the ordinary course of business, regularly participates in the decision of whether or not to extend credit. The term includes a creditor's assignee, transferee, or subrogee who so participates. For purposes of Secs. 202.4 and 202.5(a), the term also includes a person who, in the ordinary course of business, regularly refers applicants or prospective applicants to creditors, or selects or offers to select creditors to whom requests for credit may be made. A person is not a creditor regarding any violation of the act or this regulation committed by another creditor unless the person knew or had reasonable notice of the act, policy, or practice that constituted the violation before becoming involved in the credit transaction. The term does not include a person whose only participation in a credit transaction involves honoring a credit card.

(m) Credit transaction means every aspect of an applicant's dealings with a creditor regarding an application for credit or an existing extension of credit (including, but not limited to, information requirements; investigation procedures; standards of creditworthiness; terms of credit; furnishing of credit information; revocation, alteration, or termination of credit; and collection procedures).

(n) Discriminate against an applicant means to treat an applicant less favorably than other applicants.

(o) Elderly means age 62 or older.

(p) Empirically derived and other credit scoring systems—

(1) A credit scoring system is a system that evaluates an applicant's creditworthiness mechanically, based on key attributes of the applicant and aspects of the transaction, and that determines, alone or in conjunction with an evaluation of additional information about the applicant, whether an applicant is deemed creditworthy. To qualify as an empirically derived, demonstrably and statistically sound, credit scoring system, the system must be:

(i) Based on data that are derived from an empirical comparison of sample groups or the population of creditworthy and noncreditworthy applicants who applied for credit within a reasonable preceding period of time;

(ii) Developed for the purpose of evaluating the creditworthiness of applicants with respect to the legitimate business interests of the creditor utilizing the system (including, but not limited to, minimizing bad debt losses and operating expenses in accordance with the creditor's business judgment).

(iii) Developed and validated using accepted statistical principles and methodology; and

(iv) Periodically revalidated by the use of appropriate statistical principles and methodology and adjusted as necessary to maintain predictive ability.

(2) A creditor may use an empirically derived, demonstrably and statistically sound, credit scoring system obtained from another person or may obtain credit experience from which to develop such a system. Any such system must satisfy the criteria set forth in paragraphs (p)(1)(i) through (iv) of this section; if the creditor is unable during the development process to validate the system based on its own credit experience in accordance with paragraph (p)(1) of this section, the system must be validated when sufficient credit experience becomes available. A system that fails this validity test is no longer an empirically derived, demonstrably and statistically sound, credit scoring system for that creditor.

(q) Extend credit and extension of credit mean the granting of credit in any form (including, but not limited to, credit granted in addition to any existing credit or credit limit; credit granted pursuant to an open-end credit plan; the refinancing or other renewal of credit, including the issuance of a new credit card in place of an expiring credit card or in substitution for an existing credit card; the consolidation of two or more obligations; or the continuance of existing credit without any special effort to collect at or after maturity).

(r) Good faith means honesty in fact in the conduct or transaction.

(s) Inadvertent error means a mechanical, electronic, or clerical error that a creditor demonstrates was not intentional and occurred notwithstanding the maintenance of procedures reasonably adapted to avoid such errors.

(t) Judgmental system of evaluating applicants means any system for evaluating the creditworthiness of an applicant other than an empirically derived, demonstrably and statistically sound, credit scoring system.

(u) Marital status means the state of being unmarried, married, or separated, as defined by applicable state law. The term unmarried includes persons who are single, divorced, or widowed.

(v) Negative factor or value, in relation to the age of elderly applicants, means utilizing a factor, value, or weight that is less favorable regarding elderly applicants than the creditor's experience warrants or is less favorable than the factor, value, or weight assigned to the class of applicants that are not classified as elderly and are most favored by a creditor on the basis of age.

(w) Open-end credit means credit extended under a plan under which a creditor may permit an applicant to make purchases or obtain loans from time to time directly from the creditor or indirectly by use of a credit card, check, or other device.

(x) Person means a natural person, corporation, government or governmental subdivision or agency, trust, estate, partnership, cooperative, or association.

(y) Pertinent element of creditworthiness, in relation to a judgmental system of evaluating applicants, means any information about applicants that a creditor obtains and considers and that has a demonstrable relationship to a determination of creditworthiness.

(z) Prohibited basis means race, color, religion, national origin, sex, marital status, or age (provided that the applicant has the capacity to enter into a binding contract); the fact that all or part of the applicant's income derives from any public assistance program; or the fact that the applicant has in good faith exercised any right under the Consumer Credit Protection Act or any state law upon which an exemption has been granted by the Board.

(aa) State means any State, the District of Columbia, the Commonwealth of Puerto Rico, or any territory or possession of the United States.

Sec. 202.3 Limited exceptions for certain classes of transactions

(a) Public utilities credit—

(1) Definition. Public utilities credit refers to extensions of credit that involve public utility services provided through pipe, wire, or other connected facilities, or radio or similar transmission (including extensions of such facilities), if the charges for service, delayed payment, and any discount for prompt payment are filed with or regulated by a government unit.

(2) Exceptions. The following provisions of this regulation do not apply to public utilities credit:

(i) Section 202.5(d)(1) concerning information about marital status;

(ii) Section 202.10 relating to furnishing of credit information; and

(iii) Section 202.12(b) relating to record retention.

(b) Securities credit—

(1) Definition. Securities credit refers to extensions of credit subject to regulation under section 7 of the Securities Exchange Act of 1934 or extensions of credit by a broker or dealer subject to regulation as a broker or dealer under the Securities Exchange Act of 1934.

(2) Exceptions. The following provisions of this regulation do not apply to securities credit:

(i) Section 202.5(c) concerning information about a spouse or former spouse;

(ii) Section 202.5(d)(1) concerning information about marital status;

(iii) Section 202.5(d)(3) concerning information about the sex of an applicant;

(iv) section 202.7(b) relating to designation of name, but only to the extent necessary to prevent violation of rules regarding an account in which a broker or dealer has an interest, or rules necessitating the aggregation of accounts of spouses for the purpose of determining controlling interests, beneficial interests, beneficial ownership, or purchase limitations and restrictions;

(v) Section 202.7(c) relating to action concerning open-end accounts, but only to the extent the action taken is on the basis of a change of name or marital status;

(vi) section 202.7(d) relating to the signature of a spouse or other person;

(vii) Section 202.10 relating to furnishing of credit information; and

(viii) Section 202.12(b) relating to record retention.

(c) Incidental credit—

(1) Definition. Incidental credit refers to extensions of consumer credit other than credit of the types described in paragraphs (a) and (b) of this section:

(i) That are not made pursuant to the terms of a credit card account;

(ii) That are not subject to a finance charge (as defined in Regulation Z, 12 CFR 226.4); and

(iii) That are not payable by agreement in more than four installments.

(2) Exceptions. The following provisions of this regulation do not apply to incidental credit.

(i) Section 202.5(c) concerning information about a spouse or former spouse;

(ii) Section 202.5(d)(1) concerning information about marital status;

(iii) Section 202.5(d)(2) concerning information about income derived from alimony, child support, or separate maintenance payments;

(iv) Section 202.5(d)(3) concerning information about the sex of an applicant, but only to the extent necessary for medical records or similar purposes;

(v) Section 202.7(d) relating to the signature of a spouse or other person;

(vi) Section 202.9 relating to notifications;

(vii) Section 202.10 relating to furnishing of credit information; and

(viii) Section 202.12(b) relating to record retention.

(d) Government credit—

(1) Definition. Government credit refers to extensions of credit made to governments or governmental subdivisions, agencies, or instrumentalities.

(2) Applicability of regulation. Except for Sec. 202.4, the general rule prohibiting discrimination of a prohibited basis, the requirements of this regulation do not apply to government credit.

Sec. 202.4 General rule prohibiting discrimination.

A creditor shall not discriminate against an applicant on a prohibited basis regarding any aspect of a credit transaction.

Sec. 202.5 Rules concerning taking of applications.

(a) Discouraging applications. A creditor shall not make any oral or written statement, in advertising or otherwise, to applicants or prospective applicants that would discourage on a prohibited basis a reasonable person from making or pursuing an application.

(b) General rules concerning requests for information.

(1) Except as provided in paragraphs (c) and (d) of this section, a creditor may request any information in connection with an application.

(2) Required collection of information. Notwithstanding paragraphs (c) and (d) of this section, a creditor shall request information for monitoring purposes as required by Sec. 202.13 for credit secured by the applicant's dwelling. In addition, a creditor may obtain information required by a regulation, order, or agreement issued by or entered into with, a court or an enforcement agency (including the Attorney General of the United States or a similar state official) to monitor or enforce compliance with the act, this regulation, or other federal or state statute or regulation.

(3) Special purpose credit. A creditor may obtain information that is otherwise restricted to determine eligibility for a special purpose credit program, as provided in Sec. 202.8(c) and (d).

(c) Information about a spouse or former spouse.

(1) Except as permitted in this paragraph, a creditor may not request any information concerning the spouse or former spouse of an applicant.

(2) Permissible inquiries. A creditor may request any information concerning an applicant's spouse (or former spouse under paragraph (c)(2)(v) of this section that may be requested about the applicant if:

(i) The spouse will be permitted to use the account;

(ii) The spouse will be contractually liable on the account;

(iii) The applicant is relying on the spouse's income as a basis for repayment of the credit requested;

(iv) The applicant resides in a community property state or property on which the applicant is relying as a basis for repayment of the credit requested is located in such a state; or

(v) The applicant is relying on alimony, child support, or separate maintenance payments from a spouse or former spouse as a basis for repayment of the credit requested.

(3) Other accounts of the applicant. A creditor may request an applicant to list any account upon which the applicant is liable and to provide the name and address in which the account is carried. A creditor may also ask the names in which an applicant has previously received credit.

(d) Other limitations on information requests—

(1) Marital status. If an applicant applies for individual unsecured credit, a creditor shall not inquire about the applicant's marital status unless the applicant resides in a community property state or is relying on property located in such a state as a basis for repayment of the credit requested. If an application is for other than individual unsecured credit, a creditor may inquire about the applicant's marital status, but shall use only the terms married, unmarried, and separated. A creditor may explain that the category unmarried includes single, divorced, and widowed persons.

(2) Disclosure about income from alimony, child support, or separate maintenance. A creditor shall not inquire whether income stated in an application is derived from alimony, child support, or separate mainte-nance payments unless the creditor discloses to the applicant that such income need not be revealed if the applicant does not want the creditor to consider it in determining the applicant's creditworthiness.

(3) Sex. A creditor shall not inquire about the sex of an applicant. An applicant may be requested to designate a title on an application form (such as Ms., Miss, Mr., or Mrs.) if the form discloses that the designation of a title is optional. An application form shall otherwise use only terms that are neutral as to sex.

(4) Childbearing, childrearing. A creditor shall not inquire about birth control practices, intentions concerning the bearing or rearing of children, or capability to bear children. A creditor may inquire about the number and ages of an applicant's dependents or about dependent-related finan-cial obligations or expenditures, provided such information is requested without regard to sex, marital status, or any other prohibited basis.

(5) Race, color, religion, national origin. A creditor shall not inquire about the race, color, religion, or national origin of an applicant or any other person in connection with a credit transaction. A creditor may inquire about an applicant's permanent residence and immigration status.

(e) Written applications. A creditor shall take written applications for the types of credit covered by Sec. 202.13(a), but need not take written applications for other types of credit.

Sec. 202.5a Rules on providing appraisal reports.

(a) Providing appraisals. A creditor shall provide a copy of the appraisal report used in connection with an application for credit that is to be secured by a lien on a dwelling. A creditor shall comply with either paragraph (a)(1) or (a)(2) of this section.

(1) Routine delivery. A creditor may routinely provide a copy of the appraisal report to an applicant (whether credit is granted or denied or the application is withdrawn).

(2) Upon request. A creditor that does not routinely provide appraisal reports shall provide a copy upon an applicant's written request.

(i) Notice. A creditor that provides appraisal reports only upon request shall notify an applicant in writing of the right to receive a copy of an appraisal report. The notice may be given at any time during the application process but no later than when the creditor provides notice of action taken under Sec. 202.9 of this part. The notice shall specify that the applicant's request must be in writing, give the creditor's mailing address, and state the time for making the request as provided in paragraph (a)(2)(ii) of this section.

(ii) Delivery. A creditor shall mail or deliver a copy of the appraisal report promptly (generally within 30 days) after the creditor receives an applicant's request, receives the report, or receives reimbursement from the applicant for the report, whichever is last to occur. A creditor need not provide a copy when the applicant's request is received more than 90 days after the creditor has provided notice of action taken on the application under Sec. 202.9 of this part or 90 days after the application is withdrawn.

(b) Credit unions. A creditor that is subject to the regulations of the National Credit Union Administration on making copies of appraisals available is not subject to this section.

(c) Definitions. For purposes of paragraph (a) of this section, the term dwelling means a residential structure that contains one to four units whether or not that structure is attached to real property. The term includes, but is not limited to, an individual condominium or cooperative unit, and a mobile or other manufactured home. The term appraisal report means the document(s) relied upon by a creditor in evaluating the value of the dwelling.

Sec. 202.6 Rules concerning evaluation of applications.

(a) General rule concerning use of information. Except as otherwise provided in the Act and this regulation, a creditor may consider any information obtained, so long as the information is not used to discriminate against an applicant on a prohibited basis.

(b) Specific rules concerning use of information.

(1) Except as provided in the act and this regulation, a creditor shall not take a prohibited basis into account in any system of evaluating the creditworthiness of applicants.

(2) Age, receipt of public assistance.

(i) Except as permitted in this paragraph (b)(2), a creditor shall not take into account an applicant's age (provided that the applicant has the capacity to enter into a binding contract) or whether an applicant's income derives from any public assistance program.

(ii) In an empirically derived, demonstrably and statistically sound, credit scoring system, a creditor may use an applicant's age as a predictive variable, provided that the age of an elderly applicant is not assigned a negative factor or value.

(iii) In a judgmental system of evaluating creditworthiness, a creditor may consider an applicant's age or whether an applicant's income derives from any public assistance program only for the purpose of determining a pertinent element of creditworthiness.

(iv) In any system of evaluating creditworthiness, a creditor may consider the age of an elderly applicant when such age is used to favor the elderly applicant in extending credit.

(3) Childbearing, childrearing. In evaluating creditworthiness, a creditor shall not use assumptions or aggregate statistics relating to the likelihood that any group of persons will bear or rear children or will, for that reason, receive diminished or interrupted income in the future.

(4) Telephone listing. A creditor shall not take into account whether there is a telephone listing in the name of an applicant for consumer

credit, but may take into account whether there is a telephone in the applicant's residence.

(5) Income. A creditor shall not discount or exclude from consideration the income of an applicant or the spouse of an applicant because of a prohibited basis or because the income is derived from part-time employment or is an annuity, pension, or other retirement benefit; a creditor may consider the amount and probable continuance of any income in evaluating an applicant's creditworthiness. When an applicant relies on alimony, child support, or separate maintenance payments in applying for credit, the creditor shall consider such payment as income to the extent that they are likely to be consistently made.

(6) Credit history. To the extent that a creditor considers credit history in evaluating the creditworthiness of similarly qualified applicants for a similar type and amount of credit, in evaluating an applicant's creditworthiness a creditor shall consider:

(i) The credit history, when available, of accounts designated as accounts that the applicant and the applicant's spouse are permitted to use or for which both are contractually liable;

(ii) On the applicant's request, any information the applicant may present that tends to indicate that the credit history being considered by the creditor does not accurately reflect the applicant's creditworthiness; and

(iii) On the applicant's request, the credit history, when available, of any account reported in the name of the applicant's spouse or former spouse that the applicant can demonstrate accurately reflects the applicant's creditworthiness.

(7) Immigration status. A creditor may consider whether an applicant is a permanent resident of the United States, the applicant's immigration status, and any additional information that may be necessary to ascertain the creditor's rights and remedies regarding repayment.

(c) State property laws. A creditor's consideration or application of state property laws directly or indirectly affecting creditworthiness does not constitute unlawful discrimination for the purposes of the Act or this regulation.

Sec. 202.7 Rules concerning extensions of credit.

(a) Individual accounts. A creditor shall not refuse to grant an individual account to a creditworthy applicant on the basis of sex, marital status, or any other prohibited basis.

(b) Designation of name. A creditor shall not refuse to allow an applicant to open or maintain an account in a birth-given first name and a surname that is the applicant's birth-given surname, the spouse's surname, or a combined surname.

(c) Action concerning existing open-end accounts—

(1) Limitations. In the absence of evidence of the applicant's inability or unwillingness to repay, a creditor shall not take any of the following actions regarding an applicant who is contractually liable on an existing open-end account on the basis of the applicant's reaching a certain age or retiring or on the basis of a change in the applicant's name or marital status:

(i) Require a reapplication, except as provided in paragraph (c)(2) of this section;

(ii) Change the terms of the account; or

(iii) Terminate the account.

(2) Requiring reapplication. A creditor may require a reapplication for an open-end account on the basis of a change in the marital status of an applicant who is contractually liable if the credit granted was based in whole or in part on income of the applicant's spouse and if information available to the creditor indicates that the applicant's income may not support the amount of credit currently available.

(d) Signature of spouse or other person—

(1) Rule for qualified applicant. Except as provided in this paragraph, a creditor shall not require the signature of an applicant's spouse or other person, other than a joint applicant, on any credit instrument if the applicant qualifies under the creditor's standards of creditworthiness for the amount and terms of the credit requested.

(2) Unsecured credit. If an applicant requests unsecured credit and relies in part upon property that the applicant owns jointly with another person to satisfy the creditor's standards of creditworthiness, the creditor

may require the signature of the other person only on the instrument(s) necessary, or reasonably believed by the creditor to be necessary, under the law of the state in which the property is located, to enable the creditor to reach the property being relied upon in the event of the death or default of the applicant.

(3) Unsecured credit—community property states. If a married applicant requests unsecured credit and resides in a community property state, or if the property upon which the applicant is relying is located in such a state, a creditor may require the signature of the spouse on any instrument necessary, or reasonably believed by the creditor to be necessary, under applicable state law to make the community property available to satisfy the debt in the event of default if:

(i) Applicable state law denies the applicant power to manage or control sufficient community property to qualify for the amount of credit requested under the creditor's standards of creditworthiness; and

(ii) The applicant does not have sufficient separate property to qualify for the amount of credit requested without regard to community property.

(4) Secured credit. If an applicant requests secured credit, a creditor may require the signature of the applicant's spouse or other person on any instrument necessary, or reasonably believed by the creditor to be necessary, under applicable state law to make the property being offered as security available to satisfy the debt in the event of default, for example, an instrument to create a valid lien, pass clear title, waive inchoate rights or assign earnings.

(5) Additional parties. If, under a creditor's standards of creditworthiness, the personal liability of an additional party is necessary to support the extension of the credit requested, a creditor may request a cosigner, guarantor, or the like. The applicant's spouse may serve as an additional party, but the creditor shall not require that the spouse be the additional party.

(6) Rights of additional parties. A creditor shall not impose requirements upon an additional party that the creditor is prohibited from imposing upon an applicant under this section.

(e) Insurance. A creditor shall not refuse to extend credit and shall not terminate an account because credit life, health, accident, disability, or other credit-related insurance is not available on the basis of the applicant's age.

Index

acceptance, 112–14
accountants
  failure to collect, 231
  retainers, 250
accounting systems
  accrual basis, 260
  cash statement, 259
  credit limits, 90
  electronic, 114
  monitoring deposits, 250
accounts
  collection, 269
  cost of open, 258–59
  holds on, 136–37
  revolving, 271
  selling to factor, 8–9, 22, 248–49
  trust, 204
accounts receivables, 4, 22
accrual basis accounting system, 260
ACT (program), 174
agreements
  late fees, 173
  in writing, 148–49
Alabama, 177–78, 274
Alaska, 178, 274
Annual Percentage Rate (APR), 268
Antique Barn, 15
antitrust laws, 20
apparel industry, 9
applications
  See credit applications
Arizona, 178, 274–75
Arkansas, 178, 275
assets
  bankruptcy, 222–23
  collateral, 4–5
  definition, 268
  secured, 220
authorized account user, 268

bad debts, 231, 259–61
  See also nonpayment
bankruptcy
  collection agencies, 205

collection attempts, 165
  definition, 268
  filing, 166
  issuing credit after, 227
  past-due accounts, 222
  secured assets, 220
  types, 220–21
bankruptcy discharge, 268
bankruptcy dismissal, 268
banks
  credit card processing services, 252
  Export-Import, 40–41
  floor planning, 251
  as information sources, 74
  letters of credit, 34–38
  protection of interest, 37
  references, 73
  selling accounts to, 22
  source of funds, xii, 5–9
  starting a business, 2–4
Better Business Bureau, 74
billing, 112–20
  See also invoices; statements
businesses, researching, 235
business-to-business credit, xii, 20–29
  applications, 23–26
  personal guarantees, 24–25
  policies, 29

California, 178, 276
cash
  bankruptcy, 226–27
  card processing companies, 251–52
  as collateral, 37
  credit limit policy, 58, 83–85
  disputes, 148
  industry flows, 79
  limited collection, 168
  risk assessment, 68–69
  shortage, 17, 243
  timing of flow, 3
  See also C.O.D.
Cash on Delivery
  See C.O.D.

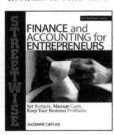

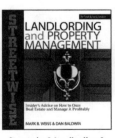
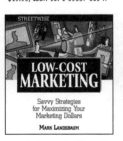
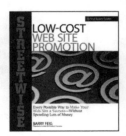

Streetwise® Managing a Nonprofit
John Riddle
$19.95; ISBN 10: 1-58062-698-X

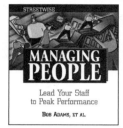

Streetwise® Managing People
Bob Adams, et al.
$19.95; ISBN 10: 1-55850-726-4

Streetwise® Marketing Plan
Don Debelak
$19.95; ISBN 10: 1-58062-268-2

**Streetwise® Maximize
Web Site Traffic**
Nobles and O'Neil
$19.95; ISBN 10: 1-58062-369-7

**Streetwise® Motivating
& Rewarding Employees**
Alexander Hiam
$19.95; ISBN 10: 1-58062-130-9

**Streetwise® Project
Management**
Michael Dobson
$19.95; ISBN 10: 1-58062-770-6

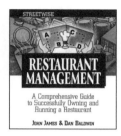

**Streetwise® Restaurant
Management**
John James & Dan Baldwin
$19.95; ISBN 10: 1-58062-781-1

**Streetwise® Sales Letters
with CD**
Reynard and Weiss
$29.95; ISBN 10: 1-58062-440-5

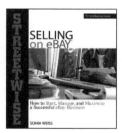

Streetwise® Selling on eBay®
Sonia Weiss
$19.95; ISBN 10: 1-59337-610-3

**Streetwise®
Small Business Book of Lists**
Edited by Gene Marks
$19.95; ISBN 10: 1-59337-684-7

Streetwise® Small Business Start-Up
Bob Adams
$19.95; ISBN 10: 1-55850-581-4

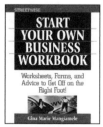

**Streetwise® Start Your Own
Business Workbook**
Gina Marie Mangiamele
$9.95; ISBN 10: 1-58062-506-1

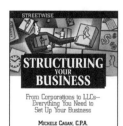

Streetwise® Structuring Your Business
Michele Cagan
$19.95; ISBN 10: 1-59337-177-2

Streetwise® Time Management
Marshall Cook
$19.95; ISBN 10: 1-58062-131-7